Management for Professionals

Annika Steiber · Sverker Alänge

The Silicon Valley Model
Management for Entrepreneurship

Second Edition

Annika Steiber ⓘ
Management Insights
Menlo Park, CA, USA

Sverker Alänge
Action Research Center for a
Resilient Society
Gothenburg, Sweden

ISSN 2192-8096 ISSN 2192-810X (electronic)
Management for Professionals
ISBN 978-3-031-48404-9 ISBN 978-3-031-48405-6 (eBook)
https://doi.org/10.1007/978-3-031-48405-6

© The Editor(s) (if applicable) and The Author(s), under exclusive license to Springer Nature Switzerland AG 2016, 2024

This work is subject to copyright. All rights are solely and exclusively licensed by the Publisher, whether the whole or part of the material is concerned, specifically the rights of reprinting, reuse of illustrations, recitation, broadcasting, reproduction on microfilms or in any other physical way, and transmission or information storage and retrieval, electronic adaptation, computer software, or by similar or dissimilar methodology now known or hereafter developed.

The use of general descriptive names, registered names, trademarks, service marks, etc. in this publication does not imply, even in the absence of a specific statement, that such names are exempt from the relevant protective laws and regulations and therefore free for general use.

The publisher, the authors, and the editors are safe to assume that the advice and information in this book are believed to be true and accurate at the date of publication. Neither the publisher nor the authors or the editors give a warranty, expressed or implied, with respect to the material contained herein or for any errors or omissions that may have been made. The publisher remains neutral with regard to jurisdictional claims in published maps and institutional affiliations.

This Springer imprint is published by the registered company Springer Nature Switzerland AG
The registered company address is: Gewerbestrasse 11, 6330 Cham, Switzerland

Paper in this product is recyclable.

Foreword from Stephen Denning

The Silicon Valley Model: Management for Entrepreneurship was published first in 2016. It was one of the first books to recognize that the industrial model of management was becoming increasingly obsolete and that a new pattern of management was already emerging in forward-looking firms particularly in Silicon Valley, but also in China.

It was one of the earliest books to recognize that these changes involved more than adding new tools and processes on top of the way the firm was currently being run. The authors were among the first to say explicitly that the entire system of management was obsolete and that new management, with new mindsets and thinking, was required. Now, agility, innovation, adaptability, and rapid response were central, not peripheral. The authors were also among the earliest to recognize that the rigid command-and-control cultures and bureaucratic structures of the late twentieth century could not succeed in the emerging digital age.

The authors truly early grasped the renewed importance of entrepreneurship, which had been suppressed in the effort of firms to achieve scale and maximize profits from existing resources ahead of creating new business opportunities.

Unlike much academic writing on management, the authors did not limit themselves to analyzing the impact of individual tools and processes. They identified a new pattern of management that includes multiple mindsets and processes, as well as the interaction of the individual elements of the pattern. They were thus able to achieve a more holistic picture of how fundamentally different management in the new model really is.

What was seen by many in 2016 as just a possibility has become the reality of 2023 that is obvious to all. The corporate giants of the twentieth century, such as GE and IBM, have given way to the giants implementing the Silicon Valley model—Apple, Amazon, Alphabet, Microsoft, Meta, Nvidia, and Tesla. The second edition of the book also covers new exemplars of the model beyond Silicon Valley: Bosch Power Tools division and Fidelity Investments. Firms that have not yet embraced the new management model are finding it increasingly difficult to compete.

The book is not just an account of the management of firms in Silicon Valley. It is a timeless guide to management of all firms who want to prosper in the rapidly changing context of the digital age.

— Stephen Denning, author of *The Age of Agile*

Foreword from Carlota Pérez

Technological revolutions deserve the name because they do indeed revolutionize, not only technology but also society and institutions, and particularly the management of companies. The process is turbulent because the successful habits of the past are deeply ingrained in all institutions and are very difficult to leave behind. Dee Hock, the innovative creator of the Visa credit system, often said that "the problem is never how to get new, innovative thoughts into your mind, but how to get old ones out." This book helps you get those old ones out and opens the way for creating the innovative organization.

We all know about the entrepreneurial spirit of Silicon Valley startups, we imagine them as young risk-takers excited about innovation and take it for granted that, if they are successful and grow into big companies, they will move to a more sedate mode. What the authors prove is that it is precisely the biggest companies, the new giants, that have kept the entrepreneurial attitude. They have remained 'young'. And what the book teaches is precisely, how to become young again.

To understand why this is so important, we need to contrast the previous mass production revolution invented by Henry Ford with the Silicon Valley Model, which responds to the requirements of the current information and communications revolution. Even if General Motors' Sloan managed to introduce variety by appealing to three different income layers and offering attractive colors, Ford's two core ideas: "you can have any color as long as it's black" and "leave your brain at home," are lurking in the background and have not completely disappeared. The information revolution, by contrast, is about constant and rapid change, about creativity, diversity, and customization.

A central notion introduced by the authors is that of 'ambidexterity': "being excellent in satisfying today's customers while working on products and services for tomorrow—ones which could even be a direct threat to today's." That requires, not only everyone bringing their brains with them, but also putting all their creativity to work every day. Keeping the entrepreneurial spirit and the types of teamwork that make constant innovation possible is a completely different mode from the one that is focused mainly on efficiency, productivity, and stability.

We are indeed in a different era, but we have not completely embraced it. For each company and for each country, making the most of the new potential of the information revolution is crucial, even more so with the geopolitical tensions, the new power of artificial intelligence and the different aspirations of the young.

This second edition is very timely. It comes after one of the authors wrote a book about the Silicon Valley model as it is applied in China. Sometimes the newcomers are more willing to embrace the new than those that are the already powerful. And that makes them strong challengers.

The model presented here is not only extremely useful for the updating of management in companies but also in governments. I trust it will achieve its purpose.

— Carlota Pérez
Honorary Professor in IIPP-UCL and SPRU,
University of Sussex, United Kingdom
Author of *Technological Revolutions and Financial Capital: the Dynamics of Bubbles and Golden Ages*

Foreword to the First Edition from David J. Teece

The competitive environment in all but the most protected economies and industries has changed radically. Global competition has rained down from diverse origins, from newly developing countries and from "disruptive" firms at home and abroad. The consequences have not been kind to firms built according to the industrial logic of yesteryear. Even those traditional firms operating efficiently using "best practices" have been swept aside.

The reason is that it is no longer enough for business firms to "optimize" and to do things right; one must also do the right things. This requires dynamic capabilities, and it is the essence of what the authors are writing about in The Silicon Valley Model.

The authors provide rich vistas into how new dynamically capable firms are organized and how they are managed. They are entrepreneurial, and they are good at not just sensing new opportunities (and threats) but also at seizing opportunities and conducting the necessary transformation or "shifting" when their newfound success is itself challenged. These firms are most visible in Silicon Valley, California, and are not just startups. They are established firms that have already scaled globally and operated profitably. They are populated by what this book calls a "special breed of people"; they have a large percentage of tech-savvy top talent as employees or independent contractors. The good news for most is that the model is no longer confined just to Silicon Valley. It has been successfully applied elsewhere too.

The book draws on the existing literature and on the authors' insightful field research in Silicon Valley and elsewhere. It should be a compelling read to academics and practitioners alike and will hopefully lead to a better understanding of what it takes to manage well in the challenging competitive circumstances which provide the allure of rapid growth in sales and profitability.

University of California David J. Teece
Berkeley, CA, USA
2015

Introduction: It's Time for a New Model — and a New Model Has Arrived

We wrote the first edition of this book, published in 2016, to help address an urgent need: the need for a fundamentally new approach to managing large firms.[1] The purpose of this second edition is to extend and update the original findings. We have done so by addressing new developments in management, and in the global business environment, during the seven-plus years between January of 2016 and the present publication date in 2023/2024.

These recent developments appear to validate the initial findings. More than ever, global currents of change are demanding that companies move to a new management model. In response, companies across a range of industries worldwide are adopting new methods which resemble the "Silicon Valley Model" that we identified at leading Silicon Valley companies in 2016. As this occurs, the Model evolves into new forms, although the underlying principles remain essentially the same. And for businesses that haven't yet joined the evolution, the need becomes increasingly urgent.

Today as in 2016, many large companies are run based on a "legacy" management system. The system is a holdover from the past Industrial Age and tends to feature a rigidly bureaucratic structure, with multiple top-down channels of command and control and tightly specified work roles and procedures. There is nothing wrong *per se* with using such a legacy system. It is well suited for holding a business to pre-existing standards of performance. The problem is that it's not very nimble or changeable—and the imperative to respond quickly to change (or better yet, to *lead* change) has permeated practically every industry.

As more than one observer puts it, the nature of change itself has changed. Already in 2016 it was evident that forces including new technologies, societal changes, and globalization had created a perpetual VUCA environment: Volatile, Uncertain, Complex, and Ambiguous. The result has been constant, unrelenting pressure on incumbents in consumer (B2C) and B2B markets alike. The new environment puts a premium on qualities like innovation, adaptability, and speed. Our 2016 research showed that highly successful firms in Silicon Valley were organized and managed to precisely achieve these qualities. Growing numbers of researchers,

---

[1] We strongly believe that not only are business firms in need of new approaches to management, so are other types of organizations, such as nonprofits, public, and government agencies. And we believe that the new management model we will describe here is applicable to them as well.

consultants, and business journalists also found that companies managed by the legacy model were greatly at risk of falling behind, *even if they adopted* the latest management tools and techniques. Typically, the upgrades didn't go deep enough; they functioned mainly as add-ons to an obsolete foundation.

We therefore concluded in the first edition of this book that the future would favor companies that can *migrate to a new management model*, better suited for the twenty-first century. Further, we argued that the Silicon Valley Model—which had evolved within the extremely fast-moving information technology industries, as well as in a geographic region accustomed to change and growth—could serve as a template for models to be used by other companies everywhere.

Events since that time have tended to support the first edition's observations. Each chapter of the current edition has a section titled "Recent Developments," summarizing activities and trends that are relevant to the research of the prior decade. Here is a brief history of how our work has unfolded, followed by a chapter outline and guide to the second edition's content.

An Expanding Web of Discovery

We first observed key elements of the Silicon Valley Model at Google, during a year of intensive research on that company. Our findings were published in an award-winning journal article and in Dr. Annika Steiber's previous book *The Google Model: Managing Continuous Innovation in a Rapidly Changing World.* Then, starting early in 2014—even as *The Google Model* was coming off the presses at Springer—we expanded our studies. The goal was to ascertain whether we were, in fact, on to something that might be widely applicable.

So, we combed through writings by a multitude of eminent business scholars, consultants, journalists, and executives worldwide, searching for evidence on what works best for managing amid rapid change. We also widened our own inquiries to look at companies which, like Google, had grown and flourished well beyond the startup stage in Silicon Valley. These companies were Tesla, Apigee, and the social-networking leaders Facebook, LinkedIn, and Twitter. Along with Google, they became the primary "case companies" for the book.

In analyzing all the results, we found a remarkable convergence. Our six case companies turned out to be using management principles and practices which not only were similar but were also congruent with the best new practices identified in our global review of the literature. Therefore, we offered the first edition of this book—and now likewise offer the second edition—as a synthesis. While it relies on a great deal of work by others as well as us, we believe it makes an original contribution in this regard: Within a single short volume, it weaves together many strands of knowledge into *a coherent and useful new model for managing in times of constant change.*

We called this new management model "The Silicon Valley Model" because that was where it appeared to be most highly developed and most thoroughly applied.

However, the model is not applicable *only* in Silicon Valley or in the IT/internet sectors. Even while preparing the first edition, we found reports of certain other companies, in the U.S. and in Europe, managing by principles that fit the model we had described. Those companies were (and still are) successfully active in industries ranging from advanced textiles to food processing.

Since 2016, Dr. Steiber has widened her research to identify still more companies using similar models. One collection of new findings was published in her 2018 book *Management in the Digital Age: Will China Surpass Silicon Valley?* As the title implies, the case companies for this book were Chinese: the global appliance maker Haier, the "big three" firms Alibaba, Baidu, and Tencent, Xiaomi, and Huawei. All were found to be implementing management approaches that strongly paralleled the Silicon Valley Model, and in some respects appeared to be even more advanced.

The most radical iterations have been made by Haier, with its perpetually evolving RenDanHeYi management system. Moreover, the system recently has been in the process of adoption at Haier's U.S. acquisition GE Appliances. Dr. Steiber described this process in her 2022 book *Leadership for a Digital World: The Transformation of GE Appliances.* Meanwhile, in additional places and industries, there are growing numbers of companies either piloting or fully adopting management methods like the Silicon Valley Model. Examples that are profiled in this second edition include the Bosch Power Tools division and Fidelity Investments. To a greater extent than the first edition was able to do in 2016, the book you are now reading presents a picture of a truly emergent global movement toward new ways of managing.

The Key to All of It

One main characteristic of the Silicon Valley Model is its emphasis on entrepreneurship. Whereas the term is typically used in a narrow sense, to mean the starting of new companies, here we define it much as Peter Drucker did: stated briefly, it is the act of *creating and exploiting new business opportunities*. We then explain its importance for older and larger firms, including major global companies.

In fact, a key to the growth of all the companies we have studied is that they *have succeeded in integrating entrepreneurship with big-firm management.* To coin a phrase, they behave like startups in large suits. They keep innovating, with good success rates, while far outgrowing their initial size and impact. And what's vitally important is that they can attract and retain the entrepreneurial people who make the model work. Thus, although the individual fortunes of these companies may vary over time, we argue that the *management approaches they use* have now passed a significant series of reality tests and are likely to represent the future of large-firm management worldwide.

A Guide to the Contents of This Book

The Silicon Valley Model is written to be read by executives from the board and CEO level on down, as well as by consultants, researchers, and others who study or work with new developments in management. There are some scholarly touches—such as formal citation of sources—but overall, we've tried to write in a style that is neither too casual nor too stuffy. We also have tried to provide *background and context* that build a case for the new model, while putting in plenty of specifics to show how the model is applied. The book is organized as follows.

- **Chapter 1—The World is Changing.** Not everyone is convinced of the need for a new management model, nor does everyone fully grasp the forces of change that are driving this need. This chapter sets the stage while providing evidence that any readers can use to persuade their more skeptical colleagues.
- **Chapter 2—Six Basic Principles for a Changing World.** The six basic management principles outlined here—dynamic capabilities, a continually changing organization, a people-centric approach, ambidexterity, an open and networked organization, and a systems approach—have been identified by many researchers as keys to managing well in today's environment.
- **Chapter 3—Silicon Valley: A Cradle of Management Innovation.** Here, we take a fresh look at the Silicon Valley region—not just as a "startup machine" or as a hub of new technology but as a center for exploring and refining new ways to manage firms.
- **Chapter 4—Entrepreneurship: What It Really Is, and Why It Must Be *Integrated* into Management of the Firm.** This chapter dispels the myth that "entrepreneurs" are only found (and can only flourish) in startup companies. It offers a broad but concise look at the realities and argues for a new synthesis of entrepreneurship with big-firm management.
- **Chapter 5—A Special Breed of People.** Every company wants to recruit top talent, but a key requirement is to first know what kinds of talented people matter the most. This chapter describes the multifaceted attributes of the "special breed" of people sought by our case companies, then examines some strategies used to attract and retain these star players.
- **Chapter 6—Culture: The New Black.** Amid all the management trends that come and go, a new constant has emerged. Companies wishing to compete in fast-changing environments must have a strong culture that's appropriate to the task. Here, we look at the cultures of our original case companies and others, identify their key set of beliefs, and describe some steps they have taken to make culture-building a priority.
- **Chapter 7—Leading for Entrepreneurship.** This chapter explores, in detail, specific measures that have been used to lead people for entrepreneurial action.
- **Chapter 8—The Entrepreneurial Firm Is Dynamic and Ambidextrous.** Two important aspects of the new management model are dynamic capabilities—i.e., the ability to sense new opportunities while reconfiguring resources and transforming the firm's structure to *seize* those opportunities—and ambidexterity, the

ability to optimize current operations while also innovating and experimenting on new fronts. The chapter describes how companies can be organized and run to achieve these abilities.
- **Chapter 9—The Silicon Valley Model.** Here is the synthesis chapter that pulls together all of the elements described thus far in the book, creating a complete conceptual model of this new approach to management.
- **Chapter 10—Implications Beyond Silicon Valley.** We wrap up the book by considering issues related to wider application of the Silicon Valley Model. The basic conclusion: this model has the potential for very wide use and global impact, so long as it is adapted well to each company's particular needs.

Throughout much of the book, we have left the first-edition text as it was when it was first published. Although several details have changed since that time, the observations and analysis are still pertinent, and many readers have found them useful. New material appears mainly in the "Recent Developments" sections near the end of each chapter. These substantial sections include both real-life events and new research findings which relate, in various ways, to the management principles described originally. In some cases, we see further validation of the principles; in others, we see elements of the Silicon Valley Model taking on new forms in response to changing times or the desires of the companies involved.

We have *not* tried to trace, in any detail, the strategic moves and changes at our original Silicon Valley case companies since 2016, nor have we attempted to analyze the results of those moves. These are dynamic companies, constantly trying new things, so there would be too much to cover and most of it is irrelevant anyway to the focus of the book—the companies' fundamental management principles and practices. However, it is worth noting some major structural and ownership changes to the original six case companies. These changes began while the first edition was going to press, and by mid-2023 the following had occurred:

Apigee ceased existing as a separate business when it was sold to Google and integrated into Google's cloud operations. Google formed a holding company, Alphabet, for itself and its various business ventures. LinkedIn was acquired by Microsoft and has continued to operate as a free-standing subsidiary. Tesla acquired Sun City, a solar energy firm, and is now active in that business (and in storage batteries) as well as in electric vehicles. Facebook re-branded as Meta Platforms to reflect its ventures into areas such as AR/VR. And, in perhaps the most controversial move, Tesla CEO Elon Musk arranged an acquisition of Twitter—not merging the company with Tesla, but rather making himself Twitter's CEO while keeping the same position at Tesla.

As of late summer 2023, Google/Alphabet, LinkedIn, Facebook/Meta and Tesla all were profitable and financially sound. Each firm remained the world's market leader in its main business while experimenting and innovating along new lines. Twitter, renamed X, was the outlier of the group, reorganizing amid a state of upheaval. Much remained to be seen in terms of how that company's future would play out.

Indeed, all companies studied in this book may eventually look quite different from their present forms. That is the nature of our modern world. More significantly, it is the nature of the companies most likely to survive and thrive through the years ahead.

Acknowledgments We hope that the synthesis we present here does justice to the work of many, by bringing it into a new light. Above all, we hope this book will prove to be provocative and useful to boards of directors, managers, consultants, and scholars everywhere, for years to come.

At this point, we would like to express our gratitude to our families, colleagues, case companies, and publisher, who have made this book possible. We thank Rikard Steiber and Sari Scheinberg, who from the very start encouraged us to write this book and who have stood behind us, literally and figuratively, during many hours at the desk. We also thank Mike Vargo, who helped us not only to write the book but also to complement our knowledge with new insights. We don't think we could have found a better, more curious, and trustworthy colleague to join us in this project. We thank colleagues such as David Teece, Gary Hamel, Kathleen Eisenhardt, Henry Chesbrough, Henry Etzkowitz, AnnaLee Saxenian, Charles O'Reilly, Homa Bahrami, Carlota Perez, Steve Denning, Hunter Hastings, Rita McGrath, Amy Edmondson, Richard Straub, Johan Roos, Peter Diamandes, Salim Ismail, Michele Zanini, Darrell Rigby, and Michael Lurie who, along with encouraging our work, have done important research of their own in key areas covered here. In addition, we appreciate all the help given to us by our original case companies—Google, Facebook, Twitter, LinkedIn, Tesla, and Apigee—as well as Haier and GE Appliances in subsequent studies. Finally, we want to thank Springer DE for choosing to publish this book and the Institute for Management of Innovation and Technology (IMIT) for supporting the administration of this project through the first edition.

Silicon Valley, California, USA
Date August 8, 2023

Contents

1	**The World Is Changing**	1
	1.1 Introducing a New Management Model	1
	1.2 The Changing Nature of Change (and What It Means for Management)	3
	1.2.1 Implications for Management: Drawbacks of the Old Way	5
	1.2.2 The New Model: Essentially Entrepreneurial	6
	1.3 Tales of Two Industries	7
	1.3.1 The Clothing Industries: Textiles, Garments, Shoes, Retail	7
	1.3.2 Telephones and Phone Services	9
	1.3.3 What Can We Learn?	10
	1.4 The High Road Versus the Missed Turn: Comparing New and Old Management Models	12
	1.4.1 Finding the High Road: The Entrepreneurial Path	12
	1.4.2 Missing the Turn: The Case of Kodak	15
	1.5 Recent Developments	16
	1.5.1 Acceleration of New Entrepreneurial Models	16
	1.5.2 Management in an AI World	17
	1.5.3 Management in a Sustainable World	19
	1.5.4 Summarizing Recent Developments	20
	1.6 Moving On	20
	References	20
2	**Six Basic Principles for a Changing World**	23
	2.1 Dynamic Capabilities	25
	2.1.1 When 'Core Competencies' Aren't Enough	25
	2.1.2 Dynamic Capabilities: A New Concept of Corporate Resources	26
	2.2 A Continually Changing Organization	28
	2.2.1 Some Practices Allowing Continual Change	28
	2.3 A People-Centric Approach	30
	2.4 An Ambidextrous Organization	32
	2.5 An Open Organization That Networks with Its Surroundings	34

	2.6	A Systems Approach	35
	2.7	Recent Findings	38
	2.8	Moving On	39
	References		39
3	**Silicon Valley: A Cradle of Management Innovation**		**41**
	3.1	The Forces That Drive Management Innovation, in Brief	42
	3.2	Management Innovation: The Influence of IT	43
		3.2.1 New Ways of Managing Emerge	44
	3.3	Management Innovation: The Influence of Regional Culture	46
		3.3.1 The Early Electronics Industry	48
	3.4	Management Innovation: New Levels of Networking	49
	3.5	Management Innovation: People Focus, from Postwar to the Present	51
	3.6	In Summary (with Remarks on 'Replicating' Silicon Valley)	53
	3.7	Recent Developments: The Resilience of Silicon Valley	54
		3.7.1 A Brief Analysis of 'Negative' Events	54
		3.7.2 The Valley's Fundamental Strength and Resilience	55
		3.7.3 Persistence of the Culture and Business Model	56
		3.7.4 Silicon Valley as a Global Innovation Hub in Transition	56
	References		58
4	**Entrepreneurship: What It Really Is, and Why It Must Be *Integrated* into Management of the Firm**		**61**
	4.1	What Is Entrepreneurship?	62
		4.1.1 A Modern Understanding (and a New Definition)	64
		4.1.2 The Company as 'Entrepreneur'	65
	4.2	The Divide Between Entrepreneurship and Management: Obstacles and Evolutionary Forces	66
		4.2.1 How Business Schools Reinforced the Split	67
		4.2.2 Toward a Re-synthesis of Entrepreneurship and Management	69
	4.3	Recent Developments	69
	4.4	What Can a Company Do?	70
	References		71
5	**A Special Breed of People**		**73**
	5.1	Focusing on the 'Special Breed,' from Google Onward	74
	5.2	On 'Multidimensional' People and the Need for Them	76
	5.3	Cornerstones of Success: Five Core Qualities of the 'Special Breed'	78
		5.3.1 Entrepreneurial	79
		5.3.2 Adaptable	79
		5.3.3 Passionate	81
		5.3.4 Constantly Questioning the Status Quo	81
		5.3.5 Collaborative	82

	5.4	Attracting the Special Breed	83
	5.5	How Do We Keep These People?	85
		5.5.1 The Ugly Duckling	86
		5.5.2 Meaningful Work, Perks and Benefits	87
		5.5.3 The Employer-Employee Alliance	89
	5.6	Recent Findings	92
	5.7	Conclusions (and a Start)	93
	References		94
6	**Culture: The New Black**		**95**
	6.1	What 'Culture' Consists Of	95
	6.2	External Influences on Culture	97
	6.3	The People Effect: How Founders Shape Culture	98
	6.4	Steps to Building a Strong Culture	100
	6.5	The '10 Commandments': Core Attributes of the Cultures We Studied	101
		6.5.1 Not an Ordinary Company	102
		6.5.2 Things Change Constantly and We Need to Be Adaptable	103
		6.5.3 Move Fast, Speed Matters	104
		6.5.4 Hiring Is the Most Important Thing We Do	105
		6.5.5 Product Excellence Is Key	106
		6.5.6 Data-Driven Decision Making and Fast Learning	107
		6.5.7 A Flat Organization with Minimal Bureaucracy	108
		6.5.8 Openness and Transparency	109
		6.5.9 Leaders, Not Managers	109
		6.5.10 Build an Ecosystem, Not Just a Company	110
	6.6	Recent Developments: The Growing Importance of Culture and the 'Ten Commandments'	111
		6.6.1 Culture in Digital Transformation	112
		6.6.2 Culture That Aligns with Generation Z	113
		6.6.3 Culture for Innovation and Growth	114
	6.7	Concluding Comments	115
	References		115
7	**Leading for Entrepreneurship**		**117**
	7.1	Top Leaders' Roles	118
	7.2	Providing Direction and Expectation Level	119
	7.3	Communication and Leader Behavior	121
	7.4	Founder Entrepreneurs	124
	7.5	The Role of Leaders on the Middle Levels	125
	7.6	Decision-Making	126
	7.7	Incentives and Motivation	127
	7.8	Hiring and Developing Leaders	129
	7.9	Recent Findings	130
	7.10	Concluding Comments	131
	References		132

8 The Entrepreneurial Organization Is Dynamic and Ambidextrous ... 135
- 8.1 Dynamic Capabilities ... 136
  - 8.1.1 Ambidexterity in Theory ... 137
  - 8.1.2 The Challenge of Ambidexterity ... 138
- 8.2 Innovation by Many, Inside Present Operations ... 139
  - 8.2.1 Top Executive Focus ... 139
  - 8.2.2 The 'Semi-Structured' State ... 140
  - 8.2.3 Small Teams ... 140
  - 8.2.4 Transparency and Openness ... 141
  - 8.2.5 Heuristics or 'Simple Rules' ... 141
  - 8.2.6 Intrinsic Incentives in Meaningful Work ... 143
  - 8.2.7 Rapid Learning Processes ... 144
  - 8.2.8 Big Data on User Behavior ... 145
- 8.3 Innovation by Separate Innovation Units ... 145
  - 8.3.1 Acquisitions ... 146
  - 8.3.2 Corporate Ventures ... 146
  - 8.3.3 Small Firm-Large Firm Ventures ... 147
  - 8.3.4 Spin-Ins and Incubation ... 148
- 8.4 Open Innovation Approaches ... 149
  - 8.4.1 University Interaction ... 150
  - 8.4.2 Suppliers as Innovators ... 150
  - 8.4.3 Crowdsourcing from Users and Communities ... 150
  - 8.4.4 External Development Platforms ... 152
  - 8.4.5 Cultivating Ecosystems ... 152
- 8.5 Concluding Comments in 2016 ... 153
- 8.6 Recent Developments ... 154
  - 8.6.1 Employment in Case Companies ... 154
  - 8.6.2 Evolving Organizational Trends ... 155
  - 8.6.3 Conclusions ... 156
- References ... 156

9 The Silicon Valley Model ... 159
- 9.1 The Evolution of a New Breed of Organizations ... 159
  - 9.1.1 The New Model's Roots in 'Adhocracy' ... 160
- 9.2 The Silicon Valley Model: 'A Startup in a Large Suit' ... 162
  - 9.2.1 Major Elements of the Silicon Valley Model ... 162
- 9.3 A Conceptual Model, Visualized ... 165
- 9.4 Differences Between a Traditional Management Model and the Silicon Valley Model ... 166
- 9.5 The Silicon Valley Model and the Six Basic Principles for a Changing World ... 168
- 9.6 Summing Up Key Points ... 170

	9.7	Recent Developments and Further Thoughts	170
		9.7.1 The Evolution of Adhocracy	171
		9.7.2 The Next Evolutionary Step?	172
	References		173
10	**Implications Beyond Silicon Valley**		**175**
	10.1	The Use of Elements of the Silicon Valley Model in Other Companies	176
		10.1.1 An Inspiring and Socially Significant Vision	176
		10.1.2 Visionary, Entrepreneurial and Growth-Oriented Top Leadership	177
		10.1.3 Belief and Investment in Entrepreneurial People	178
		10.1.4 A Culture That Guides and Motivates Entrepreneurial People	179
		10.1.5 Leaders Who Support Entrepreneurial People	179
		10.1.6 An Ambidextrous Organization	180
		10.1.7 Open Innovation	181
		10.1.8 Coordination	182
		10.1.9 Information and Communication Technologies: Do the Silicon Valley Companies Have a Unique Edge?	183
	10.2	Can the Whole System of Interlinked Elements Be Used Outside Silicon Valley?	184
		10.2.1 Startup Culture in Mature Companies	184
		10.2.2 A System of Interconnected Elements	185
	10.3	Use of the Model in an Innovation Unit Within a Large Company	186
	10.4	Recent Developments: Further Dissemination of the Silicon Valley Model	187
		10.4.1 New Models in China	188
		10.4.2 Case Study: RenDanHeYi at Haier and GE Appliances	189
		10.4.3 Case Study: Fidelity Investments	191
		10.4.4 Case Study: Bosch Power Tools	191
		10.4.5 Case Study: Fujitsu Western Europe	192
		10.4.6 A Growing Force for Change: Digital Transformation	193
	10.5	Ultimate Conclusions	194
	References		196
Index			**199**

The World Is Changing

This is a book about re-inventing management. We and many others who study the field or work in it, are convinced that the need is great. Most companies today are still managed on the basis of models developed for the Industrial Age, while the world has moved to a much faster-changing Digital Era—an era so different, that operating in the old way is like trying to apply Newtonian physics in a quantum-physics world.

Certainly, managers everywhere try to keep up with changing times. New management methods and programs are always being tried, and some may be helpful. The trouble is that most firms are using these efforts to tweak an underlying management system that isn't right. As the cliché says, they are rearranging deck chairs on the Titanic. Fundamentally new ways of navigating are required. Companies that keep steaming along, ignoring the need, may be staying afloat by luck to a greater degree than they realize.

In this book we present a new management model for the times, drawn from research on what is actually working at a number of leading companies.

1.1 Introducing a New Management Model

We have studied firms that operate in rapidly changing environments, with a specific focus on six Silicon Valley firms that served as the "case companies" for our research: Google, Tesla Motors, Apigee, and the social-networking leaders Facebook, LinkedIn, and Twitter. The principles and practices they used were strikingly similarly in terms of both what they believed in and how they did it.

These companies were, and remained, *entrepreneurial*—even as large firms. All brought an initial great new product to market, no easy feat in itself. But what they did after that is even harder. In a world where yesterday's pace-setting firms can quickly be overtaken, they not only sustained their initial successes but built on them. Consistently, these entrepreneurial companies seemed able to rise to challenges and find new opportunities; they stayed ahead of the winds of change.

The explanation to this is that they were managed radically differently from the norm.

- Their management structures and approaches were built around principles and practices that, in many respects, are 180 degrees opposite to those of the typical large firm.
- Most important, however, these companies were built on entrepreneurial *people*, and *they cultivated their skills and channeled their abilities into innovative results*. By managing in this way, the firms were able to attract and retain the entrepreneurial people they needed.

In this book, we claim that this new way of managing firms is the answer to the "paradigm shift" that the management expert Gary Hamel foresaw and called for, in 2009.

> Tomorrow's business imperatives lie outside the performance envelope of today's bureaucracy-infused management practices… Equipping organizations to tackle the future would require a management revolution no less momentous than the one that spawned modern industry.[1]—Gary Hamel

We chose to call the new management model that we observed "The Silicon Valley Model,"[2] as it seemed to be more common in that region than in other parts of the world and was explicitly operationalized in our Silicon Valley case companies. In our view, it is a model particularly fit for our modern era's unpredictable, fast-changing industries and times. The rest of this chapter will describe how and why today's economy is fundamentally different from that of the past and what implications this will have for management. The section titles and content are:

- "The Changing Nature of Change"—which sets the context by pinpointing what is different about today's economy, and what it means for management.
- "Tales of Two Industries"—a section that illustrates how the new kind of change swept through two very different fields, and how entrepreneurial firms responded.
- "Taking the High Road vs. Missing the Turn"—which highlights some new management approaches used at our case companies, then contrasts them with a negative example: the story of a distinguished global company that sailed into trouble after being unable to adjust.

---

[1] Hamel (2009), p. 92.
[2] We are not the first to talk about a Silicon Valley Model. In a 1996 article titled "Firm organization, industrial structure and technological innovation," Professor David Teece identified four archetypical firms by scope, structure and integration. One of these was labeled the "Silicon Valley Model" and was characterized by having a flatter structure, a more change-oriented culture, and being more specialized and less integrated.

Now let's begin by mapping the landscape.

1.2 The Changing Nature of Change (and What It Means for Management)

We of today's world are hardly the first to live in a time of profound change. The first decades of the Industrial Revolution, from the late 1700s through the early 1800s, brought a veritable parade of major innovations: the factory system, the improved steam engine, the mechanical loom, the coming of the railroads. Those were truly "disruptive" events. They disrupted the basic patterns of life and work for generations to come—often provoking armed conflict between the disrupters and disrupted, as well as high-stakes rivalries among firms.

Our times may not match that period for high drama, but they are extremely challenging in a different sense. As Gary Hamel wrote in his book *What Matters Now*, "change has changed."[3] The big, disruptive changes of the past were fewer in number, happened more gradually, and it was usually easier to see where they were headed. Everybody knew the race was on to build a railway from one point to another, or to win the war of currents between AC and DC systems in the early electric power industry.

Today the situation is a constantly swirling, buzzing cloud of change. In Richard Florida's words, change is "pervasive and ongoing,"[4] and business is less a matter of fighting pitched battles and more like guerilla warfare. With surprises popping up everywhere—unpredictable innovations here, sudden market shifts there—it can even be hard to tell whom you are competing against, and the strategy that worked last year may now be a blueprint for disaster.

How has the world gotten to this state of constant, swirling buzz? In her book *The Shift*, Lynda Gratton spoke of five broad "forces" that are shaping the future of work: technology, demographics, globalization, society, and energy resources.[5] Each is a source of change. Condensing our discussion of some parts for brevity, let's consider how rapid, constant change can arise from each:

Technology Technological change is said to be exponential, which isn't strictly true—some technologies (notably, computer chips) have gotten more powerful by leaps and bounds, while others have not. But the *impact* of technology grows at a faster-than-linear compounded rate, one reason being that few technologies are just single-use tools or devices. As the MIT scientist and entrepreneur Eugene Fitzgerald explained,[6] they can be combined and re-combined in new ways—as when engines, wheels, advanced metalworking, etc. were put together to make the automobile.

---

[3] Hamel (2012), p. 85.
[4] Florida (2002), p. 5.
[5] Gratton (2011), pp. 23–48.
[6] The following discussion is from Fitzgerald and Wankerl (2010), pp. 19–30.

And, Fitzgerald noted, technologies can also be combined with different business models and market applications. That is where the possibilities really proliferate.

Computer chips and software have been combined with other technologies, *and* with different business models and market applications, in areas from travel booking to brain surgery. With more people than ever in the world making combinations from an ever-growing pool of technologies, one can see how the pace of change multiplies and becomes unpredictable from this "force" alone.

Demography and Society Let's condense two of Gratton's forces into a single "people" category. The central fact is that when people change, in terms of how they live or what they value, the impacts ripple through the business world. Markets change, sometimes radically, as there can be changes in what people buy, how they buy it, and the features they want their goods to have. Meanwhile the workforce changes, too, as people enter it bringing new skills, traits, and desires. Therefore business analysts feverishly study each new generation.

But all generations from the Baby Boomers to X-Y-Z are part of a major and ongoing shift. They have grown up since World War II, during a time when economic growth keeps making more of the world's people more prosperous. And as the long-running World Values Survey has shown, prosperity correlates with changes in values. People move up the scale in Maslow's classic hierarchy of needs. In the Survey's terms, they move from a "Survival" mindset to a way of thinking that values "Self-expression" more.[7]

Florida's book *The Rise of the Creative Class* gave stunning examples of this in the U.S. The author noted that his home state had a severe shortage of young people willing to be trained for well-paid and secure jobs as machinists, at the same time there was an oversupply of young people becoming hair stylists—a lower-paying but more "creative" line of work.[8]

The impacts on market demand are tremendous. To mention just one effect that Florida and others have observed, people's lives become more complex and fragmented as they seek multiple forms of novelty and fulfillment. The result is a constant demand for any new goods that promise to (a) save time or cost or (b) help people express themselves in areas from work to active outdoor pursuits to active parenting.

Our book will have much more to say about impacts in the workplace. We'll especially focus on the highly skilled people who come to work wanting to *create change* as well as experience it: they are the entrepreneurs.

The effects of **globalization** do not need much explaining. Everyone should be familiar with the basics of how an interconnected world generates new market opportunities along with hyper-competition and volatility. And, what Gratton calls **energy resources** relates to the broad area of growing environmental concerns.

---

[7] The World Values Survey, started in 1981, is based in Stockholm and has contributors and investigators worldwide. Homepage: http://www.worldvaluessurvey.org/wvs.jsp

[8] Florida (2002), pp. 85–86.

Here, there are constraints and regulations that require changes while they also create expanding, evolving market opportunities in the green industries.

Moreover, all five forces and sources of change are operating at the same time, and they interact, adding up to the proverbial VUCA[9] world: highly volatile, uncertain, complex, and ambiguous. It is not at all apparent where the Next Big Thing, or the Next Big Threat, might be coming from.

1.2.1 Implications for Management: Drawbacks of the Old Way

Most firms are ill-equipped for this maze because they are managed by systems and principles that evolved into shape—and settled into shape—during the Industrial era. Gary Hamel's "Moon Shot" conference of business leaders and scholars in 2008 identified the system features that are major hindrances, including: formal hierarchies, with chains of command and spans of control. Tightly specified job roles, rules, and procedures. Strategic decision-making done by small groups at the top. And a narrowly defined concept of the company's purpose, with performance judged and rewarded accordingly, all up and down the line.[10] We will show later that these organizational features are more or less mirroring the characteristics of what Henry Mintzberg[11] labeled a "Machine Bureaucracy Model," still used by many large firms today.

As Hamel noted, the old system is good for coordinating large numbers of people to carry out prescribed tasks. That was its original purpose, for managing big, complex tasks like mass production. But when the task becomes to *change* the task—seeing new openings, pivoting quickly, developing new business ideas and mobilizing people around them—almost every feature becomes a negative, which was also something identified by the UC Berkeley professor David Teece in 1996.[12] The formal, more bureaucratic structures are hard to reconfigure. *The people in them* get conditioned to thinking and acting in narrow channels (whether they realize it or not). The strategists at the top are few and may have limited perspectives. In addition to the structural issue, organizations tend to become path-dependent (that is: the set of decisions one faces for any given circumstance is limited by the decisions one has made in the past, even though past circumstances may no longer be relevant). So even *firms that see themselves as innovative leaders* can therefore stumble badly.

---

[9] VUCA is an acronym used to describe or reflect on the volatility, uncertainty, complexity, and ambiguity of general conditions and situations. Common usage of the term VUCA began in the 1990s and derives from military vocabulary. It has been subsequently used in emerging ideas in strategic leadership that apply to a wide range of organizations, from for-profit corporations to educational institutions (http://www.wikipedia.org. Accessed 6 Aug 2015).

[10] Hamel (2009).

[11] Mintzberg (1980), pp. 332–333.

[12] Teece (1996).

Example Nokia was once the world leader in making mobile phones. Then it not only lost its lead but exited the market. One problem, analysts agreed, was that the firm clung too long to a key product behind its initial success, the Symbian operating system, while users were migrating to Android-based phones or iPhones, which they saw as having more advantages. At Nokia, changing the OS in a timely fashion would've been a significant and cost-incurring step that also ran counter to established thinking at the firm. The impetus for timely response—let alone for proactive change, ahead of the curve—just wasn't there.[13]

Lynda Gratton, in a blog post, made these further observations:

> Leaders must constantly acknowledge that their companies are subject to an onslaught of destabilizing forces. Being vigilant and observant about the nature and velocity of these forces is crucial …
> At Nokia, the senior leadership team was for a long time extraordinarily homogenous (mostly men, mostly from Finland, mostly software engineers, mostly educated in Helsinki). How likely was it that they would be on top of the rapid developments in Asian consumer markets, or in technology and design emanating from Silicon Valley?[14]

Firms that manage this way can become like medieval knights: formidable and fast-moving at a straight-ahead mounted gallop, but encumbered by heavy, stiff armor and peering out through narrow slits in their visors. The era of those warriors ended, and it ended badly.

1.2.2 The New Model: Essentially Entrepreneurial

Meanwhile, entrepreneurial firms thrive in a world of fast-moving change. Since they tend to be organized and managed on principles and practices that in many cases are the opposite of those described for large bureaucratic firms, they have already accomplished many of the "moon shots" that Hamel's team proposed. For instance, they have "limited the pathologies of formal hierarchy" and have flatter and more fungible structures that are easier to reconfigure.[15]

---

[13] In addition, when the choice to replace Symbian finally came in early 2011, it was to a Windows-based system instead of Android. In connection with the launch of the last Symbian-based smartphone, the new Nokia CEO, Stephen Elop (previously with Microsoft) announced that it would be replaced within a year by a smartphone with a Microsoft OS. http://money.cnn.com/ 2011/02/11/technology/nokia_microsoft/ (Accessed 5 August 2015).

In 2010 Symbian held 37.6% of the smartphone market, down from 46.9% in 2009. http://www.gartner.com/newsroom/id/1543014 (Accessed 5 August 2015).

By 2013 Symbian had disappeared from the statistics and Microsoft OS had 3.2% of the smartphone market, while Android had 78.4% (up from 22.7% in 2010 and 3.9% in 2009) http://www.gartner.com/newsroom/id/2665715 (Accessed 5 August 2015).

[14] Gratton (2013) http://lyndagrattonfutureofwork.typepad.com/lynda-gratton-future-of-work/2013/10/index.html

[15] Hamel (2009), p. 93.

Importantly, they also attract entrepreneurs into the fold—the highly skilled people who "want to create change." All told, these firms are prepared to behave entrepreneurially in every respect.

1.3 Tales of Two Industries

Pervasive, ongoing change has become a reality for firms of all kinds, not just new entrants in ICT. Let's look at an old and seemingly traditional set of industries—the clothing industries—along with an ICT industry that's more than a century old: telephones and phone service. In each we find that change has increased dramatically, with some firms profiting while others perish.

1.3.1 The Clothing Industries: Textiles, Garments, Shoes, Retail

Textile making was the first industry to be mechanized, in factories of the early 1800s. Later, finished garments and shoes also became mass-produced, and for many years this group of industries settled into a relatively stable configuration. There were far-flung supply chains feeding cotton, wool, and leather into regional manufacturing clusters where myriad firms made shirts, coats, shoes, and other items, selling them through established networks of wholesalers and retailers.

Today, everything is in flux. Upheavals began in the second half of the twentieth century, when the forces of technology and globalization came sweeping in. New synthetic materials emerged to compete with natural fibers. Industry clusters in regions like the eastern U.S. and northern Portugal (a center of contract manufacturing) were devastated as manufacturing shifted to lower-cost parts of the world and kept shifting. Sales channels were disrupted by the internet and by innovations in distribution and retailing.

And through it all, the "people" force grew more volatile, as changing lifestyles impacted market demand. The clothing industries have always had to be very market-sensitive to stay abreast of changing fashions. But now something more profound was happening: People began to want not only new styles but new *kinds* of clothing. Consider one sub-segment, the market for athletic shoes. This was a niche business until the 1970s, when the arcane sport that used to be called distance running suddenly became a booming popular activity for the public. Some companies introduced "running shoes" that were not thin-soled racing flats but a new type with much more cushioning and support. They were a mass-market hit. The firms competed (and still compete) fiercely in technical shoe design—but that was not all.

This trend in the consumer market soon triggered a secondary trend. People found the running shoes so comfortable they were wearing them for casual use. As social standards relaxed, the same happened with athletic clothing. Fashion became a factor. Sales of "athletic" goods for non-athletic purposes soared, with many of the goods designed and marketed explicitly on a fashion-and-comfort basis.

The winners were firms like Adidas and Nike that exploited the shifting trends by innovating *on many fronts at once*—diversification, multi-pronged design and marketing, reorganization of supply chains and corporate units, and retailing. (Both firms have their own branded retail stores.) Meanwhile, one big loser was the U.S. firm Converse. Up to the 1970s, Converse utterly dominated the basketball-shoe niche and competed strongly in tennis with its distinctive canvas and rubber shoes. The company had even seized on the idea of selling the shoes for everyday wear. But by staying with its traditional designs and business methods while others raced past it, Converse went bankrupt in 2001.[16]

While Adidas and Nike were winners in the more "traditional" clothing industry, an unexpected new winner was W.L. Gore. This company started as a maker of polymer-covered cables for electronics. After discovering that its polymer could be tweaked to produce a waterproof fabric, Gore shifted gears and turned Gore-Tex into its largest revenue stream. Another unexpected winner was Petratex, a contract manufacturer in Portugal. Petratex developed unique processes for bonding pieces of a garment together without bulky sewn seams—and rose to prominence, in part, by using its processes to make the advanced low-friction swimsuits worn in the 2008 Olympics.

These two "unexpected" winners are of interest for us as their success stories were not all about technology breakthroughs, but about their entrepreneurial corporate cultures and organizational structure.

Gore's "lattice" organization is a flexible structure that does not rely on chains of command but allows teams of people to organize around new projects and leaders. The company regularly shows up on lists of best places to work—which attracts good entrepreneurial people, who then are enabled to keep improving and diversifying Gore's products and searching for new markets.[17]

Petratex, a newer and smaller firm, also went with a remarkably non-hierarchical organization. As a Portuguese business magazine[18] observed in 2013:

> All major decisions are discussed in a group, and are often taken in a plenary session … Even management decisions, such as the expansion of premises [and] the definition of annual objectives … are usually subject to collective analysis.

The article noted that the CEO even had a personal policy of not being photographed: "I don't want to be recognized. I want everyone to know the company and the quality of those who work there," the CEO said. He further spoke of recruiting top-notch people who are risk-takers, not security-seekers, since the company keeps developing new processes and seeking unusual new market applications. For one client, Petratex made a high-tech undershirt with embedded microsensors and transmitters. Worn by medical outpatients, the shirt monitored their bodily functions and

---

[16] See for example Dukcevich (2001). Converse was later acquired by Nike and Converse-branded shoes are still sold, as of 2015.

[17] Nicholls-Nixon (2005).

[18] Pinto (2013) http://upmagazine-tap.com/en/pt_artigos/petratex-the-dream-factory/ (Accessed 29 June 2015).

1.3 Tales of Two Industries

could signal for aid. Petratex has done other advanced work for a global client base. The company's long-term vision, which the employees regularly reaffirm, was stated simply by the CEO as: "We want to transform the textile industry." And its philosophies reflect the principles we are discussing. In fact, the one just mentioned happens to fit the *first* item on Gary Hamel's Moon Shot list:

Ensure that the work of management serves a higher purpose.
Most companies strive to maximize shareholder wealth—a goal that is inadequate in many respects. As an emotional catalyst, wealth maximization lacks the power to fully mobilize human energies ... tomorrow's management practices must focus on the achievement of socially significant and noble[19] goals.[20]

These examples from textile-making show that even in industries outside the ICT sector,[21] definite earmarks of a new management model are emerging amid changing times.

1.3.2 Telephones and Phone Services

Here is an industry area where the pace and nature of change is vastly greater than in the past. Let's compare telephony's first 50 years with recent decades.

Commercially viable telephone technology was developed in the mid-to-late 1870s and moved swiftly to market: the first telephone exchange in Stockholm opened in 1880. There followed a period of feverish expansion in many countries, with thousands of startup companies (as many as 6000 in the U.S. alone, at one point) making or buying telephone equipment, stringing lines, and setting up service.

And yet 50 years after invention—in the mid-to-late 1920s—penetration of telephone service was still quite low in many places. In 1926, Stockholm had 28 phones per 100 people,[22] while London and Brussels had only 6 per 100.[23] Moreover, by the

---

[19] Noble goals are important in Japanese culture as well—and this point was strongly introduced by Percy Barnevik of ABB when he was seen as one of the world's thought leaders.

[20] Hamel (2009), p. 92.

[21] It can even be argued that the textile industry often leads the development when new management models emerge. Examples include the use of outsourcing, a focus on design and distribution, and the "shop-in-shop" concept that Apple later adopted in its industry.

[22] A major reason why the diffusion in Stockholm was almost five times the one in other major cities was the business strategy of the leading actors. While Lars Magnus Ericsson in Sweden viewed the telephone as something for broader groups and focused on a low-price strategy, Alexander Graham Bell, the innovator in the US, initially viewed the market in a considerably more limited way and used a high pricing strategy. The telephone was introduced by Bell in 1876 and already in 1885 Stockholm was the place in the world with most telephones: "SAT's business philosophy resulted in Stockholm having more telephones in 1885 than anywhere else in the world, both per head and in absolute figures. There were 4832 telephones in Stockholm, 4248 in Berlin, 4193 in London, 4054 in Paris and 3700 in New York." (Karlsson & Lugn, n.d.).

[23] These statistics are from Huurdeman (2003).

1950s, when finally just about every home and business had a phone, the service provided to the user had changed only in some respects: it was possible to dial most calls, rather than connect through an operator, and there were pay-phones in public places.

Now contrast that with the development and spread of mobile phones. The networks came first, to serve car phones weighing almost 40 kg. The first truly portable mobile phone—one you could carry in a briefcase—was Motorola's DynaTAC, weighing about a kilogram. It came to market in 1984 at a price of nearly US$4000.

By that time, improved networks were being built out, too (with Sweden and the other Nordic countries again leading). So, starting in the mid-1980s, a combination of a "portable" handheld phone and decent cell networks were available for the first time. And look at the state of affairs in 2015, only about 30 years later:

- Mobile phones are pocket-sized and very affordable.
- Penetration has been staggering. As of 2013, there was nearly one mobile phone for every person *in the world*—6.8 billion connections worldwide, or 97 per 100. Burkina Faso, a less-developed country, had more than 50 per 100.[24]
- The phones do more than provide a talking connection, and an ever-growing portion have been smartphones, which do much more.

This all occurred when multiple forces of change converged. The component technologies advanced by leaps and bounds. In many places, societal decisions like the deregulation of telecom or the breaking of monopolies opened the door to business advances. People in developing societies and elsewhere moved up the economic ladder (or the costs came down to their level), and they wanted phones. The product that's now considered the market standard, the smartphone, is a boundary-crossing development. It can be viewed as a handheld, connected computer as well as a phone. By channeling so many user services and activities through a single device—taking photos, playing videos and music, accessing the web, etc., etc.—it becomes both a must-have convenience and massive revenue source.

And two big winners in smartphones are firms that did not start out in any aspect of the telephone business. They are entrepreneurial firms that ventured across boundaries. One is Apple, with its iPhone and operating system linked to the iTunes and App Store platforms—highly networked systems for bringing in content and application services created by others. The other is Google [now part of Alphabet] with its Android operating system and galaxy of related online services.

1.3.3 What Can We Learn?

The pertinent question is: *What can the successes of these two companies show us about how to manage entrepreneurially in a fast-changing environment?* At present

---

[24] Global figures: UTI, Wikipedia (2015). Burkina Faso figures, Central Intelligence Agency (2013).

we'll mention just a few key points drawn from this example; they are points that will come up repeatedly and be illustrated further in the chapters ahead.

One message is that *entrepreneurial firms have big and expansive visions, not limiting visions, of what their business is*. Google's mission statement is "to organize the world's information and make it universally accessible and useful." The statement fits the company's original search business, and pursuit of this mission also led naturally to the smartphone platform, which brings search capability, Google Maps, and other services to the mobile user. All are forms of using IT to organize and deliver useful information.

Another takeaway is that these firms have *open, networked approaches to innovation*. They are able to extend their reach by making use of ideas and innovations from outside the company. Apple, through its App Store, became a primary market-maker for external developers writing new applications that run on Apple devices, while iTunes created a major market for external content creators. When both are bundled with the iPhone, they form an attractive user package that has won many new customers for Apple. Google gets similar benefits from outside developers writing applications for its Android-based devices—and its widely popular "in-house" application Google Maps was, in fact, developed largely by acquiring technology and talent from outside.[25]

Finally, although both Apple and Google had grown quite large before entering the mobile phone market, each of these big firms displayed *the flexibility and initiative of a startup* by moving into a new line of business. During an interview in 2010, Steve Jobs emphasized the importance of maintaining "startup" characteristics:

> You know how many committees we have at Apple? Zero … We are organized like a startup. One person's in charge of iPhone OS software. One person's in charge of Mac hardware … It's organized like a startup. We're the biggest startup on the planet. And we all meet for three hours once a week and we talk about everything we're doing …[26]

Jobs went on to credit Apple's dynamism to "teamwork throughout the company," with a large number of autonomous teams all "trusting the other folks to come through." He added: "And that's what we do really well. We're great at figuring out how to divide things up, into these great teams that we have … [and then we] touch bases frequently and bring it all together into a great product."[27]

As we'll see later, many companies in Silicon Valley have flat, flexible structures that consist of *teams organized around a corporate "center"*—as opposed to pyramid-style bureaucratic hierarchies, with divisions under multiple layers of control. Google even launched internal "bureaucracy buster" campaigns to detect and remove inhibiting structures or policies at their onset. Furthermore, having earned

---

[25] A key acquisition was Where 2 Technologies, whose cofounders Jens and Lars Rasmussen joined Google to continue developing their mapping technology, now known as Google Maps. See for instance Greenbaum (2011). http://6thfloor.blogs.nytimes.com/2011/04/18/who-made-googles-map-pin/?_r¼0 (Accessed 6 Aug 2015).

[26] Jobs (2010) https://www.youtube.com/watch?v¼f60dheI4ARg (Accessed 14 July 2015).

[27] Ibid.

huge revenues from its AdWords program—the company's initial chief source of income—Google invested heavily in recruiting entrepreneurial talent and in developing new businesses other than internet search. All of these steps demonstrate a *commitment to remaining entrepreneurial* and innovative, in every aspect of management from organizational structure to recruiting and investments.[28]

1.4 The High Road Versus the Missed Turn: Comparing New and Old Management Models

We round out this overview tour of the new economy by introducing our case companies, all entrepreneurial firms that kept advancing and innovating. The chapter then concludes with a cautionary tale—a story of a distinguished company, with a long history of innovation, which nonetheless missed a crucial opportunity by being caught up in its existing culture and business models.

1.4.1 Finding the High Road: The Entrepreneurial Path

There is no single way to build an entrepreneurial company. The modern business environment is far too complex and unpredictable for there to be any one "secret" to success. However, just a brief review of our Silicon Valley firms shows that they were managed by fundamental principles that were indeed polar-opposite to those of many traditional companies. Since we have just heard a good bit about Google, let's visit the rest, starting with the three personal-networking firms.

Facebook [now Meta] Anyone who has studied or worked in this company knows Mark Zuckerberg's early mantra: He told people to "Move fast and break things." The idea was to be proactive. It was also to have an environment where people are not afraid to practice the entrepreneurial art of creative destruction, by "breaking" some aspect of the Facebook web platform or business model and replacing it with a better.

On new projects, extreme speed was emphasized. But this did not mean that people were seen as mere cogs in a machine, to be put into slots and pushed solely for quick returns. Facebook showed remarkable patience and flexibility with new hires. In some cases, after being on board for a time, people were even encouraged to switch to new roles that would make better use of their abilities: a man recruited as an attorney moved into product development (and flourished); an accountant became an in-house coach and trainer.[29]

---

[28] Later chapters will explore these and other aspects of Google's management in more detail.
[29] Albergotti (2014) http://www.wsj.com/articles/facebooks-millennials-arent-entitled-they-are-empowered-1419537468 (Accessed 6 Aug 2015).

1.4 The High Road Versus the Missed Turn: Comparing New and Old Management...   13

LinkedIn At this firm, the former CEO Jeff Weiner had a management mantra of his own: "Next play!" He told the *New York Times*[30] he learned it from a successful basketball coach. According to Weiner, every time the fast-moving flow of the game changes direction—whether his players have done something brilliant or made a dreadful error—this coach "yells out 'next play,' because he doesn't want the team lingering too long on what just took place."

Weiner also commented on what he perceived as "the difference between leading and managing. Managers will tell people what to do, whereas leaders will inspire them to do it." This is a theme we'll return to later, since most entrepreneurs do *not* respond well to orders based on formal authority, but they do respond to inspiration and guidance.

Twitter [now X] Here, former CEO Dick Costolo was known for cultivating an atmosphere of competing views. He told a reporter[31] that when he arrived at the firm, there seemed to be too much emphasis on preserving group harmony. So, Costolo instructed his management team: *"You have an obligation to vocally dissent in a meeting if you disagree with what we're discussing."*[32]

Costolo also noted that being open to ideas from outside the firm does not mean mindlessly applying them. Twitter sometimes recruited people from Google, and Costolo said that when one of these introduced an idea by saying "At Google we…", he promptly reminded the person that "This isn't Google"—that is, the companies' resources are vastly different.[33] The larger point is that it's important to think carefully and entrepreneurially about the situation that one is currently in, instead of automatically jumping to thoughts of what has worked elsewhere or in the past. That point is brought home dramatically by the auto company in our study.

Tesla In 2014, after years of rolling out radically new electric cars, Tesla took the unorthodox step of opening its patent portfolio. CEO Elon Musk explained the firm knew that "Our true competition is not the small trickle of non-Tesla electric cars being produced, but rather the enormous flood of gasoline cars pouring out

---

[30] All of the following about LinkedIn is from Bryant (2012).
[31] This material about Twitter is from Costolo's remarks as reported in Gray (2012) 7 Leadership lessons from a mind-meld between Twitter's Dick Costolo and Venture Guru Ben Horowitz http://www.fastcompany.com/3002875/7-leadership-lessons-mind-meld-between-twitters-dick-costolo-and-venture-guru-ben-horowitz (Accessed 6 August 6 2015).
[32] This is almost identical to former Motorola CEO Bob Galvin's attempts to make Motorola people more aware of the risks of group thinking and the importance of counter-intuitive thinking, referring to an abridged version of Alex Osborn's 1991 book *Your Creative Power.*
[33] http://www.fastcompany.com/3002875/7-leadership-lessons-mind-meld-between-twitters-dick-costolo-and-venture-guru-ben-horowitz (Accessed 6 August 2015).

of the world's factories every day."³⁴ The patents were being shared to speed the development and acceptance of electric vehicles generally.

There are factors indicating that Tesla's move was well considered and made at the right time. The firm's prospects were indeed tied to the overall prospects for the industry; Tesla had by that point established itself as a going concern; and, with so many forces of change at work, the window of opportunity for its electric cars might not have stayed open indefinitely.

Tesla sought industry leadership going forward, Musk said, not by patenting—but "by the ability … to attract and motivate the world's most talented engineers."³⁵

Apigee [now acquired and absorbed by Google] This fast-growing IT firm provided an intelligent API platform and related services to corporate clients. The purposes were to help the client companies to do digital business faster, use their enterprise data more effectively, and give their own customers and working teams a more "connected" experience. For Apigee, the challenge was to constantly evolve the platform while adding new services that could vary widely. (For instance, Apigee offered predictive analytics, a very sophisticated service, which involves monitoring patterns of visitor traffic on the web—and it also provided clients with basic education on APIs).

To sustain such an open-ended business, Apigee had a very flat and flexible management style. Employees had no fixed schedules or rules about where they should work; most did not have closely defined job titles. There was an emphasis on recruiting highly skilled, self-motivated people and giving them room to run, with little top-down direction. Employee reviews on the public website *Glassdoor* described Apigee as a "hugely stimulating" work environment with "amazing learning opportunities" and "high employee energy and engagement." It was also described as "a company where people work on the projects they want to work on, and contribute in the manner that best fits them … There is a real effort to eliminate silos, titles, and hierarchy."³⁶

---

[34] Musk announced the move in a brief document famously titled "All Our Patent Are Belong To You": see Musk (2014). The title uses bad English grammar but apparently was written that way on purpose, as a humorous reference to a poorly translated line from an old video game which had become a running joke on the Internet: see Dubs (2009). http://knowyourmeme.com/memes/all-your-base-are-belong-to-us (Accessed 30 July 2015).

[35] Musk (2014) http://www.teslamotors.com/blog/all-our-patent-are-belong-you (Accessed 6 August 2015).

[36] Glassdoor (2015) http://www.glassdoor.com/Reviews/Apigee-Reviews-E421770.htm (Accessed 30 July 2015).

1.4.2 Missing the Turn: The Case of Kodak

We now conclude this chapter with an unhappy story—the decline of Kodak, a distinguished company with a long history of innovation, which nonetheless missed a crucial opportunity by being caught up in its existing culture and business models. For many years, Kodak[37] was the global leader in photographic films. It also led the U.S. market for cameras and was very strong in developing new products and technologies. The first modern digital camera was invented at Kodak in the 1970s, with more advances (such as in digital image sensing) soon to follow. But incredibly, for decades, the firm kept these digital inventions on the back burner, out of concern they would distract from and compete with the core business in film.

Finally, with film sales declining and the world going digital, Kodak in the early 2000s brought its own digital cameras to market. They won good reviews and quickly became the top sellers in the U.S. but could not provide the net cash flow the company now urgently needed. By that time the digital technology was being commoditized, everyone's cameras were getting cheaper and better, and Kodak had to keep prices low to compete—at one point, the firm was actually *losing* money on every camera sold.

Antonio Perez, named CEO in 2005 and charged with turning Kodak around,[38] knew the task would be immense. As *Business Week* observed a year later:

> In an era when innovation is all the rage, many CEOs, like Perez, are discovering that product innovation alone isn't enough to save sick companies or turbocharge healthy ones. For many, their core businesses are being disrupted ...*They must reinvent the company.*[39]

At Kodak, that would entail re-inventing the firm's culture. *Business Week* again:

---

[37] Kodak is, together with GE and DuPont, one of the companies that defined the modern large corporation in the US, having been a pioneer in building research labs. Kodak was the leader in creating mass-market cameras in the early 1900s, recreated this leadership with the Instamatics of the 1960s—and all of this was based on the film technology that was Kodak's backbone.

[38] Kodak's board had, however, taken measures to prepare for the digital age 12 years earlier, by recruiting Motorola's CEO George Fisher in 1993 to lead the company in a new direction. In October 1997 Bloomberg Business asked "Can George Fisher Fix Kodak?" and presented the following analysis of the situation: "But critics say Fisher has been slow to address Kodak's basic internal problems: a corporate culture mired in a mind-set left over from an earlier manufacturing age, and excessive costs. Rather than announcing a new era with tough layoffs 4 years ago and bringing in a new team to oversee the photo business, he decided to minimize cost-cutting in Kodak's traditional film business in the hope that digital revenues would grow enough to support it. Fisher is also dealing with a far more ingrained and bureaucratic culture at Kodak than he ever faced during his days at Motorola. Although he has taken steps to shake things up—such as instituting pay-for-performance standards—the old-line manufacturing culture continues to impede Fisher's efforts to turn Kodak into a high-tech growth company. 'Fisher has been able to change the culture at the very top,' says one industry executive. 'But he hasn't been able to change the huge mass of middle managers, and they just don't understand this [digital] world.'"

[39] Hamm and Symonds (2006). The following quotation and narrative are from the same article. http://www.bloomberg.com/bw/stories/2006-11-26/mistakes-made-on-the-road-to-innovation (Accessed 6 August 2015).

> ... it remains difficult to change Kodak's long-established ways. One of them is a hierarchical culture that believes in the omnipotence of leadership. It's so powerful a habit that when Perez came to Kodak from HP in 2003 as chief operating officer, he couldn't get people to openly disagree with him. "If I said it was raining, nobody would argue with me, even if it was sunny outside," he laments.

Kodak tried drastic measures. Longtime executives were let go and new ones brought in. New focus areas and target markets were defined. But once again, the moves came too late. Kodak declared bankruptcy in 2012, selling off many businesses. As of 2016 the much-reduced firm was seeking a foothold in specialty markets related to imaging and printing. That may well be a path to revival—but it's better to find the right road before going so far off course.

As the Kodak case shows, even companies that have been renowned technology innovators and industry leaders can stumble. Kodak's culture was so ingrained with its previous successes based on film technology that although the company had world-class competence in emerging digital technologies, the *entrepreneurial capability* to bring these to market was not sufficient.

1.5 Recent Developments

Since the first edition of our book in 2016, the forces of change affecting management have grown. This section highlights and discusses three key areas: the expansion of new management models along lines practiced by our case companies, the impacts of artificial intelligence, and the increasing imperatives for sustainability.

1.5.1 Acceleration of New Entrepreneurial Models

New forms of entrepreneurial management have been taking hold in companies worldwide during recent years. The expansion is happening across a range of industries. See Chap. 10 of this book for a review of how several major firms are adopting entrepreneurial management models. The firms include Haier, the global appliance maker and smart-home provider based in China, and Haier's U.S. acquisition, GE Appliances, plus Fujitsu Western Europe (active in cloud computing and networks), Germany's Bosch Power Tools, and U.S.-based Fidelity Investments. As Chap. 10 will show, these developments reflect a growing recognition of the need to manage more innovatively and proactively in fast-changing markets.

At the same time, many companies have stayed with top-down, bureaucratic management models—even while researchers and consultants cite additional reasons why change is both necessary and inevitable. This has created intensive discussions among both researchers and practitioners on how to define the new management models, and the reasons why a transformation to a new model is so hard for many companies in more traditional industries. One possible explanation is that complexity increases as the business environment evolves and management evolves along

1.5   Recent Developments   17

with it, and therefore the gap between the traditional model and the "new" seems to constantly increase over time. For example, Steve Denning pointed out that Gary Hamel's Moonshots for Management conference of 2008 missed several trends that were already starting to transform management at the time and have become major drivers of change since then.[40] One key trend, according to Denning, is the growing "significance of digital technology" and how it affects every aspect of a company's operation.[41] (This too will be addressed further in Chap. 10.) In recent years, artificial intelligence has emerged as a particularly potent form of digital technology. Therefore, its role as a driver of change deserves a closer look.

1.5.2   Management in an AI World

Artificial intelligence is not an entirely new phenomenon of the 2020s. Various forms of AI have been used increasingly over the years, in applications from marketing algorithms to speech recognition and synthesis.[42] What has happened in the early 2020s is a surge of investments in new, more advanced forms of generative AI. By combing huge datasets on the internet, these AIs can detect and "learn" patterns of behavior that allow them to generate original text, images, and computer code, as well as suggesting decisions and answers to complex problems.[43]

These new AIs thus begin to have significant powers and can also be deployed by companies in at least three different ways.

1. AI can be embedded in products and services offered to customers. Just two examples: Google in 2023 was working to merge generative AI into its online product suites, so that users could insert AI-generated text and graphics directly into documents like Gmail or Google Docs.[44] And several "deep tech" startups, such as MX Labs in Poland and Binah.ai of Israel, have developed health-and-wellness software that can read a person's vital signs and even detect levels of mental stress simply by analyzing a facial image from a smartphone camera.[45] A vast array of other applications is either possible or in development, typically combining new AI with existing technologies. These applications may come to market in a variety of ways: as standalone products, as features integrated into physical products such as smart appliances and wearables, or as back-end tools for internal use within a company.
2. AI can assist or replace human workers. Due to its ability to write code, analyze data, and compile reports, AI can either serve as a powerful aid to these functions or as a form of automation that eliminates the need for human input. And even

---

[40] Denning (2023).
[41] Ibid.
[42] Fattal (2023).
[43] McKinsey (2023).
[44] Grant (2023).
[45] See for example Binah.ai (2023).

when AI serves as an aid, the resulting efficiency gains can reduce the amount of staffing required. Many observers noted that the staff cuts in Silicon Valley during 2022–23 may in some cases become essentially permanent, with AI obviating the need to bring back as many skilled workers as were terminated.[46] For example, the firm Dropbox laid off 500 workers, attributing the move in part to AI.[47] And some have speculated that "AI could spell the end of big business," because "The leading companies in artificial intelligence tend to be small, and many big ones will use it to get smaller."[48]

3. AI can be used internally in the management of the company. In a 2019 paper summarizing research on the topic, the scholar Martin Petrin noted two big steps looming ahead. He wrote first that "the step from AI generating and suggesting expert decisions for managers (which in some areas is already common today) to AI making these decisions autonomously is hardly insurmountable."[49] The author further noted that managerial tasks can be divided into two broad categories: administrative work, such as scheduling and reporting; and judgment work, which requires "creative, analytic, and strategic skills"—with the latter including cases where "the information available is insufficient … to suggest an obvious best course of action." Also, judgment work includes interacting with other humans, in areas from making hiring decisions to leadership skills such as coaching and persuasion.[50]

One widely held view is that AI will take over administrative work, freeing up human managers to focus on judgment work. The labor-and-technology scholar Louis Hyman predicts that "embracing everyday automation" at all levels will give a company "a competitive edge" and make it "more profitable in the long run," because people will then be able to devote themselves to "more complicated, more rewarding, more human work."[51] Yet as Petrin's paper noted several years previously, some AI experts are confident "that machines will eventually exceed human capabilities in areas requiring 'soft skills.'"[52]

For the near term, at least, "algorithmic management" via AI will continue being used mainly to complement and enhance human management.[53] However, as uses of AI expand and grow more sophisticated, they will change the playing field: "[T]he introduction of algorithms into management functions has the potential to alter power dynamics within organizations, and ethical challenges must be addressed."[54]

---

[46] Turner (2023).
[47] Khare (2023).
[48] Cowen (2023).
[49] Petrin (2019).
[50] Ibid.
[51] Hyman (2023).
[52] Petrin (2019).
[53] See for example Jarrahi et al. (2023).
[54] Ibid.

1.5.3 Management in a Sustainable World

The movement toward environmentally sustainable products and business practices has been increasing. Motivating factors include the ongoing, record-level rise of carbon dioxide concentration in the atmosphere,[55] a corresponding rise in climate-related natural disasters,[56] and local factors such as the Ukraine war that have curtailed supplies of fossil fuels. Therefore, regulatory responses are increasing as well. The European Union has passed regulations mandating that by 2035, all new cars sold in the EU must be zero-emission vehicles, while several states within the U.S. have set similar standards.[57] Laws and regulations related to other aspects of sustainability are proliferating, too. Together they mark out new directions that companies are required to follow.

At the same time, there are voices suggesting that this approach is misguided. Richard Straub, president of the Global Peter Drucker Forum, argued the case eloquently in a 2023 essay. He began by invoking Drucker's precept that corporations "should nurture the long-term capacity of the firm to create value for society"—doing good while also remaining profitable, ideally in entrepreneurial and innovative ways. Straub then emphasized an inherent paradox in the regulatory approach. It is that governments are trying to get companies to achieve sustainability goals by applying outdated, top-down management 1.0 measures:

> What we have seen growing in the last decades is a culture of mistrust toward business, fanned by media and ideological groups, when it comes to sustainability. The temptation to micromanage the behaviour of business and others has led to the creation of a bureaucratic 'compliance industry' whose purpose is to police implementation. The European Commission's Corporate Sustainability Reporting Directive is a striking example of this problematic mindset.
>
> Yet if we want to achieve progress toward a more sustainable world we must move beyond the obsolete models of command-and-control management, with its focus on interdiction, precaution and coercive approaches. We must finally abandon the illusion that we can achieve our noble ends—i.e., creating the material conditions for dignified lives without destroying our natural environment—with ever more detailed micro-regulation and control. It can only be done with the distributed, bottom-up approach, nurturing a true sustainability culture in which the entrepreneurial forces in our societies are incentivized to find novel and unexpected solutions.
>
> The job of the state is then, first, to develop the conditions for entrepreneurship and innovation in economic, social and natural sustainability to thrive; and second, to draw up a legal and regulatory framework setting out positive incentives and clear responsibilities and accountability for actual negative impacts.[58]

Indeed, there are examples of alternative models that work through a more bottom-up, market-responsive approach. Corporate Knights, an independent research and media company devoted to sustainability, publishes annual lists of the world's most

---

[55] Lindsey (2023).
[56] See for example Oxfam (2023).
[57] Hernandez (2023).
[58] Straub (2023).

sustainable companies. The group's research director, Ralph Torrie, pointed out that the firms on the 2023 "Global 100" list have achieved dual goals. By responding to market factors such as rising oil prices, the firms "have stimulated growth in renewables, smart buildings, electric vehicles and other climate solutions, including circular economy measures." And, along with previous years' members of the Global 100, they have outperformed major stock indexes in terms of ROI.[59] Leading firms in the 2023 Global 100 ranged from Schnitzer Steel, a metals recycler, to the wind turbine manufacturer Vestas and the digital energy management company Schneider Electric.

1.5.4 Summarizing Recent Developments

Companies in all industries today face greater demands than ever to manage entrepreneurially. As we have seen, they must compete with other firms adopting new entrepreneurial management models. They must try to capitalize on new forms of digital technology in their products and services, as well as within their workforces and management ranks. And operating sustainably has increasingly become a requirement rather than an option, whether due to regulation or to market forces.

1.6 Moving On

This chapter has examined how and why today's economy is fundamentally different from that of the past. We've argued that conventional management approaches fail in this time of rapid, pervasive change, and have seen some characteristics of what a new and better model consists of. This new model seems to be geared to being adaptable, proactive, open, and fast; it revolves around attracting skilled entrepreneurs and employing them in ways such that the whole company behaves entrepreneurially.

In the next chapter, we'll dig deeper into six basic principles for long-term competitiveness followed by progressive, competitive firms in rapidly changing industries.

References

Albergotti, R. (2014, December 25). At Facebook, boss is a dirty word. *The Wall Street Journal*. http://www.wsj.com/articles/facebooks-millennials-arent-entitled-they-are-empowered-1419537468. Accessed 6 Aug 2015.

Binah.ai. (2023). A unique mix of signal processing and AI technologies. *Company website*. https://www.binah.ai/technology/. Accessed 22 May 2023.

Bryant, A. (2012, November 10). In sports or business, always prepare for the next play. *The New York Times*. http://www.nytimes.com/2012/11/11/business/jeff-weiner-of-linkedin-on-the-next-play-philosophy.html. Accessed 6 Aug 2015.

---

[59] Scott (2023).

References

Central Intelligence Agency. (2013). *CIA world factbook 2013*. Skyhorse Publishing.
Cowen, T. (2023). AI could spell the end of big business. *Bloomberg*, 26 April 2023. https://www.bloomberg.com/opinion/articles/2023-04-26/ai-could-spell-the-end-of-big-business
Denning, S. (2023). Five key lessons from the 2008 'Moonshots for Management.' Forbes.com, 2 April 2023. https://www.forbes.com/sites/stevedenning/2023/04/02/five-key-lessons-from-the-2008-moonshots-for-management/?sh=33a91b7d41e5
Dubs, J. (2009). All your base are belong to us. Posted on *Know Your Meme* at: http://knowyourmeme.com/memes/all-your-base-are-belong-to-us. Accessed 30 July 2015.
Dukcevich, D. (2001, January 22). Converse loses its footing. *Forbes*. http://www.forbes.com/2001/01/22/0122converse.html. Accessed 29 June 2015.
Fattal, I. (2023). Hiding behind the AI apocalypse. *The Atlantic*, 17 May 2023. https://www.theatlantic.com/newsletters/archive/2023/05/altman-hearing-ai-existential-risk/674096/
Fitzgerald, E., & Wankerl, A. (2010). *Inside real innovation*. World Scientific Publishing.
Florida, R. (2002). *The rise of the creative class*. Basic Books.
Glassdoor. (2015). Apigee reviews at: http://www.glassdoor.com/Reviews/Apigee-Reviews-E421770.htm. Accessed 30 July 2015.
Grant, N. (2023). Google builds on tech's latest craze with its own A.I. products. *The New York Times*, 10 May 2023. https://www.nytimes.com/2023/05/10/technology/google-ai-products.html
Gratton, L. (2011). *The shift: The future of work is already here*. HarperCollins UK.
Gratton, L. (2013, October 22). Leading in complex times. *On her FoWLAB Blog*. http://lyndagrattonfutureofwork.typepad.com/lynda-gratton-future-of-work/2013/10/index.html. Accessed 29 June 2015.
Gray, T. (2012, November 9). 7 leadership lessons from a mind-meld between Twitter's Dick Costolo and venture guru Ben Horowitz. *Fast Company*. http://www.fastcompany.com/3002875/7-leadership-lessons-mind-meld-between-twitters-dick-costolo-and-venture-guru-ben-horowitz. Accessed 29 June 2015.
Greenbaum, H. (2011, April 18). Who made Google's map pin? *The New York Times* 6th Floor Blog. http://6thfloor.blogs.nytimes.com/2011/04/18/who-made-googles-map-pin/?_r¼0. Accessed 6 Aug 2015.
Hamel, G. (2009). Moon shots for management. *Harvard Business Review, 87*(2), 91–99.
Hamel, G. (2012). *What matters now*. Jossey-Bass.
Hamm, S., & Symonds, W. C. (2006, November 26). Mistakes made on the road to innovation. *Bloomberg Businessweek*. http://www.bloomberg.com/bw/stories/2006-11-26/mistakes-made-on-the-road-to-innovation. Retrieved 29 June 2015.
Hernandez, J. (2023). All new cars in the EU will be zero-emission by 2035. Here's where the U.S. stands. NPR (U.S. National Public Radio), 30 March 2023. https://www.npr.org/2023/03/30/1166921698/eu-zero-emission-cars
Huurdeman, A. A. (2003). *The worldwide history of telecommunications*. Wiley.
Hyman, L. (2023). It's not the end of work. It's the end of boring work. *The New York Times*, 22 April 2023. https://www.nytimes.com/2023/04/22/opinion/jobs-ai-chatgpt.html
Jarrahi, M. H., Möhlmann, M., & Lee, M. K. (2023). Algorithmic management: The role of AI in managing workforces. *MIT Sloan Management Review, 64*(3), 1–5.
Jobs, S. (2010). Video excerpt from interview at the D-8 summit in Nigeria. Posted at: https://www.youtube.com/watch?v¼f60dheI4ARg. Accessed 14 July 2015.
Karlsson, S., & Lugn, A. (n.d.). Competition. Posted in the history of Ericsson at: http://www.ericssonhistory.com/changing-the-world/phones-for-everyone/Competition/. Accessed 12 July 2015.
Khare, Y. (2023). Dropbox lays off 500 employees as an effect of artificial intelligence. *Analytics Vidhya*, 1 May 2023. https://www.analyticsvidhya.com/blog/2023/05/dropbox-lays-off-500-employees-as-an-effect-of-artificial-intelligence/?utm_medium=email&utm_source=rasa_io&utm_campaign=newsletter
Lindsey, R. (2023). Climate change: Atmospheric carbon dioxide. U.S. National Oceanic and Atmospheric Administration website, 12 May 2023. https://www.climate.gov/news-features/understanding-climate/climate-change-atmospheric-carbon-dioxide

McKinsey & Company. (2023). What is generative AI? McKinsey website, 19 January 2023. https://www.mckinsey.com/featured-insights/mckinsey-explainers/what-is-generative-ai

Mintzberg, H. (1980). Structure in 5's: A synthesis of the research on organization design. *Management Science, 26*(3), 322–341.

Musk, E. (2014, June 12). All our patent are belong to you. Posted on *Tesla Motors Blog*. http://www.teslamotors.com/blog/all-our-patent-are-belong-you. Accessed 30 July 2015.

Nicholls-Nixon, C. L. (2005). Rapid growth and high performance: The entrepreneur's "impossible dream?". *Academy of Management Executive, 19*(1), 77–89.

Oxfam. (2023). 5 disasters that beg for climate action. *Oxfam International*, 2023. https://www.oxfam.org/en/5-natural-disasters-beg-climate-action

Petrin, M. (2019). Corporate management in the age of AI. *Columbia Business Law Review, 2019*(3), 965–1030.

Pinto, L. (2013, February 1). Petratex – The dream factory. *Up Magazine*. http://upmagazine-tap.com/en/pt_artigos/petratex-the-dream-factory/. Accessed 29 June 2015.

Scott, M. (2023). 100 most sustainable companies of 2023 still flourishing in tumultuous times. *Corporate Knights*, 18 January 2023. https://www.corporateknights.com/rankings/global-100-rankings/2023-global-100-rankings/2023-global-100-most-sustainable-companies/

Straub, R. (2023). Sustainability beyond the hype. Vienna Center for Management Innovation, 9 March 2023. https://www.linkedin.com/pulse/sustainability-beyond-hype-richard-straub/?trackingId=z%2FB48qezSZezk6niNGpLrA%3D%3D

Teece, D. (1996). Firm organization, industrial structure and technological innovation. *Journal of Economic Behavior and Organization, 31*(2), 193–224.

Turner, M. (2023). Tech giants aren't just cutting thousands of jobs – They're making them extinct. *Insider*, 27 April 2023. https://www.businessinsider.com/tech-jobs-arent-coming-back-2023-4

Wikipedia. (2015). List of countries by number of mobile phones in use. Posted at: http://en.wikipedia.org/wiki/List_of_countries_by_number_of_mobile_phones_in_use. Accessed 11 Mar 2015.

Six Basic Principles for a Changing World   2

The journey that led to this book began with an ambitious project conceived by one of us co-authors, Annika Steiber. The goal was to summarize, and synthesize, *the best thinking about what is required for companies to manage a firm successfully in a fast-changing environment.*

A vast amount is written on the subject, by management scholars and others who study companies in rapidly changing industries. Various findings are disseminated through the business media in ever-flowing streams of articles, books, speeches, webcasts, and more. There is so much material on how to keep up with the times that a manager who tried to keep up with all of it would have time for nothing else.

Thus the idea was to see if this great body of knowledge could be distilled into a few basic principles. After much effort, a review of the literature yielded the principles you will read about here. And there is more to the story. To expand on her work, Dr. Steiber conducted a year-long course of empirical research at Google, clearly one of the world's most successful and innovative companies. This confirmed that the principles were in fact applicable there. The principles were published in the book *The Google Model: Managing Continuous Innovation in a Rapidly Changing World* (hereafter referred to as *"The Google Model"*).[1]

As these principles are distilled from a greater body of knowledge, we will describe them briefly in this chapter before digging deeper into Silicon Valley as a cradle of management innovation and the elements of the alternative management model for corporations that we discovered when analyzing our six case companies. Later in Chap. 9, when summing up all findings, we will come back to these principles.

Various clusters of researchers have identified the principles as crucial in explaining how companies succeed in today's rapidly changing environment. In brief, they are:

---

[1] Steiber (2014).

1. *Dynamic capabilities*. These include the ability to sense and shape opportunities and threats, to seize opportunities, and to maintain and reorganize resources as needed.
2. *A continually changing organization.* If you delay taking action until problems arise, you will act too late. The organization should be permeated with a proactive approach to change.
3. *A people-centric approach.* This principle is based on the belief that people want and need to be creative and that a company must provide a setting in which they can exercise their creativity.
4. *An ambidextrous organization.* Entrepreneurial firms combine two different forms of organizational logic to optimize *daily production*, which works best with a conventional planning-and-control approach, and *innovation*, which requires greater freedom, flexibility, and a more open attitude toward experimentation. The firm should not only balance these two forms of logic but utilize the energy inherent in the contrast between them.
5. *An open organization that networks with its surroundings.* A company can be more or less open to integration with its surroundings. While no companies are totally closed systems with distinct borders that separate them from the world beyond, they can have more or less permeable boundaries that affect their ability to exchange information and knowledge with their surroundings. Long-term survival requires that companies develop into more openly networked systems.
6. *A systems approach.* Companies must move from a process perspective to a systems perspective in order to understand and improve their capabilities to continuously innovate. A system is "a collection of components with certain properties with connections among the components and among the properties of those components."[2]

Now for a more in-depth treatment of each. The following sections describe the "why" and "how" of the principles, by summarizing what researchers and others have noted about what they are meant to achieve, and how they are best put into action. It is important to keep in mind that the principles are interdependent. For example the first principle, dynamic capabilities, could be positively influenced by several of the following principles, e.g., a continuously changing organization and an ambidextrous and open organization.

Examples from leading firms are included. Main portions of this discussion are drawn from Dr. Steiber's previous book *The Google Model*.

---

[2] Professor Eric Rhenman, a pioneer in the systems approach, introduced this definition. We prefer to use the term "elements" for Rhenman's system "components" and will do so when discussing the systems concept in Chap. 9.

2.1 Dynamic Capabilities

> In today's environment, success may depend very little on the enterprise's ability to engage in (textbook) optimizations against known constraints, or capturing scale economies in production. Rather, enterprise success depends upon the discovery and development of opportunities ...[3]

So wrote the esteemed management scholar David Teece, in his 2007 paper "Explicating Dynamic Capabilities." To grasp its import, let's step back for a moment to consider how views of the firm have changed.

2.1.1 When 'Core Competencies' Aren't Enough

The key fact is that companies must develop in order to survive. Edith Penrose's[4] growth theory, first expounded in 1959, became the basis of "resource-based theory,"[5] which explains that a company's competitive advantages derive from its resources. Prahalad and Hamel (1990) defined "core competencies" as "the collective learning in the organization" that "provides potential access to a wide variety of markets…[The core competencies] should make a significant contribution to the perceived customer benefits of the end product… [and] should be difficult for competitors to imitate."[6] But it was later discovered that when external changes accelerate, these core competencies can lose value and may even become impediments.[7]

That seemed to be the case with IBM in the early 1990s. The company had dominated the computing age practically from the start, with its mainframe computers—which were so reliable (at a time when computers weren't always reliable), and were so regularly improved and well-serviced, that they became a near-automatic choice for businesses everywhere. Thus the common saying among purchasers: "Nobody ever got fired for buying from IBM."[8] Later, when personal computing came along, the IBM PC, released in 1980, quickly gained a huge share of that emerging market as well. Most PCs were (and still are) sold to businesses, and for the many client companies already relying on IBM mainframe systems, what could be a more logical choice?

Then the ground shifted rapidly beneath this edifice. With the advent of client–server systems plus growing individual use of PCs, mainframe sales dropped.

Meanwhile, PC buyers soon realized that while competing machines did not have the IBM label, most were IBM-*compatible*—and with competition heating up

---

[3] Teece (2007), p. 1320.
[4] Penrose (1959).
[5] Wernefelt (1984).
[6] Prahalad and Hamel (1990), pp. 82–84.
[7] Leonard-Barton (1992).
[8] The saying is still widely quoted. See for example Maycotte (2014). http://www.forbes.com/sites/homaycotte/2014/12/09/your-startup-delimma-nobody-ever-got-fired-for-buying-ibm/ (Accessed 1 Aug 2015).

on the basis of price, PCs were becoming more of a low-margin commodity business. Suddenly IBM's firmly established roost atop the computing markets had turned into a precariously teetering position. With revenues and share price declining, the company implemented the first mass layoffs in its history, and still was left grappling for positive steps back to prosperity.

2.1.2 Dynamic Capabilities: A New Concept of Corporate Resources

At one time, the value-creating resources of major, market-dominating companies retained their value because these firms were largely insulated from external change. Monopolies, licenses, advantages of scale, and government regulations made it difficult for competitors to enter a given market. Many of these obstacles are now gone, and it is therefore more difficult for companies to stay competitive with the same portfolio of core competencies. A more dynamic model is needed.

Companies that succeed on the global market detect and respond to change early. They move quickly to develop new products and/or business models, and they manage to reconfigure internal and external resources accordingly—which may entail modifying, enhancing, or re-directing core competencies. This new source of competitive advantage is what researchers such as Teece[9] have called "dynamic capabilities."

Teece described the capabilities as a matter of knowing "how to position today's resources properly for tomorrow," and said they consist of three kinds of activities—"sensing," "seizing," and "transforming"—which he defined as follows:

- *Sensing* means identifying and assessing opportunities outside your company,
- *Seizing* is mobilizing your resources to capture value from those opportunities, and
- *Transforming* is continued renewal.[10]

IBM rebounded by taking such steps and thereby developing dynamic capabilities. To condense the long story of the firm's revival to a few headlines: Since the days of IBM's crisis there continues to be plenty of opportunity in the corporate IT market. Firms have become more careful about spending on equipment, but they rely on the *uses and applications* of information technology more than ever. And a key paradigm shift for IBM management was seeing that a core competence could be applied in a new way, or at least with a major shift in emphasis. IBM still had hard-to-match competence in understanding and serving the IT needs of business. But it didn't

---

[9] Teece (2007).
[10] Kleiner (2013) http://www.strategy-business.com/article/00225?gko¼d24f3.

2.1 Dynamic Capabilities

have to get massive revenues from embodying that expertise in machinery. The company could thrive by selling the expertise in other forms. Which IBM proceeded to do. It has emphasized the providing of IT "solutions," services, and key software. To help boost competence in these areas it acquired the consulting arm of PricewaterhouseCoopers.[11] IBM still makes some mainframe computers, a type of hardware in which it excels—but the low-margin, increasingly commoditized PC business was sold to Lenovo.[12] Those steps represent a major "mobilizing of resources" to capture shifting opportunities. IBM also created systems for ongoing, continuous renewal. For example, strategic planning was greatly modified. As one white paper described it—a paper co-authored by a former IBM executive and two management scholars—

> [T]he strategy-making process [has moved] from an annual ritual to a continual process, from an emphasis on planning to one on action, from a staff function to one that line managers own, and from a concern with strategy only to a focus on both strategy and execution ...[13]
>
> In the IBM context, strategy is an ongoing, disciplined conversation between general managers and senior executives about the future of the corporation ... the strategy team itself is comprised largely of line managers who spend an 18–30 months stint deepening their strategic skills. These individuals are assigned by IBM's senior executives without the strategy unit's input. This not only broadens the perspective of the strategy group but is a valuable developmental tool for ensuring that the future senior managers of the company have deep strategic skills.[14]

And that, in a nutshell, is one instance of how a leading firm has tried to embed dynamic capabilities in its management.

Dynamic capabilities can be expected to matter differently between companies operating in environments with differing magnitudes and frequencies of change. Depending on the changeability of a market, the capabilities may vary from being detailed and analytical, with stable processes and predictable results, to being simple and experimental with uncertain processes and unpredictable results.[15] Whatever the case, dynamic capabilities should permeate the entire organization. This principle ties together the skills of management at utilizing opportunities, handling threats, and combining and reconfiguring company and shared resources with other special assets. It provides ways to meet new customer needs and enhances the company's ability to develop. In doing so, it also creates long-term value for customers, employees, and investors.

---

[11] See for example Richtmyer (2002).

[12] See for example Spooner (2004) http://www.cnet.com/news/ibm-sells-pc-group-to-lenovo/ (Accessed 6 Aug 2015).

[13] Harreld et al. (2006), pp. 33–34.

[14] Ibid, p. 29.

[15] Brown and Eisenhardt (1997).

2.2 A Continually Changing Organization

Companies in rapidly changing environments need to continually and proactively change their organization.[16] It is not enough to change things when the need arises, as with an emergency restructuring. The business must have ongoing, proactive processes of change.

In their book *Competing on the Edge*,[17] Shona Brown and Kathleen Eisenhardt described three levels of change a company should be engaged in: *reacting, anticipating,* and *leading*. Anticipating, the level above reacting, involves more than detecting early signs of change in the business environment. It includes preparing for the future by marshaling resources and creating strategic options. Leading is taking steps that "force other firms to follow," as the authors put it. This can include steps such as: developing new technologies or products, creating new markets, raising industry standards, or redefining customer expectations.

Brown and Eisenhardt cited Intel as a firm that operates on all three levels. For example, we now know—in retrospect—that the 1990s brought the start of a new epoch in computing. The Internet became a public communications channel, thanks to the then-new World Wide Web technologies, while advances in computer graphics and processing power would soon turn the PC into a versatile multimedia device. At first, it was by no means clear how these trends would play out, but Intel's managers moved swiftly to prepare:

> In the early 1990s, they launched anticipatory alliances with telecommunications, cable, and movie companies. These alliances included the development of an Internet server with MCI and the launch of a media lab with the Hollywood powerhouse Creative Artists Agency (CAA). In addition, Intel executives quietly invested more than half a billion dollars in more than fifty media, Internet, and graphics companies.[18]

Intel Capital, the firm's venture investment arm, was used to plant seeds of change and growth. Here was a chipmaker investing in companies that were developing new uses for chips. (Which is also an example of Principle 5, being "An Open Organization That Networks With Its Surroundings.")

2.2.1 Some Practices Allowing Continual Change

Brown and Eisenhardt also noted that some companies drive themselves to lead change by an approach the authors call *time pacing*. This means changing not because external events demand it, but simply because time is passing and leaders must always be doing something new.[19] Some companies set time-paced revenue targets, such as "X percent of our revenues each year should come from new

---

[16] Ibid.
[17] Brown and Eisenhardt (1998a).
[18] Ibid, p. 6.
[19] Brown and Eisenhardt (1998b).

products introduced in the past N years." (3M and Gillette are among the firms that have done this.)

Change happens in the borderlands between order and chaos.[20] The challenge for companies is not to be locked into too much orderliness, but at the same time not to become too chaotic. One solution is the complex, uncontrollable but nevertheless adjustable process called *self-organization*, which arises where structures are not so inflexible as to impede change. If everyone knows what the objective is, and if the structure so allows, individuals—working alone and in groups—can decide how to act in light of what happens.

A firm that seems to have struck this balance is Morning Star, a California-based food processing company with several hundred employees. Not only do the employees form self-organizing teams, they self-organize the terms of their working relationships by negotiating yearly contracts to provide specified services to one another, or to the firm as a whole. They even form self-organized hierarchies, wherein someone who has shown particular skills becomes recognized as an "authority" in that area (i.e., not with the power to give orders, but as an expert whose views are influential).[21]

For an article in *Harvard Business Review,* Gary Hamel interviewed Morning Star's founder and CEO, Chris Rufel, who explained his management philosophy with a metaphor:

> Clouds form and then go away because atmospheric conditions, temperatures, and humidity cause molecules of water to either condense or vaporize… Organizations should be the same; structures need to appear and disappear based on the forces that are acting on the organization. When people are free to act, they're able to sense those forces and act in ways that fit best with reality.[22]

Indeed, in a centrally governed organization where specific directives are given, problems arise when reality fails to unfold according to the data on which the management decisions were based. One crucial decision for management is thus distinguishing between what needs to be firmly laid down and what should be left open for employees to decide in light of the prevailing factors. The border between order and chaos provides two opportunities:[23]

First is *freedom to improvise*. Once management and employees agree on clear objectives, priorities, and guidelines, people can find new solutions while consistently delivering excellent products at the right time within budgetary constraints. This *planned improvisation* is based on three conditions:

- A learning culture in which everyone can adapt operations when conditions change

---

[20] Brown and Eisenhardt (1997).
[21] Hamel (2011).
[22] Ibid, p. 57.
[23] Brown and Eisenhardt (1997).

- A semi-structured organization in which deliverables, times, and priorities are monitored
- Efficient communication, so that information is accessible to everyone who needs it when they need it

The second opportunity is taking advantage of synergy effects by striving for cooperation with other units in the company.

In changing environments, one must consider *different time horizons simultaneously*: history, the present, and the future.[24] Being conscious of the entire time axis without getting locked into any one horizon is important. Time-axis thinking has two perspectives:

- Examination of past experiences (experience recycling) in order to find lessons that can be of value for the future
- Experimentation, to find various ways of obtaining knowledge and facilitating flexibility at a reasonable cost. Identifying alternative solutions and facilitating learning are important.

Finally, many events are sudden. Being a continually changing organization means choosing which events to adapt to[25] and deciding how to adapt. Not every threat or opportunity is relevant to every firm. One way of doing this is to decentralize decision-making power and assign *different roles to leaders* on different levels.[26] The first of these relates to the business unit. The strategy for this unit must be an ability to sense and seize what events are relevant for the business unit. The second role concerns synchronization on the middle level, where it is necessary to continuously reallocate among different deals and projects in order to take advantage of new events. The third role, at the level of top management, is to compile, decide, and communicate objectives and priorities for the company.

2.3 A People-Centric Approach

Many companies have used slogans or catch-phrases along the lines of "People are our most important assets." Often the statement is just an empty cliche´, but it has to be taken seriously in today's fast-changing world where the ability to innovate is crucial. Successful companies focus on tapping and releasing the innovative power of their employees—a principle grounded in the beliefs that people *want and need* to be creative and will in fact be creative if given a setting where they can exercise their skills.[27]

---

[24] Ibid.
[25] Ibid.
[26] Ibid.
[27] Richard Florida has demonstrated these points repeatedly, in his book *The Rise of the Creative Class* (Florida, 2004) and elsewhere, and so has the Danish scholar Steen Høyrup (Høyrup, 2012).

2.3 A People-Centric Approach

A key factor here is putting people into roles (or letting them find roles) that unleash their inner passions and motivations and play to their strengths. People-centric companies also strive to establish simple, well-defined structures and routines only where needed, otherwise giving people both the freedom and responsibility to make decisions and self-organize. Altogether, a successful company of this type is like a river system with unencumbered movement,[28] in which streams of work flow together powerfully.

In the previous section we mentioned the Morning Star company. This firm is people-centric in the extreme, as Gary Hamel pointed out by enumerating some of its features in his HBR article:

- No one has a boss.
- Employees negotiate responsibilities with their peers.
- Everyone can spend the company's money.
- Each individual is responsible for acquiring the tools needed to do his or her work.
- There are no titles and no promotions.
- Compensation decisions are peer-based.[29]

It is remarkable that such a model works well at Morning Star, since the company is not an experimental project-driven startup. Morning Star has been operating since 1970. Its core business is processing tomatoes and shipping the end products, such as tomato pastes and canned tomatoes—a highly focused, high-volume production business that would seem to require a more traditional command-and-control structure. Yet even this kind of work is subject to constant pressures for change and improvement. And apparently the people-centric approach pays off, by enabling Morning Star to optimize production while responding to shifting demands for products made to various specifications.

The role of management in a people-centric company is not simply to step back and get out of the way. Management plays a major role in employees' enthusiasm and level of engagement.[30] New ideas may arise anywhere in the firm, but cannot survive without the encouragement and support of management.[31] Also, the CEO and other leaders are cultural architects. They set the tone of the workplace by emphasizing the importance of innovation and continuous change. They bring out people's creative energies through challenging visions and business concepts.

In Chap. 1, with the Petratex example, we saw the value of setting "big" corporate goals that let employees know their work can make an impact on the world. The best people-centric firms have a strong, shared vision[32] that is vitalizing, attractive, realistic, and credible. In these firms we also find various soft forms of

---

[28] Tidd and Bessant (2009).

[29] Hamel (2011), p. 51.

[30] Dallenbach et al. (1999).

[31] Leifer et al. (2000).

[32] The definition of *vision* as a vitalizing, attractive, realistic, and credible picture of the future of a business is inspired by Burt Nanus. See Nanus (1992).

control— such as shared values, general guidelines, and peer accountability—replacing top-down command to a significant extent.

A company's general approach should also include delegating authority to those closest to a problem or opportunity, who often know the most about it. And, in order for employees to make good decisions, they need a culture[33] that emphasizes trust and openness, and they need access to relevant information. This requires more transparency and less secrecy than previous models have offered.[34]

There is a clear correlation between the way management treats employees, and the performance of the firm. This correlation is both positive and self-reinforcing over time.[35] Certain CEOs, such as Richard Branson at Virgin, maintain that employees are more important than customers, as satisfied employees create satisfied customers.

Releasing the energy that exists in every person requires leadership with special qualities. Inspiring, supportive leaders communicate visions and priorities but let employees choose how to perform the work. Managers reach an agreement with each employee about goals to be achieved. Leaders of innovative groups[36] have shown themselves to be both creative and disciplined. They can accept uncertainty and risk, and handle failures constructively. They also exhibit passion and enthusiasm. These leaders are curious and willing to seek out new ideas both within the company and externally. They are good at team building, modest and respectful, and have the courage to stop projects that do not meet expectations.

2.4 An Ambidextrous Organization

An ambidextrous person is skillful with either hand, and some advanced tasks (like playing the piano) require skill with both hands at once. So it is with companies in fast-moving environments. They need to conduct and improve daily operations on the one hand, while innovating significantly as well.

Harvard business professor Michael Tushman calls this the ability to "exploit" and "explore" at the same time[37]—exploiting the existing business to maximum effect while exploring new growth opportunities. Tushman, together with Charles O'Reilly of Stanford, did pioneering work on ambidextrous organizations during the 1990s.[38] The research has continued since then, drawing in more investigators. And the need for new approaches to ambidexterity is high, in part because a traditional way of being ambidextrous—devoting the operating units to operations,

---

[33] Isaksen and Tidd (2006).

[34] Hamel (2009).

[35] Tidd and Bessant (2009).

[36] Bel (2010).

[37] See for example the interview with Tushman in Cohan (2012). http://www.forbes.com/sites/petercohan/2012/02/27/how-big-companies-can-exploit-and-explore/ (Accessed 6 Aug 2015).

[38] Tushman and O'Reilly III (1997).

2.4 An Ambidextrous Organization

while major innovation is concentrated in an R&D center—has been increasingly questioned. As one observer put it:

> The idea of looking at R&D as a separate function from production is obsolete. R&D is merely one input into innovation. R&D spending in particular is a poor measure or determinant of the innovation on which the future of the firm rests.[39]

Bringing innovations from the research center to market can be a slow process (or not happen at all), and many firms have gotten low rates of return on investments in internal R&D. With speed to market becoming ever more important, internal labs will most likely be combined with outsourcing innovations and involving all employees in innovative work.

The question of course is how to structure and execute the efforts. Some commentators say that production processes and innovation are best carried on in isolation from each other (i.e., the "mainstream" and the "newstream" must be kept separated), while others argue that the mainstream and newstream must be kept within the same organization.[40] It therefore makes sense for any company to investigate the conditions under which production and innovation could coexist in its organization.[41] The model chosen, however, needs to provide the organization the ability to balance the conservative forces that oppose continuous change. This also entails a need for ambidextrous executives and managers—who can deal with both ongoing operations and innovation, and develop the company culture to promote an ambidextrous organization.

It has proved difficult to realize these intentions in practical terms, especially in connection with technological shifts. When a company or an entire industry encounters a major phase transition, one must often begin from scratch in an effort to find solutions to the major and crucial problem of how to satisfy new needs. Beginning from scratch requires avoiding building on the company's known solutions and recruiting management staff who represent the old way of thinking. It may well be that this can be done through a looser connection to mainstream operations, but also that it has to be done in a separate unit. In any case, the managers might have to accept that the traditional market is on the way to extinction and that one may need to "kill off one's darlings."

Several examples show that it is in fact possible, using an ambidextrous organization, to have both efficient production and continuous innovation: consider for example W. L. Gore, and 3M. There is also convincing evidence that ambidextrous companies succeed very well. However, to manage this strategic bifurcation, the management team and local managers must develop their ability to function within a dualistic framework. These leaders must clearly demonstrate what the

---

[39] Denning (2012) http://www.forbes.com/sites/stevedenning/2012/04/19/is-rd-really-the-secret-sauce/ (Accessed 6 August 2015).
[40] See for example Teece (2007) or Kanter (1989).
[41] Lawson and Samson (2001).

ambidextrous concept means through a continuing dialog with "both sides" internally.[42] Management thus plays an important role in launching the ambidextrous approach throughout the company.

2.5 An Open Organization That Networks with Its Surroundings

Researchers agree that companies in fast-changing environments need to have "open" boundaries, exchanging ideas and information with parties outside. Decades ago, two prominent scholars voiced a warning that had already become clear to many: "Firms that fail to exploit … external R&D may be at a severe competitive disadvantage."[43]

It is common (and often necessary) for firms in nearly all industries to *license* external technologies in the course of new-product development, but successful firms in a rapidly changing world do much more. They partner and network actively: sponsoring research at universities, investing in, or partnering with startup companies—as we noted Intel has done, through Intel Capital—and establishing modes of exchange that range from informal contacts to formal strategic alliances. In fact new modes of exchange keep emerging. For example, Lego the toymaker partnered with MIT Media Lab to develop its Mindstorm toys.[44]

Openness and networking with the external environment were well described in 2003 with Henry Chesbrough's introduction of the *open innovation* concept.[45] According to Chesbrough, there are several reasons to become more open. First, there are today powerful ways to bypass conventional limitations and benefit from ideas originating outside the firm. Second, not all the smart people are in one company; they are found in many companies and institutions. Third, innovations that arise from collaboration between various fields of endeavor, disciplines, and organizations are becoming more common. Fourth, time to market is becoming shorter, as are product life cycles. As a result, companies must shorten the time required for product development. Becoming better at discovering and adopting ideas from outside sources and integrating them into the company's own development process helps the firm to keep pace.

Companies that are operated like closed systems could dissipate their energy and finally disappear. When a company launches programs to cut costs, it may be a sign that the firm is no longer able to supply sufficient new value to earn the income it needs. A "closed" company most often focuses on cutting costs, and some companies have managed to survive on the market for many years using various types of austerity measures. Gradually, however, all of this cost cutting will impair the

---

[42] Interview July 2013 with Geoff Hollingworth, AT&T Foundry.

[43] "Innovative skills may count for a great deal less than we once thought—unless we can learn to become better imitators ourselves." Rosenberg and Steinmueller (1988), p. 234.

[44] See for example MIT News Office (1999).

[45] Chesbrough (2003).

quality of the company's products and services and eventually lead to the company's demise.

An open system has more permeable boundaries and searches beyond itself for innovations that can increase revenues. In open systems, managers and employees connect with the company's surroundings. When technological development speeds up and competition becomes intense, the company needs to use these links even more to supplement its own expertise. Under these conditions, it can be difficult for a company to keep up with developments in all relevant areas. Networks and alliances with customers, suppliers, start-ups, universities, government agencies, and sometimes even with competitors, can serve as crucial resources for a company's innovations.

Jack Welch observed, "If the rate of change on the outside exceeds the rate of change on the inside, the end is near."[46] Management and the board should decide whether the company's innovative ability is sufficient and whether increased openness to the outside world would increase that ability. How can the company benefit from new external technology and networks in order to further develop its ability to change, to be proactive, and to innovate?

2.6 A Systems Approach

Finally, a company that seeks long-term competitiveness in a changing world must be viewed (and designed and managed) as a complete *system*. A system is defined here as "a collection of components with certain properties, with connections among the components *and* among the properties of those components".[47] For companies to fully realize their innovative abilities, they must move to a "systems" perspective.[48]

Figure 2.1 shows an organization visualized from a system perspective. The system components are the company's key elements such as: the company's vision and mission, the board of directors and management team, company culture, daily managers, employees, organizational structure and processes, systems for performance evaluation, promotion and recognition, systems for learning, and the company's brand/corporate communication.[49]

In Fig. 2.1 the elements are arranged in a ring. They all revolve around the main strategic intent of the company, which is shown at the center. And this strategic intent can vary, depending on what a company considers to be its primary intent. The kind of firm that we call an "efficiency company" will pursue efficiency and

---

[46] The quotation is attributed to Welch in online sources such as Goodreads; other public figures have used the saying (or variations on it) as well.

[47] As noted earlier under (2), the definition is from Eric Rhenman.

[48] O'Connor (2008).

[49] Steiber and Alänge (2013) used similar elements when describing the corporate system for innovation at Google Inc.

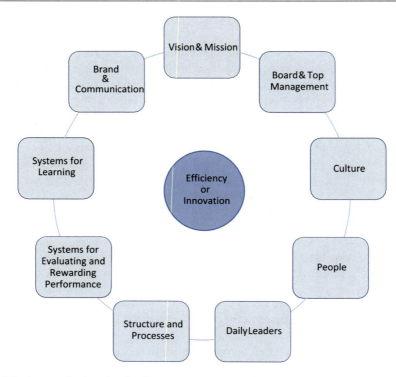

Fig. 2.1 An organization visualized as a company system

control—typically, with the purpose of maximizing near-term profits—while an "innovation company" emphasizes innovation and growth.

In order to illustrate the systems perspective, let's try a hypothetical exercise comparing two companies that are at opposite ends of the spectrum. One is very highly efficiency-oriented, like many conventional big firms today. The other more closely resembles our innovation-oriented Silicon Valley case companies. By comparing these two hypothetical firms, we can see how *all of the system elements tend to become aligned with the primary intent.*

Of course, in reality, an efficiency company must not neglect its innovation-related work, just as an innovation company must constantly mind its profitability, which after all finances its innovations. Both need to be "ambidextrous" to at least some degree. But we're exaggerating the differences here to communicate how the overarching orientation of a company ripples through the system, affecting both the behavior of people and the ultimate growth and profit or loss of the company.

Taking the individual system elements in order, our comparison would go as follows:

- The efficiency company has a **vision** that emphasizes market leadership by delivering reliable quality while cutting costs. The innovation company, by contrast,

2.6 A Systems Approach

has a bold forward-looking vision—typically, one stating a major goal or impact, which the firm strives to achieve.
- The **board and management** of the efficiency company are more internally focused. They're occupied primarily with current business, quality issues and meeting financial metrics. The board and management of the innovation company seek opportunities for growth. They are externally focused and consider different time horizons simultaneously: history, the present, and the future.
- The **culture** of the efficiency company emphasizes cost, profitability and control. The innovation company differs first of all simply by *paying more attention* to cultural issues—as we'll see in later chapters, companies of this type have an explicit focus on building a strong culture—and the culture differs in its nature as well, promoting norms such as risk taking, constant renewal, and experimentation in pursuit of growth.
- The **daily managers**, those responsible for everyday work, tend in the efficiency company to be hands-on micromanagers. They are primarily focused on execution of daily work and prescribe and control both what is to be done, and how it is done. In the innovation company, the daily leaders leave the HOW to the team members, and consciously coach them in exploring new ideas in parallel with execution of daily work.
- The efficiency company views **employees** as a resource much like any other, and work processes are standardized in an effort to coordinate their work. In the innovation company, employees are the company's most important assets. Management stimulates individuals' creativity and their mutual collaboration in order to contribute to company growth. Coordination of work is done through strong vision, culture, and clear performance goals.
- In terms of **organization**, the efficiency company is built on a "command and control" model aimed at securing lower costs and profitability while avoiding unexpected risks and disruptions. The innovation company emphasizes a dynamic balance between structure and chaos that will provide both efficiency and enough flexibility for developing new growth opportunities.
- In the efficiency company, **performance evaluation, promotion, recognition, and rewards** are all geared towards cost control, quality, and profitability. In the innovation company, these systems encourage people to constantly make new contributions—they are rewarded for innovations that serve customers in new ways, or that improve operations and lead to growth.
- **Systems for learning**: The war cry "It has to be right the first time" belongs in the efficiency company but not in the innovation company. Mistakes must be avoided and risks limited in the efficiency company. The innovation company allows risk, striving instead to learn fast and not repeat the same mistakes.
- **Communication and brand**: A company's brand is an archetype that expresses expectations about not only its products, but also about how the company's management and employees should act. At an efficiency company, the brand is mainly associated with quality and dependability. At an innovation company, the brand conveys cutting-edge excellence, in association with the company's ability to bring attractive new products and improvements to market.

To sum up, top executives must view their organizations as complex systems made up of multiple interdependent elements. Results are best when *all* elements are designed and managed to fulfill the company's strategic intent. Moreover, if there is a desire to shift the company's strategic intent—for instance, by putting greater emphasis on innovation—all elements may need to be redesigned accordingly.

2.7 Recent Findings

In 2023, the six basic principles for a changing world are still highly relevant. According to David Teece, the dynamic capabilities framework has proved fertile ground for research, and there is no evidence its momentum is slowing,[50] and the Agile movement is pushing and proving the need for a constantly changing, agile organization in a fastmoving world. In addition, Rubina Chakma et al and many others discuss the increasing importance of ambidexterity,[51] while Barbara Bigliardi et al and many of their peers restate the necessity of open innovation as the new paradigm for innovation.[52] Also, the necessity of people-centric organizations and cultures is frequently mentioned in research and media, illustrated by e.g., Larry Peters who emphasizes the increased focus on, and need for, a people-centric culture for employee engagement and commitment.[53] Finally, the large group of scholars and practitioners working for the International Organization for Standardization (ISO) with the new innovation management standard emphasize the necessity of applying a systems approach to corporate innovation in e.g., its guide 56002:2019.[54] The conclusion is therefore that the six principles remain valid for any organization that wants to be competitive in a fast-changing world.

In recent years, however, digitalization as part of the system—contributing to innovation and improvement of practices, both internally and for external collaboration—has become important for all industries. Recently also, the use and proper handling of artificial intelligence has become increasingly important for the various effects that AI can have on internal work, and on product and service innovation. In May 2023, the CEO of Google and Alphabet, Sundar Pichai, presented his view of how Google is "Making AI more helpful for everyone."[55] Digitalization and AI could therefore be expected to influence the implementation of the basic principles presented in this chapter.

---

[50] Teece (2023).
[51] Chakma et al. (2021).
[52] Bigliardi et al. (2021).
[53] Peters (2019).
[54] ISO (2022).
[55] Pichai (2023).

2.8 Moving On

In this chapter we've seen six basic principles that are widely found to be effective for managing organizations in rapidly changing environments. There is however no single standardized "formula" for success. Companies in different circumstances may apply the principles quite differently, and as was mentioned in Chap. 1, a focus on attracting, retaining, and managing entrepreneurial people is also needed. But a number of leading companies, including our Silicon Valley case companies, practice (or at least strive to practice) these principles consistently.

The principles also appear to permeate the entire Silicon Valley region. In the next chapter we look at this region from a fresh perspective. While most people think of Silicon Valley as a hub of new technology and startups, the Valley's dominance must also be credited to the innovations in big-firm management that it has produced.

References

Bel, R. (2010). Leadership and innovation: Learning from the best. *Global Business and Organizational Excellence, 32*(2), 71–87.

Bigliardi, B., Ferraro, G., Filippelli, S., & Galati, F. (2021). The past, present and future of open innovation. *European Journal of Innovation Management, 24*(4), 1130–1161. https://www.emerald.com/insight/content/doi/10.1108/EJIM-10-2019-0296/full/html

Brown, S. L., & Eisenhardt, K. M. (1997). The art of continuous change: Linking complexity theory and time-paced evolution in relentlessly shifting organizations. *Administrative Science Quarterly, 42*(1), 1–34.

Brown, S. L., & Eisenhardt, K. M. (1998a). *Competing on the edge: Strategy as structured chaos.* Harvard Business School Press.

Brown, S. L., & Eisenhardt, K. M. (1998b). Time pacing: Competing in markets that won't stand still. *Harvard Business Review, 76*(2), 59–69.

Chakma, R., Paul, J., & Dhir, S. (2021). Organizational ambidexterity: A review and research agenda. *IEEE Transactions on Engineering Management.* https://doi.org/10.1109/TEM.2021.3114609

Chesbrough, H. W. (2003). *Open innovation: The new imperative for creating and profiting from technology.* Harvard Business School Press.

Cohan, P. (2012, February 27). How big companies can exploit and explore. *Forbes.com.* http://www.forbes.com/sites/petercohan/2012/02/27/how-big-companies-can-exploit-and-explore/. Accessed 6 Aug 2015.

Dallenbach, U. S., McCarthy, A. M., & Schoenecker, T. S. (1999). Commitment to innovation: The impact of top management team characteristics. *R&D Management, 29*(3), 199–208.

Denning, S. (2012, April 19). Is R&D really the secret sauce? *Forbes.com.* http://www.forbes.com/sites/stevedenning/2012/04/19/is-rd-really-the-secret-sauce/. Accessed 6 Aug 2015.

Florida, R. (2004). *The rise of the creative class.* Basic Books.

Hamel, G. (2009). Moon shots for management. *Harvard Business Review, 87*(2), 91–99.

Hamel, G. (2011). First, let's fire all the managers. *Harvard Business Review, 89*(11), 48–60.

Harreld, J. B., O'Reilly, C. A., & Tushman, M. L. (2006, August 10). *Dynamic capabilities at IBM: Driving strategy into action* (White Paper Draft).

Høyrup, S. (2012). Employee-driven innovation: A new phenomenon, concept and mode of innovation. In S. Høyrup, M. Bonnafous-Boucher, C. Hasse, M. Lotz, & K. Møller (Eds.), *Employee-driven innovation.* Palgrave Macmillan. https://doi.org/10.1057/9781137014764_1

Isaksen, S., & Tidd, J. (2006). *Meeting the innovation challenge—Leadership for transformation and growth*. Wiley.

ISO. (2022). *ISO 56002:2019 Innovation management system*. https://www.iso.org/files/live/sites/isoorg/files/store/en/PUB100468.pdf

Kanter, R. M. (1989). *When giants learn to dance: Mastering the challenge of strategy, management, and careers in the 1990s*. Simon and Schuster.

Kleiner, A. (2013, November 11). The dynamic capabilities of David Teece. *Strategy+Business*. http://www.strategy-business.com/article/00225?gko¼d24f3. Accessed 31 Oct 2015.

Lawson, B., & Samson, D. (2001). Developing innovation capability in organizations: A dynamic capabilities approach. *International Journal of Innovation Management, 5*(3), 377–400.

Leifer, R., McDermott, C. M., O'Connor, G. C., Peters, L. S., Rice, M., & Veryzer, R. W. (2000). *Radical innovation: How mature companies can outsmart upstarts*. Harvard Business School Press.

Leonard-Barton, D. (1992). Core capabilities and core rigidities: A paradox in managing new product development. *Strategic Management Journal, 13*, 111–125. Special Issue: Strategy Process: Managing Corporate Self-Renewal, Summer 1992.

Maycotte, H. O. (2014, December 9). Your startup dilemma: Nobody ever got fired for buying IBM. *Forbes.com*. http://www.forbes.com/sites/homaycotte/2014/12/09/your-startup-delimma-nobody-ever-got-fired-for-buying-ibm/. Accessed 1 Aug 2015.

MIT News Office. (1999, October 25). The Lego Company funds $5 million lab at MIT Media Laboratory. http://newsoffice.mit.edu/1999/lego. Accessed 30 July 2015.

Nanus, B. (1992). *Visionary leadership—Creating a compelling sense of direction for your organization*. Jossey-Bass.

O'Connor, G. C. (2008). Major innovation as a dynamic capability: A systems approach. *Journal of Product Innovation Management, 25*, 313–330.

Penrose, E. T. (1959). *The theory of the growth of the firm*. Wiley.

Peters, L. (2019). *The simple truths about leadership: Creating a people-centric culture* (2nd ed.). Palgrave Macmillan/Springer.

Pichai, S. (2023). *Google I/O 2023: Making AI more helpful for everyone*. https://blog.google/technology/ai/google-io-2023-keynote-sundar-pichai/#ai-products

Prahalad, C. K., & Hamel, G. (1990). The core competence of the corporation. *Harvard Business Review, 68*(5), 79–91.

Richtmyer, R. (2002, July 31). IBM to buy PwC consulting. *CNNMoney*.

Rosenberg, N., & Steinmueller, W. E. (1988). Why are Americans such poor imitators? *The American Economic Review, 78*(2), 229–234.

Spooner, J. G. (2004, December 8). IBM sells PC group to Lenovo. *CNET News*. http://www.cnet.com/news/ibm-sells-pc-group-to-lenovo/. Accessed 6 Aug 2015

Steiber, A. (2014). *The Google model: Managing innovation in a rapidly changing world*. Springer.

Steiber, A., & Alänge, S. (2013). A corporate system for continuous innovation: The case of Google Inc. *European Journal of Innovation Management, 16*(2), 243–264.

Teece, D. (2007). Explicating dynamic capabilities: The nature and microfoundations of (sustainable) enterprise performance. *Strategic Management Journal, 28*(13), 1319–1350.

Teece, D. J. (2023). The evolution of the dynamic capabilities framework. In R. Adams, D. Grichnik, A. Pundziene, & C. Volkmann (Eds.), *Artificiality and sustainability in entrepreneurship* (FGF Studies in Small Business and Entrepreneurship). Springer. https://doi.org/10.1007/978-3-031-11371-0_6

Tidd, J., & Bessant, J. (2009). *Managing innovation: Integrating technological, market and organizational change* (4th ed.). Wiley.

Tushman, M. L., & O'Reilly, C. A., III. (1997). *Winning through Innovation: A practical guide to leading organizational change and renewal*. Harvard Business School Press.

Wernefelt, B. (1984). A resource-based view of the firm. *Strategic Management Journal, 5*(2), 171–180.

Silicon Valley: A Cradle of Management Innovation   3

It is somewhat unusual to think of Silicon Valley as a center of innovation in management. The Valley is best known as a center of *technology* innovation, and as a hotbed for breeding startup companies. Indeed, those two aspects are often thought to be the keys to the region's vitality. Economic specialists around the world have studied (and tried to replicate) the Valley's long track record of developing new technologies and forming startups to bring the inventions to market. But while the process of building new companies around technology ideas is important, it's only part of the story.

Silicon Valley Is More Than a Startup Machine We saw in Chap. 1 that the Valley's top companies do more than get off to a good start. They grow and evolve. Not only do they keep enhancing their technologies, they keep finding new ways to combine and apply them. In addition to scaling up their operations, they add new capabilities to pursue new paths to growth. They are apt to move far beyond the business models or the technical applications that led to their initial success—and they move fast.

These Companies Could Not Do What They Do If They Were Managed Conventionally They have created new organizational forms, built around new perspectives on the whole task of managing. In the pages ahead we look at how and why Silicon Valley came to be at the forefront of such innovation.

We'll also see broader themes emerging, for although these new approaches have been influenced by factors that are characteristic of the companies and their region, the situation is by no means unique. Forces that have affected Valley firms are now sweeping through the rest of the world. Thus the story of management innovation in Silicon Valley may foreshadow its future everywhere.

3.1 The Forces That Drive Management Innovation, in Brief

Companies in the Valley have developed new ways of managing that reflect two major sets of influences: the nature of their industries and the norms and values of the region. Here is a brief summary of each.

The Nature of the Industries—Silicon Valley is of course the birthplace of much of today's information technology. Most major firms are active in one or more IT-related fields, ranging from software, electronics, and telecom to e-commerce, social media, and mobile technologies. These fields, in turn, have a double-edged effect on companies. They create a *need* for constant innovation and change—because the technologies themselves change rapidly—while they also provide the *means* for building flexible, adaptive organizations.

Silicon Valley firms are immersed in the very products they create. They're able to be at the cutting edge of using IT internally, to flatten bureaucracies and speed response times, and (as we shall see) they network with their IT-intensive neighbors to achieve strategic synergies.[1]

Norms and Values of the Region—Since the mid-1800s the San Francisco Bay Area has been a highly entrepreneurial place, open to new ideas and people. Early immigrants drawn by the Gold Rush arrived in a land with virtually no pre-existing government or societal institutions, and no industries other than small farming. They built a society and economy literally from scratch and drew further waves of immigrants eager to create their own futures.

As Richard Florida noted in his studies of how high-tech regions grow, it is no coincidence that during the twentieth century the Bay Area became a center of radical social movements and a hub of experimentation in new lifestyles, music and arts: "What set Silicon Valley apart was not just Stanford University or the warm climate. It was that the place was open to and supportive of the creative, the different and the downright weird."[2]

We will see how early founders of the region's IT industries benefited from this openness, attracting investment capital and talent to companies that not only made new kinds of products, but were structured and managed along radically new lines.

The Two Sets of Influences Had Combined Effects as Well Many scholars have observed that technical and organizational innovation go hand in hand: Christopher Freeman, for instance, pointed to Henry Ford's moving assembly line as an example of a "purely organizational innovation … [which also] both entailed and stimulated a great deal of technical innovation."[3] Freeman also cited the semiconductor industry as having a rapid growth curve built on both kinds of innovation, and it was hardly surprising that both should flourish together in Silicon Valley.

Technologies developed in the Valley—from early radio transmitters and vacuum tubes to silicon chips, personal computers and more—were unprecedented

---

[1] All of this will be documented with evidence and stories from expert sources including Homa Bahrami, Annalee Saxenian, Timothy Sturgeon and others.
[2] See "The Real Legacy of the Sixties," pp. 202–207, in Florida (2002).
[3] Freeman et al. (1982), p. 217.

types of products, with very wide potential uses. There were no role models for organizing the companies that made them, or for leading those companies through iterative cycles of fast-moving change. Suitable management methods, like the products themselves, had to be newly invented. What better place could there be to do so, than in a region where self-invention is integral to the culture?

As for Implications Beyond Silicon Valley and the IT Industries: Following sections will show that new management approaches developed in the Valley are congruent with the six management principles described in Chap. 2. These principles already have been shown to apply for firms that need to innovate in constantly changing environments.

For example, management styles in the Valley are (and long have been) extremely *people-oriented*. The IT industries are knowledge-intensive. They require highly skilled people, along with structures that enable these people to be creative, collaborative, and entrepreneurial. We'll see various ways that Silicon Valley firms have learned to manage with a "people-centric approach."

Finally, the Silicon Valley/Bay Area is a place that has distinctive qualities of its own but a global character: Its industries serve global markets, since IT is used everywhere, and they attract talent from everywhere.

And as more industries and parts of the world come to resemble Silicon Valley in all these respects—driven by innovation and rapid change, increasingly reliant on skilled people and new ideas, increasingly global—it becomes ever more likely that management innovation in the Valley may represent the wave of the future.

That is a capsule summary. Now for a closer look at Silicon Valley. The following sections explore four aspects of how management innovation in Silicon Valley has developed. First are the two major sets of influences, the information-technology industries and the culture of the region, then brief treatments of two important themes, collaborative networking and people focus.

3.2 Management Innovation: The Influence of IT

> High technology obeys the iron law of revolution… the more you change, the more you have to change … you have to be willing to accept the fact that in this game the rules keep changing.[4]—Bill Joy, cofounder, Sun Microsystems.

Information technology companies in Silicon Valley are faced with dual demands on their capacity to innovate and change. They must keep up with (or better yet, keep ahead of) changes in the underlying technologies, while dealing with intense competition at every step. When Google started in 1998 it entered an already-crowded Internet search field. Facebook, a few years later, had to vie with MySpace and other competitors for the lead in social networking. Rarely in the fastmoving IT

---

[4] Excerpt from a speech by Bill Joy at the Churchill Club, Palo Alto, in 1990. Cited in sources such as Bahrami (1992).

industries has any company had a wide-open niche to exploit or a chance to rest on its laurels—and this has been true since the industries began.

The economic researcher Timothy J. Sturgeon[5] points out that Silicon Valley's true birth event came in 1909, when a Stanford-related startup called Federal Telegraph Company (FTC) was founded to refine and build a new kind of radio transmitter. The company had profound impact and a rich history, of which we'll hear more shortly. But its great new product didn't last long. FTC sold its first "arc transmitters" in 1912. By the 1920s they were obsolete—replaced by transmitters based on a vacuum tube that the inventor Lee DeForest had developed *in FTC's own research lab, at the same time those initial sales were being made*.

Nor is obsolescence the only threat. Silicon Valley—originally called the Santa Clara Valley, south of San Francisco—earned its modern nickname from the companies that were started during the 1950s and 1960s to make integrated circuits on silicon chips. The most successful has been Intel, founded in 1969. Intel prospered at first by making memory chips. They were the most commonly used type, but highly prone to being commoditized. Before long, lower-priced Asian competitors were eating up the memory business. Intel survived by shifting its focus (and re-inventing its business strategy) just in time to catch the early waves of demand for a more advanced breed of chip: the microprocessors, or CPUs, that were starting to be used as the core working units in personal computers.[6]

These ever-repeating cycles of change are why Valley companies frequently develop new product lines, alter their business models and/or migrate into new markets. They are searching for routes to survival and growth, with choices that can vary from one firm to the next. Apple, a seminal company in personal computers, still makes the machines but has come to earn most of its revenue from other sources. Along that course it crossed paths with Hewlett-Packard, which started as a maker of specialized electronic instruments, then plunged into the mass-market personal computing sector and spun off its instrument units.

But whatever path is chosen, the constant churning in these industries has required *all* the companies to think afresh about how they manage.

3.2.1 New Ways of Managing Emerge

Two Silicon Valley firms that rose to prominence after World War II set an early tone in management innovation. Both were organized and run quite differently than most companies of the time. AnnaLee Saxenian, an expert on the Valley, summed up Hewlett-Packard's approach in a few words that speak volumes:

---

[5] See Sturgeon's chapter "How Silicon Valley Came to Be" in Kenney, ed. (2000), pp. 15–47. Sturgeon and Kenney, in turn, credit Norberg (1976).
[6] For a concise summary of Intel's rebound see Saxenian (1990).

The 'H-P Way,' with its decentralized corporate structure and informal management style, its emphasis on teamwork, shared responsibility, and entrepreneurship, became the very hallmark of Silicon Valley.[7]

The other pacesetter was Varian Associates, a legendary electronics firm founded in 1948. Of this company the British consultant Steve Towers wrote:

> Varian Associates specialized in the development htm of medical linear accelerators for the treatment of cancer, a field requiring top-flight researchers… Varian attracted the very best by forming a co-operative owned by its employees with stock option agreements.
> This approach coupled with an environment where they could create without restriction spawned many important breakthroughs and won hundreds of innovation awards. Initially unprofitable, the company was sustained by its enthused employees who eventually went on to help Varian to become a world leader in the field.[8]

In both cases we see a focus on *attracting and retaining good people*—not just with high pay or promotions, but with a participatory workplace that imposes minimal rules and structures. Instead, people are encouraged to form teams, practice "entrepreneurship" and make "breakthroughs."

By the early 1990s, Homa Bahrami, a business professor at UC Berkeley, found Silicon Valley to be teeming with management innovation. In a study of 37 Valley companies, she reported that the firms "are experimenting with new organizational arrangements" which help them "manage novelty and continuous changes in product designs, competitive positions, and market dynamics."[9]

For example, Bahrami noted that the *flattening of hierarchies* was common:

> The emerging organizational system of high-technology firms is more akin to a 'federation' or 'constellation' of business units that are typically interdependent, relying on one another for critical expertise and know-how. Moreover, they have a peer-to-peer relationship with the [corporate] center. The center's role is to orchestrate the broad strategic vision, develop the shared organizational and administrative infrastructure, and create the cultural glue…However, these tasks are undertaken together *with* the line units, rather than for them.[10]

Bahrami also commented at length about what she called the companies' "Dualistic Systems." In the language of this book, we would call them systems for being *ambidextrous*. She described the firms as having a certain "bedrock structure" combined with "overlays of temporary project teams and multi-functional groups," which allowed the companies to "focus on critical assignments without causing major disruptions." In answer to the oft-heard comment that these firms simply appeared to be chaotically disorganized, she wrote:

---

[7] Saxenian (1994).
[8] Towers (2002) http://www.itstime.com/apr2002.htm (Accessed 25 June 2015).
[9] Bahrami (1992).
[10] Ibid, p. 38.

> Such an impression… only reflects one dimension of the organizational reality. Many firms we observed were both *structured and yet chaotic*; they had evolved dualistic organizational systems, designed to strike a dynamic balance between stability on the one hand, and flexibility on the other.[11]

And last but not least this researcher saw that *the use of information technologies* was making a difference. Companies were "delayering and down-sizing," a trend driven partly by efforts to cut costs but one which also

> … reflects the administrative impact of information and communication technologies. Increased use of technologies such as electronic mail, voice mail, and shared databases, has, over time, reduced the need for traditional middle management, whose role was to supervise others and to collect, analyze, evaluate, and transmit information up, down, and across the organizational hierarchy.[12]

Internal uses of IT have grown dramatically in Silicon Valley since the time Bahrami made her study. Later chapters will allude to some of these uses. Google, for instance, has a management policy of making decisions on the basis of objective measurement—a practice that is both enabled and speeded up by the company's native IT systems. Whenever a new idea or product feature is tested, its impact can be tracked in real time and communicated instantly.

For now, we've seen various ways that IT has impacted management innovation in the Valley. Let's bring in the other set of influences, the cultural norms and mindset of the region. Sources agree that these took root long before the first silicon chip was made.

3.3 Management Innovation: The Influence of Regional Culture

> The entrepreneurial culture was initially born out of a Californian history of pioneers… coupled with the legacy of the Gold Rush… Historically, Silicon Valley entrepreneurs have exhibited many of the qualities of the early pioneers.[13]—Homa Bahrami

The following paragraphs provide a whirlwind tour of nearly a century's worth of history. California's Gold Rush began in 1849. Ninety years later, in 1939, Bill Hewlett and David Packard launched the prototypical company of modern-day Silicon Valley after building their first product (an audio oscillator) in Packard's now-famous Palo Alto garage. By tracing some key events that came just before and between those dates, we can see how the basic ingredients of an innovative, entrepreneurial approach to work and management were born.

In the mid-1840s, a time when the Industrial Revolution had already swept through much of Europe and the eastern United States, the present state of California

---

[11] Ibid, p. 39.
[12] Ibid, p. 34.
[13] Bahrami and Evans (2005), p. 55.

was remote and sparsely populated. It was then a territory of newly independent Mexico. And this entire coastal area—larger than Italy—was home to no more than a few hundred thousand people. The vast majority were indigenous peoples living in scattered villages, plus some small settlements of Franciscan missionaries, Spanish or Mexican ranchers and assorted adventurers.[14]

The key fact here is that California was virtually a blank slate Newcomers would find a land with very little in the way of existing social structures or controls. Gradually, more settlers began trickling in.

Then in 1848 two things happened almost simultaneously. Gold deposits were discovered in the hills of northern California and the Mexican-American War ended, with Mexico ceding the whole territory to the U.S. This opened the gates wide for the ensuing Gold Rush, since California was now literally deregulated: Mexican rule had been fragmentary at best and no new government had yet been formed. Fortune-seekers from around the world streamed in, many coming by sea through the only good port along the northern coastline: San Francisco, at the entrance to an inner bay.

The little town quickly grew into a major metropolis, fueled by multiple sources of wealth. Some immigrants found gold (or later, silver a bit farther inland) and many more started businesses that were geared, initially, to the mining boom. They opened banks and stores; they founded engineering companies and railroads; they started food farms in the countryside and factories in the city.[15]

This tremendous growth has been attributed to the *highly entrepreneurial population* that arrived. The Gold Rush immigrants were not mere speculators with nothing better to do. As Mark Twain colorfully described them in *Roughing It*, his travel memoir of the time:

> It was a splendid population—for all the slow, sleepy, sluggish-brained sloths stayed at home—you never find that sort of people among pioneers… It was that population that gave to California a name for getting up astounding enterprises and rushing them through with a magnificent dash and daring…[16]

The immigrants also, by necessity, displayed *an openness to partnering and networking*. Diverse groups in the gold fields had to agree on the rules of engagement, such as who could look for gold where, then collaborate or compete as needed in order to mine it out. Partnering was prominent in the city, too. Levi Strauss, an immigrant who had a fabrics store in San Francisco, teamed up with a tailor to design work pants for miners and others; soon they started a factory to produce the patented Levi's blue jeans.[17] Since everything from businesses to public institutions

---

[14] There are varying estimates of the Native American population of California pre- and post- contact with Europeans, but most sources agree with the total range cited here for the years leading up to the Gold Rush. See for example PBS (2006).

[15] Ibid and many other sources; see for example Starr (1973), pp. 69, 110–139 and elsewhere.

[16] Twain (1872), Chapter LVII: http://www.gutenberg.org/files/3177/3177-h/3177-h.htm#linkch28 (Accessed 6 Aug 2015).

[17] Levi Strauss & Co (2014).

was being started anew, many people worked across conventional sector lines and boundaries. Leland Stanford started and ran multiple businesses, served a term as California's governor—and closed his career by cofounding, with his wife Jane, the university that became the nexus of Silicon Valley.

Stanford University, built on the family's horse farm south of the city and ambitiously staffed with faculty recruited from across the U.S., opened in 1891. At that time most American universities were still far inferior to those of Europe and some critics mocked the Stanfords for starting a lavish new school in a horse pasture.[18] But their effort reflected another characteristic of entrepreneurial management, which we've described in previous chapters: *creating a big vision, with inspiring goals*. That vision paid dividends remarkably soon.

3.3.1 The Early Electronics Industry

Federal Telegraph Company—the Valley's first technology firm, in 1909—was founded by Cyril Elwell, a young Stanford engineering graduate.[19] A professor had urged him to start a company in a new field that had caught his interest: radio. Radio (or "wireless") in its early days was seen mainly as a medium for sending messages in shipping and military use, and Elwell knew of a transmitter technology that promised to work better than those being used in the U.S. He traveled to Denmark to visit its inventor, returning to Palo Alto with the American patent rights and some Danish engineers to assist in starting FTC.

Seed funding for the venture came from Stanford's president, David Starr Jordan, and the head of the electrical engineering department. They also arranged for Elwell to refine the invention in Stanford's High Voltage Lab. In 1912, with further funding from San Francisco investors, Federal Telegraph Company won a contract to supply the big heavy-duty transmitters to the U.S. Navy.

Before merging with other firms in the 1920s Federal Telegraph built many more of the machines and had a powerful multiplier effect, supporting related ventures and producing spinouts. The fabled inventor Lee DeForest worked for a time at FTC and used the firm's Palo Alto facility to perfect his three-element vacuum tube—the compact device that would replace the arc transmitter and become the basis of the explosive growth of radio, television, and nearly all advanced electronics for decades to come (until it was itself replaced by transistors in integrated circuits).

The best-known FTC spinout occurred when engineer Peter Jensen left to cofound Magnavox, maker of some of the first loudspeakers, then home radios and later TVs.

---

[18] For a concise account of the founding of Stanford University, see History of Stanford at https://www.stanford.edu/about/history/. Accessed 26 June 2015. For a detailed biography of Leland Stanford and his activities, see Tutorow (2004).

[19] The following discussion is all from Timothy Sturgeon's chapter in Kenney, ed. (2000), pp. 15–47.

Other FTC spinouts included Fisher Research Laboratories (still in business) and Litton Engineering Labs (later part of a big defense-electronics firm). Meanwhile, following up on DeForest's work, the entire Bay Area became a West Coast hub for the design and manufacture of specialty vacuum tubes. Engineers migrated between firms or started their own shops, and no one minded much so long as everyone had business and the technology was being advanced, which in fact occurred.

All this activity followed the collaborative, boundary-crossing spirit of the Bay Area's formative years—and it set the patterns for the better-known events to come in Silicon Valley. The FTC era established *university-industry linkages* with Stanford, which would be repeated memorably with Hewlett-Packard's founding in 1939, and then the postwar formation of Stanford Research Park. It also established the Silicon Valley tradition of *talent mobility*, as not only were people moving around within the region, they came from outside. Jensen was a Danish immigrant, DeForest an American from back east; the Russian immigrant Alexander Poniatoff became another key person in the early industry. A core principle described in Chap. 2, *openness to innovation from outside*, was followed right from the time when Elwell brought home the transmitter technology from Denmark.

Finally, the FTC era set the tone for *a constant pursuit of new ideas and excellence*. As historians have noted, competing in electronics was not easy for the early West Coast firms. Money and talent were still concentrated in the eastern U.S., where firms such as RCA, GE, and AT&T were much bigger and held crucial patents. The Valley companies (along with their university partners) had to make their places either by creating new technologies and products or greatly improving what existed.

But after all, that has proved to be the nature of the fast-evolving electronics and IT industries generally. *And as the opening chapters of this book have shown, it is coming to be the nature of every industry. The Valley's tech industries benefited from being born to work to these conditions from the start.*

To round out the discussion we'll briefly review two key ways in which Silicon Valley companies have carried management innovation further. One is by collaborating and networking to higher degrees; the other is through increased focus on people.

3.4 Management Innovation: New Levels of Networking

In a research paper,[20] AnnaLee Saxenian described how the Valley responded to a serious threat during the 1980s: the Asian competitors that were cutting deeply into the region's chip-making industry. As already noted, Intel shifted its focus to developing a new kind of chip, CPUs for personal computers. Meanwhile other chip-making firms in the Valley responded by collaborating.

Hewlett Packard had state-of-the-art fabrication facilities that smaller, specialty chipmakers could not afford. HP opened up its fab lines to these companies on a

---

[20] Saxenian (1990).

contract basis, and even partnered with them on chip design—the latter arrangement being one that also occurred among a number of big-and-smaller firms in the Valley. Such alliances benefited everyone involved. All parties made money; they got access to resources and expertise beyond their own. They cooperated on, and shared the advantages of, new technologies.

Moreover, companies that were end-users of chips found that collaborating with their suppliers gave them better components than if they had simply written a set of specs and sent them out to be manufactured. *And the same applied to parts other than chips.* Saxenian's paper quoted an Apple purchasing director who

> …claims that good partnerships with key vendors involve not simply on-time delivery and quality control but continual extension of the relationship to new areas. He suggests that joint investment in new capital equipment, joint product development, shared funding of key engineering talent, and technology exchanges, are all ways to build suppliers that you can keep healthy and they in turn will keep you healthy… The more you can get your vendors to think about you when building new products, the better.[21]

Saxenian observed that altogether, "the resilience of the Silicon Valley economy … is a product of the region's *dense networks of social, professional, and commercial relationships*." She then elaborated as follows:

> Silicon Valley is best viewed as an American variant of the industrial districts of Europe… In these districts, technical skill and competence are widely diffused, small and medium sized firms achieve external economies through complex supplier and subcontracting relations, and the region (not the firm) is the locus of production. The result is a decentralized system, which is more flexible than the traditional vertically integrated corporation.[22]

In their book *Silicon Valley Fever*, authors Everett Rogers and Judith Larsen quoted Atari founder Nolan Bushnell, who summed up the region's vitality by saying simply "There is a tremendous amount of networking here in Silicon Valley, unmatched anywhere else." The book went on to cite European engineers who were amazed by (and sometimes beaten in competition by) the very high degree to which their Valley counterparts shared technical information and expertise.[23]

The networked character of Silicon Valley includes not only the technical side, but also business and company development through board level interaction and bridging organizations. On average, a Stanford alumni CEO is a member of 5 other company boards while a Harvard alumni CEO only sits on one other company board.[24] For startups, business angels and venture capital firms are important bridging organizations providing access to knowledge, experience and resources such as

---

[21] Ibid, p. 103. (The Apple purchasing director quoted in this passage was Jim Bilodeau.)
[22] Ibid, p. 91.
[23] Rogers and Larsen (1984), p. 80.
[24] Rubens et al. (2011) http://www.innovation-ecosystems.org/wp-content/uploads/2010/12/2011.educon.pdf (Accessed 30 July 2015).

contacts with operational business expertise in areas such as Internet, IT, mobile and media.[25]

3.5 Management Innovation: People Focus, from Postwar to the Present

As noted, Hewlett-Packard and Varian Associates were early movers in creating people-centered workplaces. The examples they set were then followed by a famous *negative* example, that of Shockley Semiconductor in 1956–1957.

William Shockley, co-inventor of the transistor, recruited a team of brilliant young scientists and entrepreneurs for his attempt to build commercial semiconductor devices. Despite Shockley's own brilliance, eight key people left *en masse* in reaction to his autocratic management approach, which was hard to deal with personally and also included strategic decisions that frustrated the team's work. This event became a powerful illustration of *the difference that top talent can make* when the eight went on to start revolutionary ventures of their own—Fairchild Semiconductor, Intel, the investment firm Kleiner Perkins and more; few groups have ever had such impact—while Shockley's venture failed.[26]

From the 1960s on, as Silicon Valley grew, the demand and competition for good people grew accordingly. Overall demand was met in several ways. The University of California in Berkeley ramped up its computing and electronics programs to match Stanford. Also, highly skilled people began pouring into the Bay Area from other parts of the U.S. and (very notably) by immigration from outside the U.S., drawn by the lure of tech activity. It was the equivalent of a second Gold Rush.[27]

Competition among companies for the best of this new talent also took several forms. Salaries climbed, and so did offers of stock options and extravagant workplace perks. But numerous studies found that one attraction trumped them all: the chance to do challenging and important work.

Richard Florida reported that this appeared to be true in high-tech industries across the U.S. He cited *Information Week* surveys in which American IT workers rated "challenge" far above any other factor in terms of what mattered most when choosing a job. ("Flexibility" came second and pay, though important, was not often a deciding factor.)[28] Florida also cited other sources showing that pay had to be good enough—skilled people would not work for pay they judged inadequate—but time

---

[25] Steiber and Alänge (2013).

[26] There are many accounts of the history of William Shockley and his company; see for example Shurkin (2006). Likewise, many sources have told the stories of the so-called "traitorous eight" defectors from Shockley, who founded Fairchild Semiconductor, which then had important spinout firms. For a "family tree" chart of companies descended from Fairchild, see *Business Week* (1997).

[27] See for example Matthews (2002), pp. 147–180 and elsewhere.

[28] Florida (2002), pp. 88–91, 99.

and again, he said, talented young people in particular said their chief desire was to work on "exciting projects" and "important stuff."[29]

In Silicon Valley, qualified young people often got the opportunity to do that very quickly. Whereas companies in other times and places would break in new recruits gradually, so they could learn how the firm operated, fast-growing Valley companies were more likely to give them all the action they could handle, in order to help rush a new product to market. The software for Apple's original Macintosh was developed by teams working the proverbial "90 hours a week," and the developers were predominately young.[30]

Throwing people into action quickly may also help to address another issue. It can allow companies to get value from good employees before they move on. Many observers have commented on the extreme mobility of people in Silicon Valley. Figures such as average length of stay, or average number of jobs per career, don't capture the reason for the mobility. A cofounder of a chip-design firm explained it this way in an interview:

> Here in Silicon Valley there's far greater loyalty to one's craft than to one's company … A company is just a vehicle which allows you to work. If you're a circuit designer, it's most important for you to do excellent work. If you can't in one firm, you'll move on to another one.[31]

The mobility of people from company to company is part of a larger phenomenon in which the companies themselves are extremely mobile and fluid—that is, they grow or contract, and emerge or merge, with unusual frequency. A report from Berkeley Research Group noted that the list of the ten largest companies in Silicon Valley changed dramatically between 1982 and 2002, and again between 2002 and 2012. For instance, Apple, the largest in 2012, was not even on the top-ten list in 1982 and had barely made it in 2002 (ranking 9th behind Applied Materials). As for Google and eBay, 5th and 7th largest respectively in 2012: not only were they absent from both previous lists, but in 1982 they did not yet exist *nor did their industries exist*. The BRG report contrasts this fluidity with the situation of Detroit's "Big Three" U.S. automakers, where the same three firms have even maintained the same size order (GM-Ford-Chrysler) over those periods.[32]

Given the re-ordering of companies in Silicon Valley, one might think that people move around just to follow the changing patterns of growth. But what occurs in the Valley is more than a matter of labor supply shifting to meet demand. It's a combination of opportunity-seeking and networking. People seek out and follow novel opportunities, forming and exploiting personal networks as they go along. And as Saxenian observed,

---

[29] Ibid.

[30] See for example a first-person account in Hertzfeld (2004) http://www.folklore.org/StoryView.py?story¼90_Hours_A_Week_And_Loving_It.txt (Accessed 25 June 2015).

[31] Saxenian (1990), p. 97. The company cofounder quoted here was Robert Walker of LSI Corporation.

[32] Teece (2014).

These networks defy sectoral barriers: individuals move easily from semiconductor to disk drive firms or from computer to network makers. They move from established firms to startups (or vice versa) and even to market research or consulting firms, and from consulting firms back into start-ups.[33]

One could add that people also move back and forth between the universities and industry, and between technology companies and investment firms. Moreover, there are benefits for the companies involved: When people move across boundaries, they bring their ideas and expertise with them. Talent mobility, strategic partnering, and networking conducted by companies *and* individuals are all mechanisms by which companies in Silicon Valley cross-fertilize and help each other to self-renew. In Saxenian's words, they help the Valley as a whole behave as a vast "productive system"—always changing and re-configuring to seize the next opportunity, and the next.

3.6 In Summary (with Remarks on 'Replicating' Silicon Valley)

Due to the interest in Silicon Valley, many companies are setting up innovation "outposts"[34] in the Valley to tap into its dynamics. One could therefore say the Valley is opening up to include the rest of the world. *Or* one could argue, as we do, that *the rest of the world and all industries are coming more and more to resemble Silicon Valley*: fast-moving, constantly changing, hyper-competitive while also being more collaborative. This offers another way of capturing the Valley's magic, besides actually locating there.

Any company can begin to see the business environment and manage within it from a Silicon Valley perspective, and that perspective can best be summarized by re-stating something that's been pointed out already. The new management approaches that have evolved in the Valley dovetail closely with the management principles we expounded in the previous chapter.

- This chapter has shown that industries in Silicon Valley operate on a basis of *dynamic capabilities* and *continually changing organizations*. In example after example, we've seen companies reconfiguring their resources and changing radically in response to threats and opportunities.
- The region is *essentially people-centric*, with a special focus on entrepreneurial people and providing settings for them to exercise their creativity.
- It is *ambidextrous* in the sense that innovation and production are always occurring simultaneously, on a large regional scale, and also in the sense that companies have developed Bahrami's "Dualistic Systems" to do both tasks at once.

---

[33] Saxenian (1990), p. 97.
[34] For a good overview of this topic see Trondsen (2015) http://siliconvikings.com/blog/2015/4/6/innovation-outposts-a-growing-element-in-silicon-valleys-dynamic-innovation-ecosystem (Accessed 25 June 2015).

- Silicon Valley is most definitely built around *openness and networking*.
- Because the whole region operates as a system—Saxenian's "productive system"[35]—it invites *systems thinking* on the part of the firm.

And ultimately, since highly *entrepreneurial people* are the heart of the system, the message is that managers must look deeply into the best ways of attracting and managing them. The chapters ahead provide that look. However, first will a short chapter clarifying what "entrepreneurship" really is. Then we will get into understanding the special breed of people who can practice it, and how our case companies lead and organize their firms in order to attract and retain this breed of people.

3.7 Recent Developments: The Resilience of Silicon Valley

In 2022 and 2023, many people expressed concerns that Silicon Valley was entering a state of decline. This was due to the simultaneous appearance of several, seemingly ominous trends, and events. They included mass layoffs at Valley companies, a net outflow of skilled workers from the region, and the failure of Silicon Valley Bank, a key financial asset of the region. However, a closer look tells a different story. The Valley remains as fundamentally strong and resilient as ever. Its unique culture persists. And the Valley's major companies, along with their distinctive approaches to culture and management, may grow even stronger as they continue to evolve.

3.7.1 A Brief Analysis of 'Negative' Events

The layoffs of 2022-23 reached far and wide. Most companies (including our case companies) reduced staffing, and the total number of jobs cut throughout the Valley climbed into tens of thousands.[36] But there were underlying factors involved. Some companies had over-hired too optimistically during the Covid pandemic, when people's isolation drove a surge in demand for online services;[37] and the growing use of AI within companies has led to efficiency gains that reduced the need to keep staffing at previous levels.[38] Thus the layoffs might best be seen not as a sign that companies are weakening, but rather as part of a cyclical change in employment patterns—the kind that tend to happen from time to time in practically every industry and region.

The net out-migration of skilled workers can be attributed mostly to one factor: people seeking more affordable places to live, because of high living costs throughout the San Francisco Bay Area. In 2022, a World Economic Forum survey ranked

---

[35] Saxenian (1990).
[36] Avalos (2023).
[37] Thorbecke (2022).
[38] See for example Turner (2023).

San Francisco as the city with the eighth-highest living costs in the world.[39] And, when looking at entire metropolitan areas instead of just cities, some sources rank the Silicon Valley metro (which includes San Francisco) as the most expensive, slightly higher than the New York metro area.[40] This issue is common in many vibrant places. A dynamic economy attracts people to the area, and since space is finite, demand for housing pushes the limits of supply, and housing costs soar up.[41] Silicon Valley appears to be going through an adjustment period in this regard, but the adjustment cannot be said to signal any decrease in its fundamental dynamism.

As for the failure of Silicon Valley Bank: This did not devastate the region's startup ecosystem as some had feared it might. The U.S. government stepped in to insure the deposits of all account holders; the bank's business was purchased by another bank; and although the collapse of Silicon Valley Bank was definitely admitted to be a "challenge" to the region, by mid-2023 the shocks were being absorbed and most tech business was proceeding as usual.[42]

3.7.2 The Valley's Fundamental Strength and Resilience

Now for the positive evidence. Despite layoffs, Silicon Valley's unemployment rate dropped to just 2.8% in the spring of 2023—a figure that is generally seen as equivalent to full employment.[43] And the employment picture was only one sign among many that reflected the region's ongoing dynamism.

As of this writing, Silicon Valley remained the world's leading innovation hub by almost every conceivable measure. According to Startup Genome—which uses multi-factor analytic methods—the five leading innovation ecosystems in the world during 2022 were Silicon Valley, followed by New York City, London, Boston, and Beijing.[44] During the period measured, Silicon Valley had a staggering total "ecosystem value"—a figure combining the worth of startup exits and valuation of those not yet exited—of approximately $2.4 trillion. Over a four-year survey period, the region had 251 unicorns—individual startups valued at $1 billion or more—and an accumulation of venture capital funding that totaled $344 billion.[45]

Furthermore, the region's dynamism appears to be very much alive in terms of being at the forefront of new technologies and businesses. In the 1980s, Silicon Valley pioneered the personal computer; in the 1990s, public use of the internet, and in the 2000s, the mobile smartphone and the suites of applications built on it. Next, the region took a lead in AR/VR and Web3, and now Silicon Valley companies are

---

[39] Broom (2022).
[40] See for example Zetlin (2023).
[41] Ibid.
[42] Hetler (2023).
[43] Joint Venture Silicon Valley (2023).
[44] Startup Genome (2023a).
[45] Startup Genome (2023b).

at the forefront in generative and applied artificial intelligence.[46] At the same time, not only has Tesla remained the leader in electric vehicles, but it has also expanded into solar energy while becoming a diversified physical-technology company.

All evidence therefore points to Silicon Valley as a truly dynamic region, and to its major companies as exhibiting the dynamic capabilities required for constant innovation.

3.7.3 Persistence of the Culture and Business Model

As part of the region's Big Data and AI gold rush, unicorns such as Nuro, Lacework, and others were among the Valley startups listed as having valuations over $1 billion as of mid-2023.[47] Interestingly, these new unicorns expressed their culture in ways that mirror the entrepreneurial Silicon Valley mindset described earlier in this chapter.

One example is Nuro, a firm that is pioneering fully autonomous vehicles for local deliveries of goods. The company has a bold, challenging vision, stated on its website as follows: "We are trying to do something that has never been done before. We are working to solve a problem that so far has no solution." Nuro also places high value on people: "In striving to create the future, we need the very best people doing their very best work." Also, in the spirit established by early Valley companies like Varian and HP, Nuro grants its people high degrees of autonomy and flexibility: "Our team members are the owners of the Nuro mission and vision. This inspires a culture of proactive problem solving, creative solution seeking, and readiness and willingness to step outside of the lanes of our typical roles."[48] In a similar vein, the cloud computing unicorn Lacework boasts of recruiting and empowering "world class people" to build the definitive security platform for the cloud, while adopting "a mindset for lightspeed growth."[49]

3.7.4 Silicon Valley as a Global Innovation Hub in Transition

In general, it seems best to characterize Silicon Valley as a strong and resilient innovation hub, but also one in a state of evolutionary transition. This should not be surprising, since the region and its industries have been marked by constant change throughout their existence. We therefore close by noting just three trends, out of many, which could impact the ongoing evolution of both the Valley's entrepreneurial culture and its role in the global economy.

One is the use of remote work. The Covid pandemic forced Valley companies to shift to a virtual-work basis with employees working remotely from their homes.

---

[46] Ghaffary (2023).
[47] Fallory (2023).
[48] Zhu (2019).
[49] Lacework (2023).

Although many people liked this arrangement—and about 35% of the Valley's workforce continued to enjoy it, as of 2023—some observers voiced concern that it could threaten an organization's culture. One management scholar wrote that "there is often no substitute for co-presence when communication, problem-solving, and creativity are called for," and that furthermore, the physical separation involved in remote work can erode the social cues and bonds sustaining the culture.[50] After the pandemic, some Valley companies tried to capture the best of both worlds by instituting a "hybrid" policy. For example, Google/Alphabet required employees to be on-site in their offices at least three days per week.[51] It remains to be seen whether the changing patterns of work location will have long-term effects on company culture and management models.

A second and potentially much more impactful trend is the focus on artificial intelligence. If generative AI indeed turns out to be the next big breakthrough in technology, the Silicon Valley companies that have led R&D in this field may become even more influential than they have been so far. They will also play a major role in determining the status of the United States versus competition from other nations:

> While the USA is currently leading the AI arms race, China is quickly becoming a close second. In fact, the government of China has been investing heavily in AI research and development ... Major corporations including Alibaba, Baidu and Tencent are all actively involved in pushing China's AI capabilities to new heights, with many of their efforts creating groundbreaking results.[52]

And this in turn leads us to the third trend. Patterns of global alliance and collaboration between countries are shifting. After China joined the World Trade Organization in 2001, Silicon Valley became a center of growing interchanges between that nation and the U.S. Major Chinese firms established R&D centers in the Valley; Chinese venture funds opened Silicon Valley offices; the flow of Chinese students and immigrants to the Valley increased; and foreign direct investment between the U.S. and China surged.[53] Since 2016, however, "the accelerating deterioration of US-China relations has dramatically altered this pattern ... FDI fell to its lowest level since 2009 ... China's investments in Silicon Valley dropped due to capital controls by China's government and U.S. government's concern with leakage of critical technologies," and research collaborations began to suffer as well.[54] Meanwhile, the Valley continued to maintain strong relations with firms and governments in other Asian countries, notably Japan, Taiwan, and South Korea.[55] Perhaps most significantly, while ties with China receded, investments and collaboration *increased* with the nation that is now the world's largest—India:

---

[50] Howard-Grenville (2020).
[51] O'Loughlin (2023).
[52] InvestGlass (2023).
[53] Bay Area Council Economic Institute (2023).
[54] Ibid.
[55] See for example Widakuswara (2023).

> ... through the first seven months of 2022, FDI was on track to be the largest in recent history in terms of dollars and deals. In fact, the U.S.-India relationship could lead to a new innovation corridor in which Silicon Valley would play a key role. As India continues to shift from being a global back office to becoming a technology co-creator, the partnership that could be intensified could represent a great economic opportunity for both regions in the coming decade.[56]

In the report quoted above, this growing partnership was described as a potential "seismic shift" in global economic relations. The fact that Silicon Valley is seen as playing a key role serves to underscore the Valley's continuing importance. And it raises some interesting questions for the future. For example, how might the Valley's entrepreneurial culture influence (or be influenced by) Indian culture and management approaches? Strong connections already exist, built in large part through TiE, The Indus Entrepreneurs, a networking organization that was founded in Silicon Valley and now is established in major cities across India. (TiE 2023).[57]

But we are getting ahead of ourselves if we try to speculate on further evolution of the distinctive culture typified in Silicon Valley. First, we must look more closely at what this entrepreneurial culture and its associated management model really consist of. The next chapter begins the process by inquiring into a core concept: What exactly does "entrepreneurship" mean?

References

Avalos, G. (2023). Bay Area tech layoff plans in 2023 already top the total for all of 2022. *The Mercury News*, 4 May 2023. https://www.mercurynews.com/2023/05/02/bay-area-tech-job-layoff-facebook-google-twitter-cisco-economy-covid/

Bahrami, H. (1992). The emerging flexible organization: Perspectives from Silicon Valley. *California Management Review, 34*(4), 33–52.

Bahrami, H., & Evans, S. (2005). *Super-flexibility for knowledge enterprises*. Springer.

Bay Area Council Economic Institute. (2023). Technology, China, and the new U.S. industrial policy: A Bay Area view of economic relations with China in 2023. *White Paper*, February 2023. http://www.bayareaeconomy.org/files/pdf/Technology-China-NewIndustrialPolicy-2023-2.pdf

Broom, D. (2022). These are the most expensive cities in the world. *World Economic Forum*, 22 December 2022. https://www.weforum.org/agenda/2022/12/world-most-expensive-cities/

Business Week. (1997, August 25). Fairchild's offspring. *Business Week*, p. 84. Viewable at: https://www.yumpu.com/en/document/view/5533025/fairchilds-offspring-pdf-businessweek

Fallory. (2023). *The 63 unicorn companies in Silicon Valley in 2023*. Updated 18 May 2023. https://www.failory.com/startups/silicon-valley-unicorns

Florida, R. (2002). *The rise of the creative class*. Basic Books.

Freeman, C., Clark, J., & Soete, L. (1982). *Unemployment and technical innovation*. Frances Pinter.

Ghaffary, S. (2023). Silicon Valley's AI frenzy isn't just another crypto craze. *Vox*, 6 March 2023. https://www.vox.com/technology/2023/3/6/23624015/silicon-valley-generative-ai-chat-gpt-crypto-hype-trend

---

[56] Randolph (2023).
[57] TiE (2023).

References

Hertzfeld, A. (2004). 90 hours a week and loving it! in *The Original Macintosh*. Archived at: http://www.folklore.org/StoryView.py?story¼90_Hours_A_Week_And_Loving_It.txt. Accessed 25 June 2015.

Hetler, A. (2023). Silicon Valley Bank collapse explained: What you need to know. *TechTarget*, 20 April 2023. https://www.techtarget.com/whatis/feature/Silicon-Valley-Bank-collapse-explained-What-you-need-to-know#

Howard-Grenville, J. (2020). How to sustain your organization's culture when everyone is remote. *MIT Sloan Management Review*, 24 June 2020. https://sloanreview.mit.edu/article/how-to-sustain-your-organizations-culture-when-everyone-is-remote/

InvestGlass. (2023). *Which countries are leading the AI race?* 6 February 2023. https://www.investglass.com/which-countries-are-leading-the-ai-race/

Joint Venture Silicon Valley. (2023). *Silicon Valley unemployment rate decreases to 2.8%.* 19 May 2023. https://jointventure.org/2023-news-releases/2525-silicon-valley-unemployment-rate-decreases-to-2-8#

Kenney, M. (Ed.). (2000). *Understanding Silicon Valley*. Stanford University Press.

Lacework. (2023). About us. https://www.lacework.com/about-us/

Levi Strauss & Co. (2014). History of the Levi's 501® Jeans. http://www.levistrauss.com/wp-content/uploads/2014/01/History-of-Levis-501-Jeans.pdf. Accessed 25 June 2015.

Matthews, G. (2002). *Silicon Valley, women, and the California dream: Gender, class, and opportunity in the twentieth century*. Stanford University Press.

Norberg, A. L. (1976). The origins of the electronics industry on the Pacific coast. *Proceedings of the IEEE, 64*(9), 1314–1322.

O'Loughlin, H (2023). Google's return to office policy & timeline (June 2023). *Build Remote*, 8 June 2023. https://buildremote.co/return-to-office/google/#

PBS. (2006, September 13). The California Gold Rush in web pages for the PBS *American Experience* TV series. http://www.pbs.org/wgbh/amex/goldrush/peopleevents/e_goldrush.html. Accessed 25 June 2015.

Randolph, S. (2023). Seismic shift: Economic growth and strategic alignment between the Bay Area and India. Bay Area Council Economic Institute White Paper, March 2023. http://www.bayareaeconomy.org/files/pdf/SeismicShift-India2023.pdf

Rogers, E. M., & Larsen, J. K. (1984). *Silicon Valley fever: Growth of high-technology culture*. Basic Books.

Rubens, N., Russell, M., Perez, R., Huhtamäki, J., Still, K., & Kaplan, D. (2011). *Alumni network analysis*. http://www.innovation-ecosystems.org/wp-content/uploads/2010/12/2011.educon.pdf. Accessed 30 July 2015.

Saxenian, A. (1990). Regional networks and the resurgence of Silicon Valley. *California Management Review, 33*(1), 89–112.

Saxenian, A. (1994). *Regional advantage: Culture and competition in Silicon Valley and route 128*. Harvard University Press.

Shurkin, J. N. (2006). *Broken genius: The rise and fall of William Shockley, creator of the electronic age*. Macmillan.

Stanford University. (n.d.). *History of Stanford*. https://www.stanford.edu/about/history/. Accessed 26 June 2015.

Starr, K. (1973). *Americans and the California dream 1850–1915*. Oxford University Press.

Startup Genome. (2023a). *The global startup ecosystem report 2022*. https://startupgenome.com/article/global-startup-ecosystem-ranking-2022-top-30-plus-runners-up

Startup Genome. (2023b). *Silicon Valley*. https://startupgenome.com/ecosystems/silicon-valley

Steiber, A., & Alänge, S. (2013). The formation and growth of Google Inc.: A firm-level triple helix perspective. *Social Science Information, 52*(4), 575–604.

Teece, D. (2014). Regional clusters, ecosystems and dynamic capabilities: Lessons from Silicon Valley. Presentation from Berkeley Research Group to the iKuben conference in San Francisco, 1 December 2014.

Thorbecke, C. (2022). Silicon Valley's greatest minds misread pandemic demand. Now their employees are paying for it. *CNN Business*, 10 November 2022. https://www.cnn.com/2022/11/10/tech/tech-layoffs-analysis/index.html

TiE. (2023). About – TiE – Global entrepreneurship organization. *The Indus Entrepreneurs Website*. https://tie.org/about

Towers, S. (2002, April). The Silicon Valley management style. *Institute for Management Excellence Online Newsletter*, http://www.itstime.com/apr2002.htm. Accessed 25 June 2015.

Trondsen, E. (2015, April 6). Innovation outposts: A growing element in Silicon Valley's dynamic innovation system. *At Silicon Vikings*. http://siliconvikings.com/blog/2015/4/6/innovation-outposts-a-growing-element-in-silicon-valleys-dynamic-innovation-ecosystem. Accessed 25 June 2015.

Turner, M. (2023). Tech giants aren't just cutting thousands of jobs—They're making them extinct. *Insider*, 27 April 2023. https://www.businessinsider.com/tech-jobs-arent-coming-back-2023-4?

Tutorow, N. E. (2004). *The Governor: The life and legacy of Leland Stanford*. Arthur H. Clark Company.

Twain, M. (1872). *Roughing it*. American Publishing Company. Available from Project Gutenberg. www.gutenberg.org/files/3177/3177-h/3177-h.htm. Accessed 25 June 2015

Widakuswara, P. (2023). US, Japan, South Korea launch forum to cut off chips to China. VOA (*Voice of America*) News, 28 February 2023. https://www.voanews.com/a/us-japan-south-korea-launch-forum-to-cut-off-chips-to-china-/6984483.html

Zetlin, M. (2023). Here's the salary you need to live comfortably in America's 10 most expensive cities. *Inc.*, 16 April 2023. https://www.inc.com/minda-zetlin/heres-salary-you-need-to-live-comfortably-in-americas-10-most-expensive-cities.html

Zhu, J. (2019). What drives Nuro's culture. *Medium.com*, 13 August 2019. https://medium.com/nuro/what-drives-nuros-culture-cd53d269105c

Entrepreneurship: What It Really Is, and Why It Must Be *Integrated* into Management of the Firm

It is time for a fresh look at the whole concept of entrepreneurship. In recent decades the term has been used most frequently in a narrow sense, to mean the starting of new companies. That was not its original meaning, and the problem is more than how the word is used. *The attention that is paid* to entrepreneurship has followed the same line, leading to a division of thought and action. People think and act as if it is a function separate from the management of big, existing companies or other organizations.

In this chapter we argue that a new synthesis is now needed. Companies[1] need to reclaim the broader concept of entrepreneurship—which has to do with creating new sources of wealth and new value streams, not only new firms—and integrate it into a management approach for today's economy.

Doing so will require a measure we have emphasized all along: attracting and employing entrepreneurial people, in positions throughout the firm. But it may also require a shift in thinking, which isn't easy. Because of how the business world has evolved, the management ranks at many companies are filled largely with people who do not have an entrepreneurial background or outlook. And this, combined with other factors, can put the company into a bind. Everyone assumes they are managing in a way that is normal and right for the times, when in fact the firm has a bias against acting entrepreneurially (or is not equipped to do it well)—and moreover, will have trouble attracting entrepreneurial people for the road ahead.

So the first step is just to understand entrepreneurship in its broadest sense, and to see why it must be part of a new management synthesis. There are several key points to be grasped but a simple summary, based on a definition of entrepreneurship that we develop in this chapter, might read as follows:

---

[1] We use the term "company" frequently here, but entrepreneurship is equally important for organizations in the not-for-profit and government sectors.

Entrepreneurship is recognizing and seizing new business opportunities. Every firm needs to practice it regularly because in today's VUCA environment—volatile, uncertain, complex, ambiguous—current business lines can change dramatically, and revenue streams can be quickly eroded or lost. The good news is that the constant changes in this environment keep opening new windows of opportunity. It's a world in which proactive, entrepreneurial companies can thrive.[2]

In a paper on "Strategic Entrepreneurship," the scholar Michael A. Hitt and his colleagues put this last point nicely. Noting that business has entered an age of discontinuous change and high uncertainty, they wrote:

> Uncertainty can be used to your benefit if you create and employ an entrepreneurial mindset—a way of thinking about your business that captures the benefits… [for] there are opportunities in uncertainty.
> The firm's focus must be on identifying and exploiting those opportunities.[3]

There you have the heart of the message from two angles, ours and Hitt's. To fill out the picture, the sections below delve into the situation from several more angles. We'll start by looking at how various experts have described entrepreneurship, to convey a rich sense of all that it involves. Then we will briefly trace the evolution of modern business (and of business education) to see how this vital function became identified solely with startups, to the exclusion of big-firm management. The chapter closes by reiterating the call for a new synthesis and examining some issues related to it.

4.1 What Is Entrepreneurship?

As far as records show, the first person to write about entrepreneurship in business was the Irish-French banker and merchant Richard Cantillon. His *Essai sur la Nature du Commerce en Ge'neral* (*Essay on the Nature of Trade in General*), written in the 1730s and published in 1755, is now considered a foundational work of economics. The word "entrepreneur" comes to us from the French language because Cantillon wrote in French—although some English translations of his *Essay* give the word as "undertaker," referring to a class of people who undertake risky or uncertain activities.

Cantillon pointed out that while there are risks in any activity, most economic actors know (at least approximately) the returns they can expect before doing work

---

[2] Again, this summary applies not only to business firms but also to not-for-profit and government related organizations. They too can (and often must) dramatically change how they operate, and/or enter new lines of activity, in order to deliver maximum value. (For example, the International Committee of the Red Cross was founded in 1863 to treat those wounded in battle, and still does so—but Red Cross and Red Crescent teams now work in many other areas of humanitarian aid as well, from disaster relief to economic development). So, wherever this chapter speaks of "companies" or "business," please know that the basic concepts apply to organizations of all kinds.

[3] Hitt et al. (2001), p. 479.

or making a transaction. Wage earners agree to a specified pay rate; producers and traders of standard goods usually know the range of prices they can get for them in current markets, and so on. But entrepreneurs are willing to try something more adventurous. As Cantillon wrote, "They pay a fixed price" for goods or materials that will bring "an uncertain price" when resold as end products—or they may get no returns, for "These entrepreneurs never know how great the demand will be ...."[4] Although modern entrepreneurs can use methods to try to minimize risk,[5] the *willingness to deal in uncertainty* remains a hallmark of entrepreneurship to this day. And as Hitt observed, since today's markets are chronically uncertain, this trait can be an advantage.

About a century after Cantillon the French economist Jean-Baptiste Say added more dimensions to the emerging picture. He described an entrepreneur as someone who *"shifts economic resources out of an area of lower and into an area of higher productivity and yield."* A modern scholar further paraphrased one of Say's key insights in these words:

> The entrepreneur uses the ideas of a *philosopher*, that is new knowledge, which has not yet been applied in the economy to produce a new product.[6]

Joseph Schumpeter in the 1900s then elaborated further, focusing on entrepreneurs starting new companies in 1934[7] and then in 1942 emphasizing the importance of entrepreneurship and innovation also for large corporations, noting that entrepreneurs come up with *"new uses and combinations"* of resources which they apply in the marketplace. And in an oft-quoted passage, Schumpeter wrote:

> The function of entrepreneurs is to reform or revolutionize the pattern of production by exploiting an invention or, more generally, an untried technological possibility for producing a new commodity or producing an old one in a new way, by opening up a new source of supply of materials or a new outlet for products, by reorganizing an industry and so on.[8]

This function produces the "creative destruction" that the economist famously described. It displaces old ways of doing business; it can even displace old notions of the kinds of business that are possible to be done. During Schumpeter's own lifetime (1883–1950), electric lighting displaced gaslights, and the new automobile companies destroyed the horse-and-carriage trade (with some former carriage makers changing their "patterns of production" to make auto bodies). Also, the new radio industry was "reorganized" into a major broadcast medium after starting as a

---

[4] There are various English translations of Cantillon's *Essay*; these quotations are from Cantillon, Saucier (trans), and Thornton, ed. (2010), p. 74. https://mises.org/library/essay-economic-theory-0. Accessed 6 Aug 2015.

[5] E.g., Lean Startup methodology to increase efficiency in the innovation process.

[6] Sledzik (2013), p. 92.

[7] Schumpeter and Nichol (1934).

[8] Schumpeter (1942), p. 132.

point-to-point communication business—thus opening up "a new outlet for products" of the industry—and many more events of these types occurred.

4.1.1 A Modern Understanding (and a New Definition)

An aspect of entrepreneurship that emerges clearly from Schumpeter's work is as follows: it typically consists of *more than incremental innovation.* Incremental steps are important, such as always improving internal processes in order to gain efficiency and stay competitive, but entrepreneurial activity in its highest form is aimed at a larger goal. It is aimed at creating and capturing *new avenues to growth*, by taking substantially different approaches to one's business.

Writing in 2000, Scott Shane and Sankaran Venkataraman described the difference in terms of the kinds of opportunities being pursued:

> Entrepreneurial opportunities differ from the larger set of all opportunities for profit… because the former requires the discovery of new means-end relationships, whereas the latter involve optimization within existing means-end relationships.[9] — The authors credit this insight to the economist Israel Kirzner.

A very simple example of discovering new means-end relationships would be adapting a technology for sale into a new market, where customers would use it in new ways. More complex examples might entail finding "new combinations" of technologies, business models, target markets, etc. In some cases—such as Google developing AdWords, and Apple developing the iTunes platform to go with the iPod (and later the iPhone)—the companies combined a variety of means to achieve new ends. The returns in these cases were high and also gave the companies a big jump on competitors. As Schumpeter put it years before, in another of his well-known passages, entrepreneurial competition "strikes not at the margins of the profits and the outputs of the existing firms but at their foundations and their very lives."[10]

Meanwhile, late in the twentieth century—with the pace of change accelerating, and with markets of all kinds becoming global and more complex—Peter Drucker made this observation:

> Entrepreneurs see change as the norm and as healthy… *the entrepreneur always searches for change, responds to it, and exploits it as an opportunity.*[11]

We think Drucker has provided the final piece of the puzzle. Our definition—the one we'll use implicitly for the rest of this book—is in line with the spirit he identifies. We also believe it concisely reflects the other facets that have been mentioned:

---

[9] Shane and Venkataraman (2000), p. 220.
[10] Schumpeter (1942), p. 84.
[11] Drucker (1985), p. 28.

> Entrepreneurs are people who *create and exploit business opportunities. They create value by serving customers (or the company itself) in new ways, and by generating new revenue streams.*[12]

If you do these things, wherever you do them, you are an entrepreneur. And please note something else. What entrepreneurs do, by this definition, is exactly what companies must do to thrive in a fast-changing economy.

4.1.2 The Company as 'Entrepreneur'

In his book *Innovation and Entrepreneurship,* Drucker made two additional points that now should be emphasized.

- "Not every new small business is entrepreneurial," he wrote. Many are just like existing firms; they don't try anything substantially different or disruptive. And the converse:
- "An enterprise also does not have to be new and small to be an entrepreneur."[13]

To reiterate: *Large older companies, and the people in them, can (and in today's environment, must) do all the things that we've just seen entrepreneurs described as doing.*

This includes not only taking risks but embracing uncertainty and learning how to turn it to one's benefit. It includes applying new knowledge, to develop new uses and combinations of resources. And beyond incremental innovation, it means aiming to "reform or revolutionize" businesses, capitalizing on inventions and exploring untried possibilities in order to find "new outlets" and avenues to growth—always "searching for change" and "exploiting it as an opportunity," in order to "serve customers in new ways" and generate "new revenue streams."

However, they are stated, these functions would appear to be integral (and indeed necessary) parts of the job of managing *any* healthy, dynamic company.

Entrepreneurship inside large corporations has been studied under various headings, such as "corporate entrepreneurship",[14] corporate venturing,[15] and "intrapreneurship."[16] Intrapreneurship[17] has been defined as

---

[12] This definition can be adjusted to the nonprofit and public sectors. "Business opportunities" become opportunities for the society or citizens, and "new revenue streams" become new value streams, i.e. new ways of benefiting people.

[13] Drucker (1985), p. 20.

[14] Burgelman (1983), Guth and Ginsberg (1990), Granstrand and Alänge (1995).

[15] MacMillan (1986).

[16] Antoncic and Hisrich (2001, 2003), Menzel et al. (2007), Parker (2011).

[17] Intrapreneurship can be classified into eight dimensions: (1) New ventures, (2) New businesses, (3) Product/service innovativeness, (4) Process innovativeness, (5) self-renewal, (6) Risk taking, (7) Proactiveness, and (8) Competitive aggressiveness (Antoncic and Hisrich 2003), p. 19.

emergent behavioral intentions and behaviors that are related to departures from the customary ways of doing business in existing organizations.[18]

There have even been authors addressing the question of how to make engineers active in intrapreneurship, including what kinds of managerial and organizational support are required to facilitate their efforts inside the company.[19]

Yet "entrepreneurship" has in many cases become separated from "management" and identified with startups, to the extent that founders of new firms typically learn and practice the skills much more than managers of established firms are likely to do. This has happened (and still happens) in a variety of ways, which we will now explore.

4.2 The Divide Between Entrepreneurship and Management: Obstacles and Evolutionary Forces

To begin with, it is widely observed that companies have a tendency to become less "entrepreneurial" as they grow beyond the startup stage, for a couple of reasons. One reason, often stated informally, is simply that bureaucracy sets in—that is, structures and routines are put in place that interfere with experimentation and trying new approaches.

Max Weber commented on this transition long ago. In his terms, it would be a transition from "charismatic authority"—wherein a relatively small startup is ruled and inspired by the charisma of the founder(s), who set the norms for behavior by others—to a state of "legal-rational" governance by bureaucracy.[20] Weber didn't see this as a necessarily bad thing, though, pointing out that bureaucracies have virtues and benefits. They define people's roles and positions clearly (and, ideally, on the basis of merit rather than patronage); and as many have noted, some degree of "bureaucratic" structure is needed just to keep order in a big organization.

But other forces are at work besides imposing order. When a dynamic founder leaves the firm or is replaced by a professional executive in the top spot, the power of that founder's enterprising spirit (along with his/her expertise and guidance in entrepreneurship) may indeed be lost as well. One example that's often mentioned is Apple slumping after Steve Jobs left the company, then being re-energized when he returned.

Also, as a startup succeeds and grows it may become "path-dependent"—that is, its future tends be shaped by the path it has taken thus far. The structures that are put in place are organized around the business model and product lines which led to the success. People in the company become inclined to do "what worked" before and grow skeptical of other approaches.

---

[18] Antoncic and Hisrich (2003), p. 20.
[19] Menzel et al. (2007).
[20] Waters and Waters ed. and trans. (2015).

4.2 The Divide Between Entrepreneurship and Management: Obstacles…

And since a big organization has many needs and goals, it may institute special purpose systems that turn out to conflict with entrepreneurship. This happened at 3M when the company adopted the Six Sigma quality program. Entrepreneurial engineers and managers found it more difficult to implement new ideas, because all the steps had to be run through the program's quality-assurance protocols. Eventually 3M dropped the program, confident that it could maintain quality by other means.[21]

All of the above are ways that entrepreneurship can be lost or diminished *within an individual firm as it matures*. It is possible to counteract these effects, and a good way to begin is just by watching out for them. Top management at Google, for instance, has been mindful of the need to keep obstacles from creeping in. But this is not the place for a detailed discussion of how to do that. We would call your attention to another, longer-running force that has led to a separation between entrepreneurship and management: the force of history.

4.2.1 How Business Schools Reinforced the Split

As the business world has evolved over time, business *education* has evolved, and the programs for educating future leaders have split into forking paths: entrepreneurship programs (targeted to the founding of new firms) on one hand, conventional management programs (targeted to preparing big-firm managers) on the other. Here is a brief summary of how this occurred and what the present status is. There have long been "business schools" in the sense of formal or informal programs to teach basic skills such as accounting. As the Industrial Age progressed, the first university-level business schools appeared during the 1800s. The *Ecole Supérieure de Commerce* (now ESCP Europe) was co-founded by a group of scholars and businessmen in Paris in 1819, followed much later by other such as the Pest Academy of Commerce (now Budapest Business School) in present-day Hungary and the University of Pennsylvania's Wharton School in the U.S.[22] These schools were few in number, and they granted the equivalent of a modern bachelor's degree, teaching economics—then a new field—along with practical business skills and some core academic subjects.

The real expansion of high-level business education began in the late 1800s and early 1900s, especially in the U.S. with the founding and proliferation of MBA programs. And this happened to be a time when business itself was undergoing a profound expansion. As Carter A. Daniel wrote in his book *MBA: The First Century,* until about the 1860s, "businesses had been one-shop and owner-managed … [but then] everything changed."[23] Massively integrated oil and steel companies, big railroads, and retailers, and Fordist mass-production lines carried division of labor to a new level: they required division and specialization of management. According to Daniel,

---

[21] See for example Hindo (2007).
[22] See "Business school" with footnoted list of "Notable firsts" at Wikipedia (2015).
[23] Daniel (1998), p. 40.

an entire category of employment — the 'middle management ranks' — rose from nonexistence to ubiquitousness… Universities everywhere cited this development as the single major reason for having a school of business.[24]

Daniel went on to quote from early school catalogs which stated, for instance, that their mission was "to fit young men more thoroughly and definitely for the successful management of large manufacturing and commercial enterprises." Adding to this trend was the fact that "scientific management" methods had been developed by Frederick Taylor and others, and business schools went beyond these methods, studying and teaching business in ways that were "overwhelmingly mechanical and descriptive."[25]

So it continued—and though Taylorism eventually fell out of vogue, another tool came along that reinforced the emphasis on teaching highly detailed optimizing techniques for the management of big companies. After World War II, the advent of computing enabled sophisticated quantitative modeling of big-firm operations and sped the growth of operations research.[26] This new trend remained dominant in many schools for decades.

And in the meantime, the teaching of entrepreneurial skills and behaviors—such as opportunity recognition and all that must follow, in order to develop and implement new ideas—gravitated into special "entrepreneurship" programs focused on new-firm formation. These programs began fitfully with a few scattered courses at various business schools in the mid-twentieth century. They started proliferating in the 1980s, mainly at first in the U.S., where new cohorts of young people were being inspired by the successes of high-tech founder-entrepreneurs like Jobs, Bill Gates, et al. As more and more students dreamed of starting their own firms, they created a growing demand for education in that *particular* form of entrepreneurship, and the supply grew accordingly.[27]

By the first decade of the 2000s, according to research from the Kauffman Foundation,[28] virtually every major university in the U.S. (and many smaller colleges) had not only courses in entrepreneurship, but full-fledged academic programs, entrepreneurship support centers, and extracurricular programs for entrepreneurs such as business-plan competitions—all of them focused on the startup process. Much the same was coming to be true in other countries as well.

---

[24] Ibid, p. 41.

[25] Ibid, p. 82.

[26] For instance Carnegie Mellon's Graduate School of Industrial Administration (now Tepper School of Business), founded in 1949, was an early champion of computer-based analytic methods and operations research, and in 1958 was the first business school to teach decision making via computer simulation—its "Management Game" was elaborately modeled on actual businesses at Procter & Gamble. See for example Phillips (2007).

[27] See for example Henricks (2003).

[28] See for example Ewing M. Kauffman Foundation (2013).

4.2.2 Toward a Re-synthesis of Entrepreneurship and Management

Some of the academic activity is now migrating over into the realm of big-firm management. There are courses with titles like "Entrepreneurship Inside Organizations." Babson College, for one, has offered such a course, and has posted materials on its website with statements like the following:

> Most of today's organizations were built through entrepreneurship but ironically are not built for entrepreneurship... while we're supportive of entrepreneurial behavior in the world of start-ups, we haven't successfully leveraged that behavior inside organizations.[29]

Babson and other institutions have conducted seminars and conferences on the issue. A growing cadre of business researchers (including those quoted earlier in this chapter) are paying attention to entrepreneurship as a phenomenon in existing firms as well as startups.

Gradually, one hopes, the situation will evolve to an appropriate state that reflects reality. Both the academic world and the business world will treat entrepreneurship as a set of activities to be studied and practiced everywhere, with the only "divisions" being in the form of considering how the practice differs in different settings. (Of course, the startup process in a small firm is not identical with big-firm entrepreneurship; each has particular challenges. The point is that both are *important* and need to be treated as such—with attention to the interactions and potential synergies between big and new firms, as well as to the differences between them.)

For now, though, the reality is that many young people are graduating from business schools without much formal preparation for managing entrepreneurship in big firms.[30] And, many are entering big firms where entrepreneurship isn't valued as highly, or supported as diligently, as it is in the realm of startups.

4.3 Recent Developments

The re-synthesis of entrepreneurship and management has continued since the book's first edition. Still, there is a lack of a common definition of entrepreneurial management, and a wide knowledge gap on how to develop the attributes of an

---

[29] Babson College http://www.babson.edu/executive-education/blended-learning/webinars/archives/Pages/Entrepreneurship-Inside-Your-Organization.aspx. Accessed 12 Dec 2015.

[30] The same situation has existed within most engineering education as well—although here also, programs focusing on entrepreneurship inside large corporations have been started, such as the one at Chalmers University of Technology, described on the Chalmers website as follows: "The Corporate Entrepreneurship track offers the students [the opportunity] to develop entrepreneurial skills to handle large scale of complexities in large firms, in enabling innovative new products and services to be developed. The students work hands on in a real and innovative project of a large firm, where they will be able to develop and reflect on entrepreneurial behaviour and skills. In those projects the students will work in close collaboration with management from industry."

entrepreneurial manager and leader.[31] What is known, however, is that entrepreneurship is becoming increasingly important in a global and fast-changing world,[32] and that embedding it in educational practices is key.[33] Further, entrepreneurship is now studied and discussed from multiple perspectives. These include but are not limited to women's entrepreneurship,[34] the digitalization of entrepreneurship,[35] family-business entrepreneurship,[36] founder-CEO entrepreneurship,[37] and entrepreneurship in developing countries.[38] This diversification into many sub-fields might be seen as an indicator of the subject's universal and growing importance. The pattern therefore tells us that entrepreneurship within the context of a firm, including management of the firm, is here to stay and will most probably accelerate in importance throughout the twenty-first century.

4.4 What Can a Company Do?

It is more important than ever to integrate entrepreneurship with big-firm management. Prospects are dim for companies that do not build an effective new synthesis. Many will continue to be reactive and path-dependent in a world where being entrepreneurially proactive matters greatly and the past matters not at all.

There is currently no dominant model for how to build the required new synthesis. However, the chapters ahead examine how six case companies in Silicon Valley have created and sustained a management model for entrepreneurship, while still being excellent at scaling and operational efficiency. We believe these companies represent a new breed of large firms that are fast, responsive, and able to do both innovation and core business in parallel—making them prototypes of a breed well fitted for today's rapidly changing world.

To start filling out the new model these companies exemplify, the next chapter describes the kind of people they recruit. This reiterates a theme that has run through the book: the focus is on attracting and employing entrepreneurial *people*. (As the chapter will note, it is not necessary for everyone in the firm to have the complete skill set and characteristics of an entrepreneur. But entrepreneurs are needed "all over the firm"—at every level and in every part—and everyone should have the flexibility to fit well with entrepreneurial activity.)

We will then continue with a discussion of culture and how the companies are led, in order to attract entrepreneurial people and enable them to do their best work.

---

[31] Clark et al. (2019).
[32] Pauceanu et al. (2021).
[33] Ratten and Jones (2021).
[34] See for example Cardella et al. (2020).
[35] See for example Kraus et al. (2019).
[36] E.g., Minola et al. (2021).
[37] Abebe et al. (2020).
[38] Hoang et al. (2020).

But let us now start by meeting this "special breed of people" who are central to the task of building a great entrepreneurial company.

References

Abebe, M. A., Li, P., Acharya, K., & Daspit, J. J. (2020). The founder chief executive officer: A review of current insights and directions for future research. *Corporate Governance: An International Review, 28*(6), 406–436.

Antoncic, B., & Hisrich, R. D. (2001). Intrapreneurship: Construct refinement and cross-cultural validation. *Journal of Business Venturing, 16*, 495–527.

Antoncic, B., & Hisrich, R. D. (2003). Clarifying the intrapreneurship concept. *Journal of Small Business and Enterprise Development, 10*(1), 7–24.

Babson College. (undated). Entrepreneurship inside your organization on Babson College website: http://www.babson.edu/executive-education/blended-learning/webinars/archives/Pages/Entrepreneurship-Inside-Your-Organization.aspx. Accessed 29 Apr 2015.

Burgelman, R. A. (1983). Corporate entrepreneurship and strategic management: Insights from a process study. *Management Science, 29*(12), 1349–1364.

Cantillon, R., Saucier, C. (Trans.), & Thornton, M. (Ed.). (2010). *An essay on economic theory*. Ludwig von Mises Institute. https://mises.org/library/essay-economic-theory-0. Accessed 30 June 2015.

Cardella, G. M., Hernández-Sánchez, B. R., & Sánchez-García, J. C. (2020). Women entrepreneurship: A systematic review to outline the boundaries of scientific literature. *Frontiers in Psychology, 11*, 1557.

Clark, C. M., Harrison, C., & Gibb, S. (2019). Developing a conceptual framework of entrepreneurial leadership: A systematic literature review and thematic analysis. *International Review of Entrepreneurship, 17*(3), 347–384.

Daniel, C. A. (1998). *MBA: The first century*. Bucknell University Press.

Drucker, P. (1985). *Innovation and entrepreneurship*. Harper Business.

Ewing M. Kauffman Foundation. (2013, August). Entrepreneurship education comes of age on campus. Kauffman Foundation white-paper report: http://www.kauffman.org/~/media/kauffman_org/research%20reports%20and%20covers/2013/08/eshipedcomesofage_report.pdf. Accessed 30 June 2015.

Granstrand, O., & Alänge, S. (1995). The evolution of corporate entrepreneurship in Swedish industry – Was Schumpeter wrong? *Journal of Evolutionary Economics, 5*(2), 133–156.

Guth, W. D., & Ginsberg, A. (1990). Guest editors' introduction: Corporate entrepreneurship. *Strategic Management Journal, 11*, 5–15.

Henricks, M. (2003, April). Can entrepreneurship be taught? *Entrepreneur*. http://www.entrepreneur.com/article/60244. Accessed 30 June 2015.

Hindo, B. (2007, June 10). At 3M, a struggle between efficiency and creativity. *Bloomberg Business*. http://www.bloomberg.com/bw/stories/2007-06-10/at-3m-a-struggle-between-efficiency-and-creativity. Accessed 29 Apr 2015.

Hitt, M. A., Ireland, R. D., Camp, S. M., & Sexton, D. L. (2001). Guest editors' introduction to the special issue 'Strategic entrepreneurship: Entrepreneurial strategies for wealth creation'. *Strategic Management Journal, 22*, 479–491.

Hoang, G., Le, T. T. T., Tran, A. K. T., & Du, T. (2020). Entrepreneurship education and entrepreneurial intentions of university students in Vietnam: The mediating roles of self-efficacy and learning orientation. *Education + Training, 63*(1), 115–133.

Kraus, S., Roig-Tierno, N., & Bouncken, R. B. (2019). Digital innovation and venturing: An introduction into the digitalization of entrepreneurship. *Review of Managerial Science, 13*(3), 519–528.

MacMillan, I. C. (1986). Progress in the research on corporate venturing. In D. L. Sexton & R. W. Smilor (Eds.), *The art and science of entrepreneurship*. Ballinger.

Menzel, H. C., Aaltio, I., & Ulijn, J. M. (2007). On the way to creativity: Engineers as intrapreneurs in organizations. *Technovation, 27*(12), 732–743.

Minola, T., Kammerlander, N., Kellermanns, F. W., & Hoy, F. (2021). Corporate entrepreneurship and family business: Learning across domains. *Journal of Management Studies, 58*(1), 1–26.

Parker, S. (2011). Intrapreneurship or entrepreneurship? *Journal of Business Venturing, 26*(1), 19–34.

Pauceanu, A. M., Rabie, N., Moustafa, A., & Jiroveanu, D. C. (2021). Entrepreneurial leadership and sustainable development—A systematic literature review. *Sustainability, 13*(21), 11695.

Phillips, D. (2007). Management game. Carnegie Mellon University website at https://www.cmu.edu/corporate/news/2007/features/mgmt%20games.html. Accessed 29 Apr 2015.

Ratten, V., & Jones, P. (2021). Entrepreneurship and management education: Exploring trends and gaps. *The International Journal of Management Education, 19*(1), 100431.

Schumpeter, J. (1942). *Capitalism, socialism and democracy*. Harper & Brothers.

Schumpeter, J. A., & Nichol, A. J. (1934). Robinson's economics of imperfect competition. *Journal of Political Economy, 42*(2), 249–259.

Shane, S., & Venkataraman, S. (2000). The promise of entrepreneurship as a field of research. *Academy of Management Review, 25*(1), 217–226.

Sledzik, K. (2013). Schumpeter's view on innovation and entrepreneurship. In S. Hittmar (Ed.), *Management trends in theory and practice*. Faculty of Management Science and Informatics, University of Zilina & Institute of Management by University of Zilina. http://poseidon01.ssrn.com/delivery.php?ID¼0191210240260850100951120821031221110540250700850220920 8.70210800911220770230660160751141170550440510600150720841010140900821180160 8.4042033015116110102080005027122104019077079093086096118123012126111116010 10.4071096002123089025085115104103085008001073&EXT¼pdf&TYPE¼2. Accessed 6 Aug 2015.

Waters, T., & Waters, D. (Eds. & Trans.). (2015). *Weber's rationalism and modern society*. Palgrave Macmillan.

Wikipedia. (2015). Business school with footnoted list of "Notable firsts" at: https://en.wikipedia.org/wiki/Business_school#Notable_firsts. Accessed 29 Apr 2015.

A Special Breed of People

5

> Great vision without great people is irrelevant.—Jim Collins (2001), p. 42

In the book *Good to Great*, Jim Collins reported some findings that surprised him and his research team. Executives who transformed their companies from good to great did not first figure out the direction in which the company should be developed, and then get people to take it there.

Instead, they first recruited the right people (and got rid of the wrong people), then they worked on direction. According to Collins, great leaders understand three simple truths. One is to begin with *who* rather than *what*, which makes an organization more adaptable in a changing world. Second, if a company has the right people on board, they are highly self-motivated by the intrinsic rewards of their work, so the problem of how to motivate employees largely goes away. And third, if you have the wrong people, it doesn't matter which direction you take; you still won't have a great organization.

Collins published those observations in 2001. We were able to update and expand upon them in our research, by focusing on the key practical questions that arise:

> What kinds of people are "the right people" for today's fast-moving business world? And what can a company do to attract and keep them?

This chapter presents the answers we learned from studies of successful Silicon Valley companies over the period 2010–2015. All of our case companies— Google, Facebook, LinkedIn, Twitter, Tesla Motors and Apigee—placed an extraordinary emphasis on hiring and retention. Furthermore, they looked for similar qualities in the people they recruited, and there were common threads in the approaches they used to attract and select such people.

A profile of the companies' ideal employees would read briefly as follows: The best people have more than superb technical skills. They are *entrepreneurial* by nature, and *passionate* about their work. They are change-seekers who *constantly question the status quo*. And though they can be quite individualistic, as well as persistent in following up on their ideas, they're also highly *adaptable* and *collaborative*.

People who combine all these qualities could be labeled as "a special breed". One might be tempted to call them a "new breed" simply because so many workers at our case companies were young, but there were middle-aged or older people who fitted the profile equally well—including founders and top executives at some of the firms! The members of this special breed could not be defined by generational stereotypes, and in some respects they were the opposite of the classic corporate stereotype. Rather than seeking personal advancement by being yes-men or players in office politics, they sought personal *fulfillment* by being strong-minded and highly engaged team players that want to be part of a greater mission.

Two other characteristics of the special breed should be noted. They are relatively rare, and they tend to be mobile, not staying with one firm for a lifetime. This means that competition for them is intense. It also means that companies must face the paradox of trying to build and maintain staffs of excellent people, each of whom may only be around for a few years at most. In the pages ahead we will describe how our case companies dealt with these issues. But let's begin at the beginning. Below is a short recap of how our research originated, followed by a more detailed description of the people who constituted the special breed.

5.1 Focusing on the 'Special Breed,' from Google Onward

Our Silicon Valley research started in 2010 with a nearly year-long series of site visits and interviews at Google. The initial purpose was to investigate what drives innovation within Google. We found that Google's management model supported well the six basic principles described in Chap. 2. Google in fact exhibited dynamic capabilities, a continually changing organization, a people-centric approach, an ambidextrous and open organization, and a systemic approach to innovation.[1]

However, one factor stood out as being central to Google's innovativeness, namely its *people*. Most of the interviewees asserted that Google's greatest strength came from its employees, and again and again the importance of the right individuals was mentioned. The value of focusing on people is supported by leading researchers like David Teece, who wrote:

> In recent decades, expert talent has become more important than ever for the creation and management of technology in the global economy.[2]

Our Google interviewees didn't label the type of people they were searching for as "experts," but described them in some detail. Among other things they were called

---

[1] Steiber (2014).
[2] Linden and Teece (2014), p. 87.

incredibly smart, curious, never satisfied with status quo, team players, and very "humble".[3] One person said:

> Every single one here is remarkable…Everybody feels that the others are better. Still, the amount of ego is very small… [and] this creates an incredible strength—excellent people without ego and politics.

Google's emphasis on people was addressed by Executive Chairman Eric Schmidt and former Senior VP Jonathan Rosenberg in their 2014 book *How Google Works*.[4] In one general statement they said

> Smart coaches know that no amount of strategy can substitute for talent…Googlers made it a priority to invest the time and energy to ensure they got the best possible people.[5]

To us, as external researchers, the finding that Google saw people as being so central to innovation and long-term competitiveness was interesting in itself. Then, when we continued our research by interviewing at other successful Silicon Valley-based companies—and they all expressed the very same thing—the role of people became even more interesting. It gave birth to the idea for the book you're now reading.

We were struck by noticing that the six companies in our study all seemed to search for a very specific breed of people. Moreover, it was a breed that differed markedly from most people we had met in other large corporations we've visited. Adding further interest, these six companies in the Valley seemed to have created and sustained a management model that fit this breed of people. So not only were our case companies searching for a particular type of people to hire, but they had also apparently designed their leadership and organizational structure—and ultimately, their corporate culture—with a view to attracting and retaining this type of people. In short, the companies seemed to be performing a balancing act that some researchers have described as *necessary*. As Greg Linden and David Teece of UC-Berkeley stated it:

> In today's global business context, the business enterprise must accomplish the difficult but essential tasks of delivering intellectual stimulation to its experts, keeping them financially satisfied, fostering collegiality and collaboration among them and allowing them the guided professional autonomy they seek (and that their work demands) while holding them accountable to the enterprise.[6]

Chapters after this one will delve more deeply into the aspects of corporate culture, leadership and organizational design that help attract great entrepreneurial people. Let's now focus on the characteristics that make these people desirable.

---

[3] Steiber (2014), p. 56.
[4] Schmidt and Rosenberg (2014), p. 96.
[5] Ibid., pp. 96–97.
[6] Linden and Teece (2014), p. 89.

5.2 On 'Multidimensional' People and the Need for Them

...the ideal is to hire someone who is better than yourself.[7]—Interviewee at Google

In our 2010 study of Google, it became clear that the company's hiring process was very selective. Each new employee was chosen after a long multi-stage evaluation. The individual was evaluated on four basic sets of characteristics: cognitive abilities, knowledge and expertise in the field he or she will be working in, "Googliness," and leadership abilities.[8] Googliness meant how well the individual's values and personal character fit with Google's culture. According to our interviewees in 2010 the company wanted employees who had excellent academic track records and were entrepreneurial ("scrappy"), curious and questioning. Further, they were also to be energetic, driven, nonpolitical, humble, and change-oriented self-starters who had a passion for the internet and the mission of the company.

That is a long list of desirable attributes. In *How Google Works*,[9] Schmidt and Rosenberg sketched out the core qualities in somewhat simpler terms and coined a name for people who possess those qualities. The authors described them as "Smart Creatives."

Interestingly, they differentiated Smart Creatives from the people generally labeled as "knowledge workers"—a category introduced by Peter Drucker in his 1959 book *Landmarks of Tomorrow*.[10] In Schmidt and Rosenberg's view, most knowledge workers have tended to build expertise in a narrow (or shallow) set of skills. Either they develop deep technical expertise but little breadth, or wide-ranging management expertise but not technical depth.[11]

Smart Creatives stand out because they are *multidimensional*, usually combining *business competence* with *creativity* and *technical depth*. According to the authors, these people make up a new breed in the sense that they are key to achieving success in the Internet Century. Schmidt and Rosenberg cited several reasons why such people will be increasingly needed and valuable.

The reasons stem mainly from the development of information and communication technologies. Progress in ICT has led to cheap experimentation; it has made data and computer power into non-scarce resources, and it makes collaboration easier than ever, whether across a room or a continent. All this creates the possibility for people to have an "inordinately big impact."[12] As we saw in Chap. 3, the effects of ICT in broadening the powers and roles of people in a company were recognized years ago by researcher Homa Bahrami. She found that use of ICT was decreasing the need for middle management, and noted that the "potential consequences" for

---

[7] Steiber (2014), p. 59.
[8] Ibid.
[9] Schmidt and Rosenberg (2014), pp. 16–20.
[10] Drucker (1959).
[11] Schmidt and Rosenberg (2014), p. 17.
[12] Ibid., p. 16.

employees generally could include "larger spans of control, increased workloads, and a broader range of assignments and roles for individuals and groups".[13]

But there is another side of the coin. This potential to have greater impact also puts new and more complex demands on the personalities and skills of people working in organizations. Hence the list of requirements cited by our Google subjects, along with Schmidt and Rosenberg's call for multidimensional people who combine business and technical understanding with creative flair. Furthermore, as Schmidt and Rosenberg pointed out, Smart Creatives demand to be treated in ways that fit their multidimensional capabilities—for instance, not confined to specific tasks nor limited much in their access to the company's information and computing power. They are unafraid to take risks and do not wish to be hemmed in by role definitions or organizational structures. They don't keep quiet when they disagree with something; they are easily bored if new challenges are lacking, and they are prone to shift jobs.[14]

Issues of managing this special breed of people will be discussed a bit later. First, we must fill out our description of the breed. The Google findings gave a good initial picture but they represented just one company's views. And while the other companies we studied in the Valley looked for people with substantially similar characteristics—nobody said they wanted a different breed—the sources at these firms added some instructive details to the profile.

All of the other five case companies (Facebook, Twitter, LinkedIn, Apigee and Tesla) wanted people who were entrepreneurial or "scrappy" and who dared to take risks. Further, they looked for people who can handle and do well in an environment with a high degree of ambiguity and rate of change. In connection with fast-paced change, sources at these firms spoke of wanting people who are adaptable and agile learners, especially in situations where learning must occur more as "on the job training" than in classrooms. Also, the candidates should exhibit fresh new thinking and question the status quo more or less continuously. They should be both strategic and operational, have a strong drive and be self-organized. Finally, they must be excellent at working in teams and collaborating with other people, both internally and externally.

When looking over the list of desired qualities, you get the impression that this is quite a mature and experienced class of people who are being recruited. Maybe they've started their own companies or projects, have been drilled in teamwork, and have worked in both strategic and operational roles. Surprisingly, however, the average age of these people is rather low. The median age at Facebook was 28, compared with 30 at Google.[15] This meant that a majority of the companies' employees were so-called Millennials or even Generation Z. Despite their youth, they were given unusual freedom to choose and change assignments—even outside their areas

---

[13] Bahrami (1992), p. 34.
[14] Schmidt and Rosenberg (2014), p. 17.
[15] Albergotti (2014).

of expertise—and managers were urged to put them in roles that catered to their strengths.[16]

So, was employing Millennials the secret sauce behind these companies' success? Probably not. According to an IBM study of 1784 multigenerational employees in organizations across 12 countries and six industries, Millennials want many of the same things and exhibit many of the same traits that their older colleagues do. The IBM report—released in 2015 and titled "Myths, Exaggerations and Uncomfortable Truths"—found little substance behind the stereotypes that portrayed Millennials as dramatically different from members of Generation X (aged 35–49 at the time of study) or postwar Baby Boomers (aged 50 and up).[17] IBM's researchers found that the only fundamental distinction between Millennials and older employees was their digital proficiency, as Millennials were the first generation to grow up immersed in a digital world. The study concluded that "good management" of a company entails seeing people as individuals, not as generational stereotypes, *and* it includes leveraging the capabilities of the "digital natives." The secret sauce is therefore most likely not the share of Millennials *per se*, even if you might be able to benefit faster from their digital capabilities. What's more important is skill in managing individuals generally and in using their digital capabilities overall.

Meanwhile, we now have a fairly well-developed picture of the "special breed" of people that successful Silicon Valley companies have sought to employ. To make the picture more useful, the following section condenses the many desired attributes that have been mentioned into five "cornerstone" qualities and elaborates on each one.

5.3 Cornerstones of Success: Five Core Qualities of the 'Special Breed'

Sources at our case companies agreed widely on these fundamental points: In a fast-changing business world where firms must innovate to survive, people are the main ingredient for success, and a particular type of people are needed the most. Not surprisingly, different companies in our sample had somewhat different lists of attributes that they looked for in recruiting. But five core qualities were mentioned repeatedly across the board.

All of the companies wanted employees who are *entrepreneurial, adaptable, passionate, constantly questioning the status quo,* and *collaborative.* Calling these the cornerstone qualities of success, let us now take a closer look at what each quality entails.

---

[16] Ibid.
[17] IBM Institute for Business Value (2015).

5.3.1 Entrepreneurial

> People must be both strategic and scrappy…be big picture thinkers and roll up their sleeves and get things done.—Interviewee at Twitter

Naturally, companies that strive to be entrepreneurial want employees who fit the agenda. In Chap. 4 we saw entrepreneurs described as people (or groups of people) who create and exploit business opportunities. They create value by serving customers (or the company itself) in new ways, and by generating new revenue streams.

Here, a question presents itself. Does everyone in the company have to become a full-fledged entrepreneur in the sense of originating new business ideas and carrying them to fruition? That may be too much to expect, but *everyone must be willing and able to be part of the entrepreneurial process*. For instance: Our case companies had engineers who specialized in operating areas such as product reliability. Firms that make physical goods have manufacturing specialists, and all sizable firms have various kinds of internal service providers. Understandably, many people who play these critical roles may not originate a new-business idea.

However, *in an entrepreneurial company, they all may at some points be members of new-product or new-business development teams—or at least, they will need to support such efforts to the fullest*. Specialists who work on reliability or manufacturing systems must be able to tailor their systems to new offerings, and scale them up quickly as the ventures grow. The same holds true for employees (and managers) in every role. Certainly, they must not resist the new, as often happens in bureaucratic firms. Their "scrappiness" should be channeled into fighting *for* positive change rather than obstructing it.

Moreover, employees throughout the company must act entrepreneurially in the sense of being opportunity-seekers. They should *always be open to innovating how they do their jobs—looking for a competitive edge, looking for a better wa*y. And if, in the course of their work, they come across a potential new business idea, they should be able to recognize it as such. Many new ventures spring from unexpected sources, a prime example being 3 M's Post-it Notes, which were literally invented by accident and then were used internally at 3 M before succeeding as a massmarket product. Entrepreneurial people are primed to notice opportunities of this kind, wherever they may occur.

5.3.2 Adaptable

> The profile of a Twitter employee is someone who is forward-thinking, a team player and clear about what they're focused on. And of course being agile is a requirement.—Interviewee at Twitter

Adaptability can be defined as "the ability and willingness to prepare for change and to implement an effective response when change occurs."[18] Building on leadership and change research, referring to adaptability practices in hedge funds[19] and their own long-term experiences from adaptability training and research at the Institute for Defense Analysis (IDA), William R. Burns and Drew Miller commented:

> To be more adaptive, leaders at all levels, and particularly senior leaders, need to apply well-developed skills of critical and creative thinking, intuition (pattern recognition), self-awareness and self-regulation, and a variety of social skills…in varying combinations and across a wide range of situations…research found that while training is important, education, career development, and organizational culture are even more vital in developing senior leaders able to adapt to a changing environment. For most companies, we believe adaptability is not just an issue of developing personnel who are more adaptable, but freeing employees from central regulation and restrictions without losing the efficiency and effectiveness of common purpose and central direction.[20]

What was found is that adaptability refers to an ongoing process, that it can be trained and learned, and that it is influenced by an organization's environment and culture. Adaptive performance[21] depends on three main factors:

1. Individual differences.
2. Knowledge, skills and attitudes gained through education, training and reflecting upon experiences.
3. An environment that calls for and/or permits adaptive performance.

---

[18] Burns Jr. and Miller (2014).

[19] Taleb (2010).

[20] Burns Jr. and Miller (2014), pp. 2–3.

[21] Burns and Miller argue that in order to build adaptability in your organization, you need to: (1) Hire, educate and promote to grow critical thinkers in your organization with the requisite relational skills, providing them with time to reflect upon experiences, developing cognitive skills (intuition and critical and creative thinking) and self awareness to be able to recognize when past experiences are counterproductive for changed circumstances, as well as self-regulation and relational skills; (2) Encourage humility, unlearning, and abandonment, to be able to have the integrity and courage to admit that a great idea didn't work, cut losses, and move on; (3) Conduct training and exercises in adaptability where the complexity and difficulty progress so participants reach a failure point in dealing with uncertainty and impossible situations; (4) Improve your organization's Observe-Orient-Decide-Act loop to react faster and more effectively than competitors in an iterative learning process; (5) Empower lover level managers' ability to adapt by telling them what to do but not how (referring to Lord Nelson and General Patton); (6) Reward initiative and prudent risk taking, including promoting risk-takers and showing no tolerance for passivity; (7) Institute "radical openness" to promote challenging superiors, which (with reference to the hedge fund Bridgewater) "does not just allow but requires employees to question anything and anyone, with total disregard to personal feelings or hierarchy, to probe for weaknesses and get at the truth"; (8) Demand accountability for results without punishing failures for thoughtful experimentation that through an iterative learning process of trial and error is essential in adapting; and (9) Change the culture, or your organization will revert to conservative standard operating procedures and business as usual. (Burns Jr. and Miller 2014), pp. 7–19.

Almost by definition, the special breed of people sought by our six case companies were accomplished critical thinkers and self-aware, and they had been well equipped in terms of social skills. In addition, these people were used to adapting, maybe based on experience from their childhood, schooling, and/or previous workplaces. However, it also mattered that their median age was low. Younger people are usually more amenable to being shaped to fit the culture and skills of the company.[22]

Finally, the fact that the environment influences the adaptability of people meant that the six companies emphasized this attribute as a key aspect of their culture, which we will discuss in the next chapter.

5.3.3 Passionate

> A fine marker of a smart creative is passion ... Passionate people don't wear their passion on their sleeves; they have it in their hearts. They live it ... If someone is truly passionate about something, they'll do it for a long time even if they aren't at first successful.[23]— Eric Schmidt and Jonathan Rosenberg (2014), p. 100

People who were attractive to our case companies cared about and *shared passion for* the company's mission. They wanted to be part of something *bigger* than themselves. At the Silicon Valley firms, they also tended to believe that technology can make the world better, and they were eager to take part in the quest. As a person at Apigee put it, "They must have a passion for digital."

5.3.4 Constantly Questioning the Status Quo

> The key is to have a team that does not accept current standards but continually asks the question, "If we were to start from scratch, what would we do then?"—Interviewee at one of our case companies

It is interesting that this quality was mentioned explicitly by so many sources at our six case companies. Essentially, it meant that people must seek to develop the company and its offerings beyond existing standards on the market, even if doing so disrupts the firm's own successful practices. Various interviewees expressed the quality in different ways, such as:

- People at the company must "participate and create new things."
- Everyone should "continually think about new ideas."

Questioning the status quo means that an individual can't be a victim of inertia (resistance to change) or path dependency (the limitation of decision-making by

---

[22] According to our own knowledge both Toyota and IKEA, two different companies from two different sectors, hire young people who are then shaped and formed in the company culture.
[23] Schmidt and Rosenberg (2014), p. 100.

decisions that have been made in the past, even though past circumstances may no longer be relevant).[24] Inertia and path dependency can influence not only an individual's but also an organization's decisions and behavior to a high degree.[25] Therefore, questioning the status quo usually demands *active and conscious* work on the part of the individual.

In his book *Thinking, Fast and Slow*,[26] Daniel Kahneman, a winner of the Nobel Memorial Prize in Economics, described two modes of thought. "System 1" thinking is fast, emotional, and instinctive, based on past experience; while "System 2" thinking is slower and more conscious, deliberative, and logical. Kahneman conducted a number of experiments showing that with the same input, people arrived at different results depending on whether they used System 1 or System 2. Kahneman explained that System 1 thinking involves associating new information with existing patterns or thoughts, rather than creating new patterns for each situation. A person who constantly questions the status quo would therefore need to more frequently use System 2, deliberately reflecting and analyzing. The thought processes for System 2 could, according to psychologists, be influenced by persuasion or education. Over time this should in turn affect System 1 with its basis in previous experience. All of this might mean that the people our six companies were looking for had learned to frequently use System 2, which over time had created a normal inclination of questioning the status quo. The inclination can be strengthened further by the organizational culture.

5.3.5 Collaborative

> We want a WE culture, not a ME culture.—Interviewee at Twitter
> Everyone can talk with anyone…You don't need to be a top executive to matter; your work matters.—Interviewee at one of our case companies

Groups of people are increasingly acknowledged as the source of knowledge construction.[27] It is expected that bringing together people with different perspectives and knowledge will lead to improved results on the order of 1 + 1 = 3. However, research has shown that it is not that simple. Merely assembling a team of people with relevant experience and skills is not enough for successful collaboration. Coordination of the team members' *understanding* is required as well.[28] The shared understanding is in turn affected by factors such as interdependence (the degree to which team members are mutually dependent on the others), task cohesion (shared commitment among members to achieving a goal), psychological safety (team members feeling accepted and respected, so the group is "safe" for interpersonal

---

[24] Praeger (2007).
[25] Alänge et al. (1998).
[26] Kahneman (2011).
[27] Van den Bossche et al. (2006).
[28] Ibid.

risk taking), and group potency (a collective belief that the group can succeed and be effective).[29]

The people that the six case companies wanted to attract and keep must be good team players. They should therefore have knowledge of the basic requirements for fostering the processes and beliefs that promote team learning. Here again, we could assume that an environment conducive to these processes and beliefs was present at the companies in the form of culture and leadership.

Having now explored the "cornerstone" qualities of our special breed of people, let's turn to the next subjects: how the case companies found and attracted these people, and just as important, how they kept them.

5.4 Attracting the Special Breed

We've already seen that offering good pay and perks is not enough to attract this breed of people. The company's mission, culture, and way of working (as expressed by leadership and organization) all play crucial roles. Interviewees at the six case companies expressed these facts in various terms, such as:

- "People are drawn to us as they see the value of doing good in the world."
- "You compete on culture."
- "We attract people because they like our energy, that everyone is smart, that it is fun, and because you are not put in a box but have freedom".

In a digitally connected world with a high degree of visibility, the culture also must be mirrored in the company's brand, which can become a magnet for attracting great people. This was very clear in the case of Google,[30] where several interviewees felt that the company's brand image was crucial for its innovative energy. Google's profile was, and is, that of a company creating and realizing big ideas that can change the world. The brand therefore has attracted innovative and gifted people from all over the world. Further, the employees become physical manifestations of the company's brand. The brand was also thought to influence employee opinions and expectations, which, in turn, affect employee behavior; this eventually renders the brand a self-fulfilling prophecy.[31]

Another factor that seems to play a role in talent attraction is what Eric Schmidt and Jonathan Rosenberg in their book call "the herd effect".[32] By this they mean that *a workforce of great people not only does great work, it attracts more great people.*

---

[29] Ibid.
[30] Steiber (2014).
[31] Ibid.
[32] Schmidt and Rosenberg (2014), p. 99.

The hiring process as such was seen by all six case companies as *strategically important*. Schmidt and Rosenberg called hiring the most important thing you can do.[33]

As we saw earlier, these authors said a smart leader knows that no amount of strategy can substitute for talent and Googlers therefore had invested time and energy in getting the best possible people. However, this priority was not specific to Google, but something repeated over and over among all the case companies. In fact, at several companies it became clear that the CEO personally invested time in recruitment. Some of our sources mentioned figures like 25–30% of the CEO's time being spent on organizational development and hiring people.

> Businesspeople in general are not comfortable with organizational development...Our CEO spends 25% of his time on culture and organizational development.—Interviewee at Apigee

This is quite unique. Normally, the higher up you go in a traditional organization, the more detached the executives are from the hiring process. Further, the traditional hiring process is hierarchical. In contrast, Google used a process inspired by academia, where hiring is peer-based and done by committees.[34] Committees at the company decided whether a candidate should be presented to Larry Page, who then would make the final decision to hire or not hire the individual.[35]

A reason for taking this approach is that once a person starts at Google, the way of working is collaborative. If a single hiring manager were to make the decision, it would impact numerous teams besides her or his own. Another reason is that leaders should hire people smarter than themselves, which rarely happens as human nature gets in the way. By having committees focused on bringing the best people into the company, Google constantly tried to increase the "standard" among employees. Committees were used as a tool to emphasize people not organization, the individual characteristics more than the role, and the company more than the manager.[36] Ideally, the result should be that "next generation employees" are always better than "this generation employees." However, while all six of our companies shared the view that the job of finding people belongs to everyone in the company, not all used hiring committees. For example, a source at one company said:

> Google's hiring process is more centralized...Here everybody hires... [We have] loose groups making decisions.

In order to find the right people, all companies but one had a quite large group in the human resources department with only one task, searching for the right people. One company said that the HR department is

---

[33] Ibid, p. 96.
[34] Ibid., p. 98.
[35] Steiber (2014).
[36] Schmidt and Rosenberg (2014), p. 98.

> ... 80–90% a giant search function. People working here are extremely talented in finding people with specific experience, skills, and knowledge areas.

In the case of Google, the company had changed its recruitment approach from passively waiting for applicants to actively seeking individuals with the right profile.[37] The company determined which talents it would need in the future, and continually developed and refined its search strategy.

At all the companies, recruitment was taken very seriously and was moving from a passive to a more active, conscious activity, as the number of people that the firms desired was limited and all seemed to perceive that the "battle for talent" was intensifying.

Once good candidates were located, the next steps were actually interviewing and hiring them. Exactly what the companies asked for in interviews was clearest in the case of Google, where we spent most of our time as researchers. As noted earlier, Google evaluated people on four basic dimensions: cognitive ability, knowledge and expertise related to the position, Googliness, and leadership ability.[38] Googliness is how well the individual's values match those of the company, and the importance of such a match has been emphasized in research. In the words of Greg Linden and David Teece: "Individual hires must be assessed for compatibility with the prevailing corporate culture".[39]

According to Eric Schmidt and Jonathan Rosenberg, interviews should be kept to 30 minutes as the shorter time drives a focus on the most important issues and a substantive discussion.[40] The authors also believe that the incremental cost of conducting more than four interviews outweighs the value that additional feedback can contribute to the hiring decision.

If the job has been done well in the search and interview phases, the risk of recruiting someone who drops out of the company within the first 2 years is low according to Reid Hoffman,[41] one of the founders of LinkedIn. Let us now turn our focus to talent retention.

5.5 How Do We Keep These People?

Hoffman, along with Ben Casnocha and Chris Yeh, co-authored an excellent book titled *The Alliance: Managing Talent in the Networked Age*. He confirmed that talent is the most valuable resource a company or organization can have today, and in line with our other sources he said it can't be just any talent but talent that is entrepreneurial and can drive change when their companies need to adapt and grow.[42]

---

[37] Steiber (2014), p. 58.
[38] Ibid.
[39] Linden and Teece (2014).
[40] Schmidt and Rosenberg (2014), pp. 118–119.
[41] Hoffman et al. (2014).
[42] Ibid., pp. 12–14.

However, entrepreneurial people are in great demand. Presumably they will be most attracted to companies that can meet their desires for a good entrepreneurial environment, with great people and interesting projects and tasks.

This means a company must design a management model that fits entrepreneurial behavior; otherwise, good entrepreneurs will not consider the firm or stay for very long.

5.5.1 The Ugly Duckling

During our research on companies outside Silicon Valley, we found a prime example of what can happen when a traditional large firm tries to squeeze an entrepreneur into its ranks. One of our interviewees was a woman who worked at a large corporation in the beverages sector—and before that, had been a serial entrepreneur. In fact, the job at the beverage corporation was the first non-startup position she had ever held. Soon after joining that firm, she identified an opportunity that could lead to an entirely new future business area. But when she presented her idea to an internal steering committee it was turned down as too risky. The corporation had never built new businesses organically, choosing instead to buy the businesses or technologies it needed.

So instead, the woman then worked with external entrepreneurs to develop her idea as a startup company, while still holding her full-time job at the large corporation. She kept the steering committee informed of the startup's progress, and within a year, the committee became positive about investing time and resources in the new company. The startup had now proved the business model. It had clients, suppliers, and a production plant up and running. According to the woman, the reasons the big firm finally decided to invest were her persistence and confidence in the business idea, together with tangible proof that it worked.

However, despite succeeding on that venture, she said she continued to feel different from others at the firm—often to the point of feeling like someone whom others had problems dealing with. Just the fact that she approached senior decision makers in the hallway instead of waiting for a formal meeting to take place 3 weeks later was perceived as breaking the internal rules. She was clearly a pain in the ass as she not only didn't follow rules and routines, but also brought in a different way of thinking that was not shared by many others in the corporation.

Therefore, even after the success of the new business, the woman still thought frequently of leaving the company.

However, now the company has started to use her entrepreneurial strengths to its benefit, in respects that range from heading up new businesses to supporting human resources in attempts to recruit more entrepreneurial people.

Drawing from the example above and from other observations, we find that putting an entrepreneur into an organization not adjusted to entrepreneurs will lead to one of four things: (1) the individual becomes conformed to the corporation's way of seeing and doing things, (2) the individual continues to be entrepreneurial by learning how to go around the system, (3) the person leaves the company, or (4) the company learns to use and benefit from the entrepreneurial individual. In this specific case the firm learned to appreciate the woman's entrepreneurial skills and started to benefit from them before she decided to leave.

We will discuss culture and how our six case companies are led and organized in Chaps. 6, 7 and 8. For now, we simply leave you with the points that existing firms must offer engaging work—and *an appropriate work environment*—to have any hope of drawing and *keeping* entrepreneurs in the fold.

5.5.2 Meaningful Work, Perks and Benefits

As an entrepreneurial person you can choose whether to work with a startup or join an existing large company. The work done at the big firm must then be equally attractive, if not more so. Thus, it is not odd that all six of our case companies promoted their desire to change the world, or to revolutionize how things are done in a certain area. Such a mission is more or less needed in order to recruit and retain the best entrepreneurial people!

A bigger company can also sometimes offer the chance to have more impact than one might have at a startup. Google, for instance, promoted the notion that "Talented people are attracted to Google because we empower them to change the world, [with our] large computational resources and distribution that enable individuals to make a difference."[43] Mark Zuckerberg said in one interview with *Business Insider* that great people want to make impact, and Facebook therefore measured impact by counting the number of users that each developer actually could affect by his/her work.[44]

In addition to promising meaningful work, our case companies invested heavily in attracting and developing human capital, even with the understanding that most people would probably leave after some years. One may ask: What exactly do these firms "invest" in?

The investment is multidimensional. First, all of our case companies offered stocks or stock options for employees. Second, as the border between work and free time becomes increasingly blurred, the companies invested in providing a "good experience" for employees. According to one company it should be fun to work there, and according to another the goal is to make life easier and better for employees. Great offices with free meals and drinks, game rooms, workout facilities, dry cleaning and medical services made up only part of the package. Facebook had even planned a housing community near its campus for employees.[45] Such a community would offer affordable employee homes (which are very hard to find in Silicon Valley), along with stores and pubs, services from hair styling to dog care, etc. Google offereds on-campus childcare and most of the tech companies offered new

---

[43] Page and Brin (2004) https://investor.google.com/corporate/2004/ipo-founders-letter.html
[44] Blodget (2009).
[45] Alsever (2013).

moms and dads competitive (for Silicon Valley) maternity and paternity leaves of 4–5 months with full pay, plus "baby cash."[46]

These perks—together with the chance to have a pool of work colleagues who are not only highly skilled, but also share the same beliefs as oneself—can be very attractive. They may tip the balance for good candidates who are trying to choose between forming or joining a startup versus joining one of our case companies. Therefore, the creation of such packages was a vital dimension of the human-capital investment that the companies made.

Another dimension is investment in the knowledge, skills, and training of employees. Our interviews with Google identified a "smorgasbord" of courses and training programs offered internally.[47] According to our research study, Google in its early days did not know much about what drove various people, so each person was offered a choice of the full panoply of courses and programs. This also meant that employees had to take responsibility for their own development. The weakness in the system was that not everyone understood what would suit him or her, and it was then difficult for the company to straighten things out later. Since then, Google furnished managers with resources to help them better support employees' development.[48] Because employees are busy but still need to update their skills frequently, the company further aimed to embed training modules in normal work routines. In this way the training could become even more efficient for all concerned.[49]

But as noted, companies know that the most valuable learning can occur on the job, *from* the job itself. One good way to learn on the job is by conducting experiments. And all of our case companies "experimented" regularly through their pursuit of fast, frequent learning cycles, whereby they developed a new product or feature, tested it, learned, modified it, tested it again, and kept learning. In fact, a number of the companies emphasized the achievement of short learning cycles as a critical goal in its own right. These cycles allow a firm to move fast generally and therefore be competitive. As one interviewee at Google told us:

> Organizational learning is what we do at Google; we just learn and improve—that's the core of what we do.[50]

Other learning mechanisms that were mentioned in our studies at Google were post-mortem analysis (learning from historical projects) and internal networks.[51] In relation to the latter, there was a widely held belief that informal, unplanned meetings were useful for learning and developing new ideas through interaction. Workplaces at all of our case companies were designed to facilitate unplanned meetings.

---

[46] Ibid.
[47] Steiber (2014).
[48] Ibid.
[49] Interview at Google Inc. in 2012.
[50] Steiber (2014), p. 73.
[51] Ibid.

Learning can also take place through external networks. All six companies frequently scheduled visits by outside experts or interesting people with new, alternative views on things. Another component of such learning is that external developers and employees may meet at industry events, or through cooperation with leading research universities. Transfer of knowledge then occurs through joint research in which, for example, university professors are invited to take part in a company project for some time. The knowledge transfer is two-way, with ideas moving from external parties to employees and vice versa.

5.5.3 The Employer-Employee Alliance

As mentioned in Chap. 3, the Silicon Valley labor market is fast-moving, with entrepreneurial individuals moving frequently to new positions both inside the same firm and at new firms. To keep great people and get maximum value from them, there were different approaches favored by the companies studied. An obvious one was to make the work itself as satisfying as possible and most companies had, together with HR, developed routes for internal development and career planning. As Reid Hoffman wrote:

> The real secret of Silicon Valley is that it's really all about the people. Sure, there are plenty of stories in the press about the industry's young geniuses, but surprisingly few about its management practices. What the mainstream press misses is that Silicon Valley's success comes from the way its companies build alliances with their employees. Here, talent really is the most valuable resource and employees are treated accordingly. The most successful Silicon Valley businesses succeed because they use the alliance to recruit, manage, and retain an incredibly talented team of entrepreneurial employees.[52]

Drawing on his experience as cofounder and executive chairman of LinkedIn, Hoffman described three different kinds of *learning "tours"* a company can offer,[53] which do not necessarily entail a conventional hierarchical path to a management position.

The first one most of us know very well. It is a *rotational tour of duty*, in which employees are rotated to different functions, positions and geographies in order to get a broader portfolio of knowledge and skills. Hoffman believes this kind of learning tour is not very individualized but is good for building *scalability and flexibility* in a firm because it enables more people to learn about, and to handle, more tasks.

The second one is a *transformational tour of duty*. One solution to employee mobility practiced at LinkedIn was to create a temporary agreement for a transformational tour of duty between the company and a valued employee, to the benefit of both parties.

---

[52] Hoffman et al. (2014), p. 13.
[53] Ibid., pp. 28–40.

> In the context of the alliance, the tour of duty represents an ethical commitment by employer and employee to a specific mission…LinkedIn…offered an explicit deal to talented employees. If they signed up for a tour of duty of between two and four years and made an important contribution to some part of the business, Reid and the company would help advance their careers. Most importantly, a realistic tour of duty lets both sides be honest, which is a necessity for trust.[54]

A transformational tour of duty is valid for a specified time period (commonly 2–5 years), and though it can be ended earlier by mutual agreement, both parties have strong incentives not to break the deal unilaterally.[55] According to Hoffman, the transformational tour of duty creates *adaptability* for a firm.

To put the rotational tour and the transformational tour of duty in perspective: According to one of our case companies, most new employees tended to stay for at least 2–3 years if selection and recruiting were done well at the start. During this time, it was quite normal for a person to take part in a rotational tour at least once or twice. For example at Google, employees were expected to change position, function, or geography every 18 months.[56] If an employee then wanted to stay at the company beyond the first 2–3 years, *and* the company wanted to keep the person, a transformational tour of duty could be a good strategy to further develop, but also retain, the key individual.

The third kind of tour is the *foundational tour of duty*, which is important for the company's *continuity*. A foundational tour of duty is not offered to everyone. It is exclusively for cases where there is an *exceptional alignment* between the individual and the company. Individuals who merit a tour of this type might currently hold key positions at the firm—for example, they could be someone like Jonathan Ive, Apple's Senior VP of Design, or even a founder or CEO—or they could be rising stars who have been identified as key people for the company's future.

The fact that the foundational tour of duty is aimed at building continuity may seem a paradox in a context where companies want to become more adaptable. However, it is not. In our own research, previous to the Silicon Valley studies, we found that firms or organizations that want to conduct organizational change need a certain degree of continuity in their top leadership.[57] In fact one of Google's success factors, according to our own study, was the continuity found not only in the management team, but also in the board whose beliefs and ambitions matched well with those of the founders. This created more than continuity of personnel; it made for

---

[54] Ibid., pp. 23–25.

[55] An employee who "breaks the employment alliance" by leaving a tour early faces a "major hit to his credibility and reputation," and will also "forgo future benefits, such as distinguished alumni status… and favorable references." And if the company unilaterally "lays off the employee in the middle of a tour," it faces similar negative consequences, as "an employer … who makes a habit of breaking alliances is warning both current and prospective employees that it isn't trustworthy." (Hoffman et al. 2014), pp. 86–87.

[56] Steiber (2014).

[57] Alänge and Steiber (2009).

5.5 How Do We Keep These People?

continuity of vision.[58] Reid Hoffman also pointed to continuity at Apple, Amazon and Google in the form of the average tenures of executives who report to the CEOs of these firms.[59] He asserted that a shared background of experience (which the next chapter will show is the basis for the company's culture) becomes the "intellectual and emotional foundation of the organization." Also, according to Hoffman, this common background of experience enables the company to communicate and make decisions more rapidly—i.e., it increases the firm's dynamic capabilities, which was described in Chap. 2 as one of six basic principles for long-term competitiveness in a rapidly changing environment.

One important part of the "alliance" between the employer and employee is to support people in building their personal networks, through social networking or physical meetings.[60] The reason is that the company acts in an ecosystem, and in a healthy ecosystem, *"there are more smart people outside your company than inside it."* Management therefore needs to mobilize the collective knowledge and networks of all its employees. In a working alliance, *"growing their professional networks helps employees transform their career;* [and] *"employee networking helps the company transform itself."*[61]

In cases where an employee and/or the company concludes that a next tour is not appropriate, but rather that the employee should leave, our six case companies were quite aligned as to what should be done. They all helped the person to *successfully go somewhere else*. According to one case company, the milestone for making this decision usually came at around 4–5 years, which typically correlated with the full vesting of employee stock options. This indicates that stock options do play an important role in both hiring and retaining great people.

Supporting employees who leave is important because the companies act in an open and networked society in which rumors travel fast. Another reason is that valuable relationships should last for a lifetime.[62] One way to maintain these relationships after an employee has left is through corporate alumni networks. LinkedIn's alumni network is based on a continued alliance with the same principles as the working relationship: mutual trust, mutual investment, and mutual benefit. The benefits for the company include customer and employee referrals, the hiring of "boomerang" talent (previous employees who have gained valuable experience by working somewhere else), and the fact that current employees can tap the alumni network for help in solving business challenges.

---

[58] Steiber (2014).
[59] Hoffman et al. (2014).
[60] Ibid.
[61] Ibid.
[62] Ibid.

5.6 Recent Findings

During Covid restrictions it became quite common for employees to work remotely from home instead of in the office. Many employees found advantages to working that way or in a hybrid remote/on-site arrangement, and our case companies introduced policies in which the hybrid approach was approved by management even after the pandemic had eased up.

Some Silicon Valley companies had a previous tradition of working from home. As an example, when we interviewed Google employees in 2010–2014, they mentioned that in several cases, part of their work in developing individual ideas under the 20% principle was done while they were in their homes. They also had a long tradition of collaborating online with individuals in other locations, including in other countries.

As of 2023, however, leaders at some of the case companies have indicated that it's equally important for employees to spend time in the office every week. For example, Facebook/Meta changed its policy to state that employees living within travelling distance of their office need to work on site at least 3 days every week. Also, whereas the Covid pandemic had led to a surge in people using online services, that trend did not persist after lockdowns ended. This and other factors prompted significant layoffs at Silicon Valley companies from 2022 into 2023, which in turn affected relations with employees.

Nonetheless, the people dimension has continued to be highly relevant,[63] as the right kind of people are still eagerly sought. However, peoples' impact on innovation and entrepreneurship could be understood on a more granular level. For example, George Martinidis et al. divided the general concept of human capital into three distinct forms of capital: a person's human, social, and psychological capital. Human capital refers to the individual's education, knowledge, and skills; social capital refers to the strength and coherence of their social links, and psychological capital encompasses values, attitudes, and behaviors.[64] As was described in this chapter, all three of these "capitals" have been emphasized among the case companies.

The importance of a supporting *system* that fosters people's creativity and innovativeness is also emphasized in recent twenty-first-century research. For example, George S. Day and Gregory Shea found that organizations that achieve faster growth need to have a narrative for their employees about innovation, from growth-denying to growth-enabling. This narrative requires a change of the support system in the form of leadership commitment to innovation talent, culture, and aligned metrics and incentives.[65] As has been stated in this chapter our case companies had all invested in an innovation-oriented environment. Further, Chap. 2 described the importance of a systemic approach to accelerate innovation.

---

[63] Tajeddini et al. (2020), Martinidis et al. (2021).
[64] Martinidis et al. (2021)
[65] Day and Shea (2020).

Finally, although companies are still looking to hire special individuals, new advances in AI (artificial intelligence) mean that the innovation process could be expected to change. At the heart of the innovation process, the fundamental ingredients are the ways in which people create ideas and solve problems.[66] Traditionally, people also have made the key decisions in this process. All of this may change, however, as AI algorithms for tasks like creative problem-solving grow more sophisticated and more widely used. The role of humans may then shift toward tasks such as sense-making, that is, understanding which problem should be addressed.[67] Further, AI might enable companies to overcome limitations in human decision-making by improving the scalability of the process, broadening its scope across traditional boundaries, and enhancing the ability to learn and adapt continuously. Problem-solving might therefore be automated into learning loops that operate without limitations of volume and speed.[68]

Summing up this trend, we could say two things. Since there is no realistic prospect of replacing human input entirely, at least not in the foreseeable future, having the right people on board will continue to be both necessary and valuable in innovative organizations. But, given the disruptive potential of today's AI, a great deal of further research and experimentation will be needed in order to arrive at optimal ways of managing people within this changed context.

5.7 Conclusions (and a Start)

In this chapter we've covered a great deal of territory—identifying and describing the "special breed of people" that the leading companies in our Silicon Valley studies deemed crucial for success in business; outlining the many different measures that were used to attract and retain these people; and delving into how the companies went about developing top talent internally. All of the factors are essential, because employing the right people is essential. To come back to Jim Collins' observation, it is best to start with *who* instead of *what*.

Yet everything that's been discussed here is, indeed, just a start. We still have only a partial view of the larger picture: the entire Silicon Valley Model that describes how best to manage for long-term competitiveness in a rapidly changing world. The chapters ahead will fill out the rest of the picture. In the next chapter we examine what our interviewees (and others) considered to be a key *differentiator* between firms that compete successfully for top talent and market leadership, and those that struggle: the company's culture.

---

[66] Verganti et al. (2020).
[67] Ibid.
[68] Ibid.

References

Alänge, S., & Steiber, A. (2009). The board's role in sustaining major organizational change: An empirical analysis of three change programs. *International Journal of Quality Service Sciences, 1*(3), 280–293.

Alänge, S., Jacobsson, S., & Jarnehammar, A. (1998). Some aspects of an analytical framework for studying the diffusion of organisational innovations. *Technology Analysis & Strategic Management, 10*(1), 3–21.

Albergotti, R. (2014, December 25). At Facebook, boss is a dirty word. *The Wall Street Journal.* http://www.wsj.com/articles/facebooks-millennials-arent-entitled-they-are-empowered-1419537468. Accessed 15 Apr 2015.

Alsever, J. (2013, October 14). Which tech company offers the best child care? *Fortune.com.* http://fortune.com/2013/10/14/which-tech-company-offers-the-best-child-care/. Accessed 2 Aug 2015.

Bahrami, H. (1992). The emerging flexible organization: Perspectives from Silicon Valley. *California Management Review, 34*(4), 33–52.

Blodget, H. (2009, October 1). Mark Zuckerberg on innovation. *Business Insider.* http://www.businessinsider.com/mark-zuckerberg-innovation-2009-10?IR¼T. Accessed 2 Aug 2015.

Burns, W. R., Jr., & Miller, D. (2014). *Lessons in adaptability and preparing for black swan risks from the military and hedge funds* (NSD-5215). Institute for Defense Analysis.

Collins, J. (2001). *Good to great.* Harper Business.

Day, G. S., & Shea, G. (2020). Changing the work of innovation: A systems approach. *California Management Review, 63*(1), 41–60.

Drucker, P. (1959). *Landmarks of tomorrow.* Harper & Brothers.

Hoffman, R., Casnocha, B., & Yeh, C. (2014). *The alliance: Managing talent in the networked age.* Harvard Business Review Press.

IBM Institute for Business Value. (2015). *Myths, exaggerations and uncomfortable truths: The real story behind millennials in the workplace.* IBM. http://www-935.ibm.com/services/multimedia/GBE03637USEN.pdf. Accessed 20 June 2015

Kahneman, D. (2011). *Thinking, fast and slow.* Penguin.

Linden, G., & Teece, D. (2014). Managing expert talent. In P. Sparrow et al. (Eds.), *Strategic talent management.* Cambridge University Press.

Martinidis, G., Komninos, N., & Carayannis, E. (2021). Taking into account the human factor in regional innovation systems and policies. *Journal of the Knowledge Economy, 13*(3), 1–31. https://doi.org/10.1007/s13132-021-00722-z

Page, L., & Brin, S. (2004). An owner's manual for Google's shareholders. *Google Investor Relations.* https://investor.google.com/corporate/2004/ipo-founders-letter.html. Accessed 19 May 2015.

Praeger, D. (2007, June 15). Our love of sewers: A lesson in path dependence. *Daily Kos.* http://www.dailykos.com/story/2007/06/15/346883/-Our-Love-Of-Sewers-A-Lesson-in-Path-Dependence#. Accessed 2 Aug 2015.

Schmidt, E., & Rosenberg, J. (2014). *How Google works.* Grand Central Publishing.

Steiber, A. (2014). *The Google model: Managing continuous innovation in a rapidly changing world.* Springer.

Tajeddini, K., Martin, E., & Altinay, L. (2020). The importance of human-related factors on service innovation and performance. *International Journal of Hospitality Management, 85*, 102431.

Taleb, N. N. (2010). *The black swan: The impact of the highly improbable* (2nd ed.). Random House.

Van den Bossche, P., Gijselaers, W. H., Segers, M., & Kirschner, P. A. (2006). Social and cognitive factors driving teamwork in collaborative learning environments. *Small Group Research, 37*(5), 490–521.

Verganti, R., Vendraminelli, L., & Iansiti, M. (2020). Innovation and design in the age of artificial intelligence. *Journal of Product Innovation Management, 37*(3), 212–227.

Culture: The New Black

> *Many people, when considering a new job, are primarily concerned with their role and responsibilities, the company's track record, the industry, and compensation. Smart creatives, though, place culture at the top of the list. To be effective, they need to care about the place they work. This is why, when starting a new company or initiative, culture is the most important thing to consider.*
>
> Eric Schmidt and Jonathan Rosenberg (2014), p. 29

In management as in fashion, fads come and go, but one element has now emerged as the business equivalent of the essential basic black. More and more firms now recognize corporate culture as the key determinant of success in both recruiting and long-term competitiveness. This certainly proved to be true of our six case companies. The pages to come will describe the cultures they built, which turn out to have many features in common.

Since the notion of "culture" in a company or organization can have different meanings to different people, we will begin with a short introduction to the concept.

6.1 What 'Culture' Consists Of

A concise definition comes from Chet Kapoor, CEO of Apigee, who says culture is

> what we value and how we do things here.

For a deeper look we can turn to Edgar Schein, a professor emeritus at MIT's Sloan School of Management. Schein, a long-recognized expert on company cultures, has studied how they originate and propagate. He defined culture as

> A pattern of shared basic assumptions that the group learned as it solved its problems of external adaptation and internal integration, that has worked well enough to be considered valid and, therefore, to be taught to new members as the correct way you perceive, think, and feel in relation to those problems.[1]

Company cultures are thus seen primarily as *belief systems*. They are sets of beliefs about the realities of the business world and "what works." Not only do they shape how a company does a particular task, they influence what the company pays attention to and deems important to begin with. Cultures also govern employee expectations. As Schein has noted, they influence how members of the firm relate to each other, to other parts of the company, to outside parties such as suppliers and customers, and to the society in which the company functions.[2]

Of course many observers other than Schein have studied culture. Out of the vast body of writing on the subject, we will share just a couple more general insights that may be useful. For example, consultant and author Tom Peters has found that successful companies have *strong* cultures[3]—and a marker of a strong culture is that it is well integrated. Its components work in harmony with each other. The thoughts and actions of employees are based on mutually shared beliefs, with which each employee identifies. Identifying with a set of beliefs means that each person accepts personal responsibility for maintaining them.

Further, new employees are introduced into a culture through two parallel processes: a *socialization* process[4] and an *individuation* process.[5] Socialization makes people "similar" as they learn the shared beliefs and begin to act congruently; this process is meant to support collaboration. The individuation process makes people "different" by supporting the development of each employee as an *independent*[6] person within the culture. Both processes require experience-

---

[1] Schein (1984), p. 3.

[2] Ibid.

[3] In 1982, *In Search of Excellence* was published. This work analyzed more than 40 companies that had been very successful for a very long time. The common denominator was a *strong culture*. During the latter part of the 1980s, all of these successful companies were on the skids, and some questioned whether the conclusion about strong culture had been wrong.

Naturally, a strong culture at that time meant one focused on stability, which militates against conditions that require the company to change. This is what prevailed until the end of the 1970s when the authors, Tom Peters and Robert Waterman, worked on the documentation of the book. In the 1980s, external changes rose to a level that rendered a stable culture a handicap. This is why the successful trends were broken for these formerly successful companies.

[4] Socialization means an individual's growing to be part of society. During this process, values, attitudes, norms, etc., are absorbed and become part of one's personality. The term *socialisering* is also used in Swedish articles. For many people, *socialisering* means nationalization (of banks, for example), which is why we chose the term socialization.

[5] Individuation has several definitions. In this context, individuation means liberation from dependency on the collective, such as from the liberation from the traditions and customs of society and the development of an individual personality (Egigius, 1994).

[6] Independence means the ability and willingness to choose opinions and actions, and take responsibility for one's choices. The definition comes from Wiberg (1999).

based learning. One can inform others *about* the set of beliefs, but what these *mean for each person* can only be understood through the person's own experiences, which elicit *feedback*. When a new employee interprets a situation "correctly" and acts according to the set of beliefs, he or she receives positive feedback that reinforces the behavior. Persons who violate the set of beliefs, or show that they haven't understood them, receive negative feedback that stops and corrects the behavior.

Now let's get more specific, homing in on our case companies to see how their cultures in fact originated and took shape. Cultures don't arise from nowhere or exist in a vacuum. Many observers agree that there are two main sources of influence from the very start: the external environment (both national and regional) in which the company originates … and the founders of the company. We will look at each in turn.

6.2   External Influences on Culture

There may be substantial differences between a company founded and based in Japan, one in an EU country, and one in the United States, for a variety of reasons. The laws and regulations pertaining to business are different; the social cultures are different; the national "innovation systems" are different.

And within each country there are regional variations as well. For example, Annalee Saxenian, author of *Regional Advantage*, pointed out some key differences between two major high-tech industry regions in the U.S.: the Route 128 corridor in the Boston metro area on the East Coast, and Silicon Valley, where our six case companies were founded. She described the Route 128 industry cluster as having an "independent firm-based system," whereas Silicon Valley has a "decentralized regional network-based structure" that's more fluid: people, capital, and technologies move around and regroup more readily in response to changing opportunities.

This is very much in line with what we described in Chap. 3. Behaviors and beliefs in e.g., "openness" and "networking" are valued in Silicon Valley, as are traits such as "thinking big." They are part of a distinctive regional culture that influences any company based there, including our case companies.

In addition, company cultures are influenced by the kinds of industries they are in, and Silicon Valley has been a cradle of information technologies. As described previously, these technologies are by nature fast-changing, and their administrative impacts include a reduced need for traditional management structures along with a preference for flatter, more flexible organizations.

There is more to be learned about how various external influences show up in the cultures of the case companies. But the next step is to drill down to a level that's much more specific than either the nation or the region—the level of the individuals who started these companies.

6.3 The People Effect: How Founders Shape Culture

A company's culture is heavily influenced by the founders and the first waves of employees they choose to hire. The founders often start with a theory of how to succeed and have a set of assumptions and beliefs in their heads, based on their own prior experiences in the business culture in which they "grew up."[7] With this in mind, let's look at the founders and cofounders of our case companies.

The first thing to notice is that many are serial entrepreneurs, and/or had worked in other startups before starting their own. For instance, Tesla's Elon Musk previously cofounded the web software companies Zip2 and XCom (which merged with another firm and became PayPal) plus the space vehicle firm SpaceX. Reid Hoffman of LinkedIn cofounded an earlier personal networking company—SocialNet, one of the first of its kind—and then was a key executive at PayPal. Apigee's founder Raj Singh is currently the founder and managing director for Redwood Ventures but also a serial entrepreneur and has started companies such as: Advanced Logic, Fiberlane Communications (later split into Cerent, Siara Systems, and Cyras Systems), and StratumOne.

This kind of background reflects a passion for exploring new ideas and building businesses around them. As shown in Chap. 5, these founders' case companies seek to recruit people who have a similar passion and mindset. Thus it is not surprising that the same mindset shows up in various aspects of the companies' culture, as the rest of the present chapter will show.

Google's cofounders had no prior startup experience, nor did Mark Zuckerberg of Facebook. But they did have distinctive kinds of experience that carried over into the cultures of their firms. For Google's Larry Page and Sergey Brin, a big factor was their Stanford and even earlier education. Both, as children, attended Montessori schools, which emphasize independent thinking. And both have said that what they learned there helped to shape their unconventional approach to business. As Page said in a TV interview:

> I think it was part of that training of not following rules and orders, and being self-motivated, questioning what's going on in the world, and doing things a little bit different.[8]

Other observers also have noted the Montessori influence on Google's founders and the company itself.[9] Zuckerberg, meanwhile, has a notable trait that he shares with other founders of our case companies—*deep knowledge of software development, grounded in hands-on coding experience from an early age.*

Already known for his software skills when he entered college at Harvard, Zuckerberg developed and launched the Facebook site at age 19, then left school to

---

[7] Schein (1983), p. 3.

[8] Excerpt from Larry Page's remarks on the Barbara Walters ABC-TV special "The 10 Most Fascinating People of 2004" (Walters, 2004).

[9] E.g., former Google executive Marissa Mayer said that Montessori thinking "is really baked into how Larry and Sergey approach problems." This was quoted in Steven Levy's book *In the Plex* (Levy, 2011), p. 122.

6.3 The People Effect: How Founders Shape Culture

incorporate the startup a few months later. Elon Musk sold his first software, a video-game program that he'd written when he was only 12. Twitter cofounders Jack Dorsey, Evan Clark Williams, "Biz" Stone and Noah Glass were all software prodigies—Dorsey wrote an open-source program for taxi dispatch routing while in his early teens—and on through the rest of the case companies, we find cofounders with significant direct experience in creating computer programs.

In terms of influence on company culture, this has at least two implications.

- The founders were persons steeped in *product development*. While they may also have proved to be highly capable in other areas, such as marketing, they were "product people" at heart. And as we'll soon see, a focus on product excellence is one key cultural marker of the case companies.
- People who get deeply into writing software are bound to be exposed to the so-called hacker ethic. This is a set of beliefs that have emerged in the software community over the years, especially among those who see themselves as free-thinking. Although not every software writer ascribes to the hacker ethic or interprets it the same, there is general agreement on what its basic tenets are. They include open sharing of information, decentralized and collaborative work structures (with a dislike of authority for authority's sake), and a striving to do great work that improves the world.[10] This same set of beliefs turn up in the cultural profiles of our six companies.

Last but not least, the cofounders of the case companies were united by something they did *not* have. *None of them had an MBA degree.* In an era when the MBA has become a standard credential for anyone aspiring to business leadership, particularly in the U.S., this is extraordinary.

The cofounders' higher education backgrounds vary widely. Some never finished undergraduate school, some have done PhD work, and some have degrees in unusual fields: LinkedIn cofounder and VP Allen Blue holds a bachelor's in scenic design for theater. Yet not a single one formally studied business in an MBA program—most of which, as noted in Chap. 3, are focused on teaching standard big-firm methods of analysis and control. None of them even pursued an entrepreneurship-track MBA!

Certainly, many of these cofounders had the chance to learn basic business principles and practices in the course of their previous work. And certainly, their companies have employed, or been advised by, people with MBAs. But if the founding team members themselves are the chief early architects of company culture, it seems very significant that no founders of the *highly successful, cutting-edge firms* in this

---

[10] See for example Steven Levy's book *Hackers* (Levy, 1984)—the book credited with first identifying and naming the "hacker ethic"—or later works such as *The Hacker Ethic and the Spirit of the Information Age* (Himanen et al., 2001).

sample felt the need to study, or propagate, the typical MBA program assumptions about how to run a business.[11]

Since founders by nature tend to attract and hire people who share their own assumptions on the nature of the world, the role which their organization will play in that world, the nature of human nature, etc., the initial culture takes shape as a result of wave 1, wave 2, and maybe wave 3 of employees who join the company during its first few years. However, the culture of that group is not fully formed until the group has a shared history of overcoming various problems and crisis.[12] An interviewee at one case company observed:

> Culture is how you approach problems and interact…Everyone feels responsible for bringing in people who could be good colleagues… people like themselves.

6.4 Steps to Building a Strong Culture

Google, Facebook, LinkedIn, Twitter, Tesla and Apigee had two major traits in common. All believed in the importance of a strong culture and had taken some unusual measures to create one.

At Google, the founders had no intention to build a conventional company,[13] and a critical component of an *un*conventional company was to create and sustain a unique culture.[14] The founders believed that one requirement for building and retaining such an environment was to be extra selective in the choice of employees. According to one of our interviewees at Google, each candidate's fundamental values were personally examined by the founders during the company's first 2 years, when its culture was primarily evolved.[15] The focus then became to sustain the unique culture,[16] which is why Larry Page, as late as 2014, was still directly involved

---

[11] However, according to a 2013 article by Eric Jackson in Forbes.com, there was pressure 10 years ago on founders of various firms to pass the reins over to the "professional managers." Jerry Yang and David Filo stepped aside at Yahoo and Pierre Omidyar handed over the keys for eBay to Meg Whitman. According to Jackson's report, all these handovers of power worked out well in the beginning but as time went on the "professional manager" somehow became unhooked from the company's core and the company got off track from its core operating principles. Mark Zuckerberg changed all this at Facebook, the article claims: He stayed in charge, determining that his founder mindset could be more valuable to the company in the long run as CEO (Jackson, 2013).

[12] Schein (1984).

[13] Steiber (2014).

[14] Schmidt and Rosenberg (2014).

[15] Steiber (2014).

[16] According to Mark Pincus, the founder and CEO of Zynga, a company reaches a critical inflection point at around 300–400 people, as the number of "original" employees then is usually much fewer than the number of new employees. At this inflection point it will be critical to sustain enough people from wave 1, wave 2 and wave 3, if the firm wants to sustain its original culture. See Jackson (2013). http://onlinecareertips.com/2013/03/the-difference-between-the-mindsets-of-founders-and-professional-managers/ (Accessed 2 Aug 2015).

in recruitment, something that also several of the other case companies applied as a practice.

The founders also wished to avoid importing what they considered bad habits from other companies. As a result, during its early years, Google recruited many new employees directly from universities rather than from industry where they would have gained work experience.[17] Then in 2005—shortly after Google's IPO—the position of Chief Cultural Officer was created.[18] The reason was to emphasize the importance of the culture, and to sustain and develop it in light of the new demands that would come with being a publicly traded company.

At another of our case companies, similarly to Google, culture was the extension of the belief set of the founders and earliest employees. According to sources there, culture is what a company in the Valley competes on. It is so highly valued that when the current CEO [as of 2016] came aboard, he spent 6 months aligning the company around strategy, culture, and operations by developing a joint language that described the three, and had speeches written that could easily be understood and repeated.

At a third case company, people believed that in order to make different and unique things, *they* had to be different and here again culture played a major role. Like Google in the beginning, the company hired many people directly from school, as they wanted employees who didn't have pre-conceived ideas on how companies should operate and were more willing to think in new ways.

In order to secure a strong culture, one firm had a high-ranking executive whose role was to observe and give guidance on the overall "experience" of working there. Finally, people at yet another firm in our study viewed culture simply as *the company*, and referred to the famous saying "culture eats strategy for breakfast".[19] The CEO encouraged the employees to sustain the culture, while viewing revenues as oxygen: necessary but something they shouldn't think about too much.

6.5 The '10 Commandments': Core Attributes of the Cultures We Studied

Our case companies had several specific cultural traits in common. In fact, the commonality was surprising, given how much the firms varied in some basic ways. As mentioned previously, for instance, Google was much larger than the other software-intensive firms, while Tesla made and marketed complex physical products. Yet when it came to culture, they were remarkably similar—and *their cultures, based on our experience, differed from the traditional cultures of many other large companies worldwide.*

All six shared certain core beliefs about *what the business world is like* and *what a company should be like* in order to be competitive. Our studies identified ten such beliefs found across the case companies. Since they can be framed as cultural "mandates" we've called them the "10 Commandments." Stated very simply, they are:

---

[17] Jackson (2013).

[18] Ibid.

[19] Attributed to Peter Drucker; used by various executives and business consultants.

1. We are not an ordinary company.
2. Things change constantly and we must be adaptable.
3. Move fast, speed matters.
4. Hiring is the most important thing we do.
5. Product excellence is key.
6. Data-driven decision making and fast learning.
7. A flat organization with minimal bureaucracy.
8. Openness and transparency.
9. Leaders, not managers.
10. Build an ecosystem, not just a company.

Let's now look at each in a bit more detail.

6.5.1 Not an Ordinary Company

> How will we create different, unique products if we are not different ourselves? — a question posed at Tesla

The first cultural marker of the six case companies was an explicit desire to be different or unconventional. Google is famous in this regard for the "Founders' IPO Letter" that was included with the prospectus for its initial public stock offering in 2004. Cofounders Larry Page and Sergey Brin began their letter to prospective shareholders with the warning:

> Google is not a conventional company. We do not intend to become one.

They noted that Google's initial success was based in "an atmosphere of creativity and challenge," and that its "ability to innovate" had to be protected from the pressures of being publicly traded. Thus, for instance, the firm would continue to focus on longer-term exploratory projects rather than trying to maximize quarterly revenues:

> Many companies are under pressure to keep their earnings in line with analysts' forecasts. Therefore, they often accept smaller, predictable earnings rather than larger and less predictable returns. Sergey and I feel this is harmful, and we intend to steer in the opposite direction...
> We will not hesitate to place major bets on promising new opportunities... Do not be surprised if we place smaller bets in areas that seem speculative or even strange when compared to our current business...By investing in Google, you are placing an unusual long-term bet on the team ... and on our innovative approach.

The Founder's Letter also noted that Google would not try to economize by cutting employee benefits, since employees are central to the company's work, and that the stock offering was structured to keep voting power and strategic direction under the control of the management team. In short, the document argued that Google's distinctive culture was inseparable from its success—and it laid out a series of steps to preserve that culture from the conformist influences of the stock market.

6.5 The '10 Commandments': Core Attributes of the Cultures We Studied

In a similar vein, interviewees at the other case companies said a distinctive culture was not only desirable but necessary. As one person said, "To be different allows us to make different things." Another emphasized that to move ahead, one always has to be creating something new—not just in terms of bringing out new products, but in terms of re-thinking and re-inventing the company itself. One company preferred not to hire people from typical large corporations because "their norms don't work here." Instead, the firm recruited directly from universities, as we've noted Google did during its early years. In our previous research on Google, we were told that "Google is a calling" and the goal is to recruit people who see it as such. An executive at another company said:

> We hire people that are curious and want to be part of something bigger … They have to have the passion…They have to care, not just about the paycheck.

The intent, in each case, was to attract people who wanted to help build and/or sustain a new and different culture.

Part of being different is to have a unique, bold, and socially significant mission. All our case companies referred to their higher mission when discussing the firm. For example, Google's is "to organize the world's information and make it universally accessible and useful." And at LinkedIn the mission is to "connect the world's professionals to make them more productive and successful." The other companies had similarly bold missions, all of which guided employees as they strove to develop the company, its offerings, and its larger ecosystem. As we learned in Chap. 5 the mission was also used in the hiring process, as a common belief among the case companies was that there must be a good match between the company's mission and a candidate's personal mission.

6.5.2 Things Change Constantly and We Need to Be Adaptable

> Our products are upgraded constantly [and] our organization changes frequently as teams and individuals shift based on priorities…Technology companies are used to doing this, as the technology landscape changes fast. — Interviewee at Twitter

The six companies studied for this book all recognized that they operated in constantly changing times and markets. This might have seemed obvious, but the fact that the companies acknowledged it as a fundamental fact of existence made it a key part of their culture. As one company's executive noted, functions like strategic planning became vastly different: "We don't have a 5-year plan but rather try something for 3 to 6 months."

One consequence of this commandment is that the companies need to construct some sort of long-term framework for stability and operational efficiency, in parallel with a highly flexible organization around this stable core. Some of our case companies called the long-term framework for stability a "lightweight platform". How it is achieved in practice will be discussed more in Chaps. 7 and 8.

Knowing that things constantly change also dictates a *proactive* culture. At our case companies, the old philosophy that "if it's not broke, don't fix it" was replaced with an opposite set of views. These companies knew they could not rest on their laurels and strove to change even things that were working well, in order to stay ahead of the curve. An interviewee who was part of our research on Google told us:

> We don't stick to what works so much. We actually go out and change, even if it makes people feel uncomfortable or unhappy in the short term.[20] — if we are convinced that it was the right thing for users in the long run

Another person commented that Google reinvents itself every couple of years, beginning from scratch with a new platform, and justifying it by how it benefits the customers.[21] This continuous re-invention of the firm was also supported by the CEO and founder of Zynga, who said that companies in Silicon Valley looked over their business models every second year due to the fast pace of change.[22]

Some quotes from other case companies on this topic:

> The company drives itself to disrupt itself…We went from a desktop company to a mobile company in one year.
>
> The real risk is if you stop developing yourself, you stagnate … Then you have hired all these people with great potential that now start to look for other jobs.

Similarly, at another of our case companies, the need for constant change was stated simply as a desire to keep the company ahead of its industry. "If clients are buying your products to gain an edge for themselves, why would they want anything that isn't the latest and best?"

6.5.3 Move Fast, Speed Matters

> In an accelerated world…to grow your business you must exceed the pace of change. — Anders Berglund, Google's country director in Sweden

An interesting cultural aspect of all six companies was their focus on speed. Two of the firms sought these qualities by adjusting strategy and priorities every quarter; one of them even reallocated resources as frequently as every month. A couple of the companies emphasized that speed requires having employees who are willing to be flexible and agile, as they need to cope with both rapid change and uncertainty, often moving forward without all information at hand. As one firm put it, "the culture attracts people who are comfortable with being uncomfortable."

Facebook had a widely known internal mantra that said, "Move fast and break things." In the other case companies the importance of speed was also emphasized

---

[20] Steiber (2014), p. 51.
[21] Ibid.
[22] Jackson (2013).

and expressed in statements like: "Speed is very important; a flat organization is therefore needed to shorten reaction time." Speed includes "fast decision-making, fast development and implementation." "Speed is a comparative advantage." And furthermore: "Speed drives efficiency. We learn more quickly what is working and not, then make a judgment."

What's especially interesting, culturally, is that people at our case companies talked about the quest for speed and efficiency in *positive* terms. This is quite different from what occurs at most companies. There, these subjects are typically framed—and acted upon—in negative and reactive terms. People are told to work faster because a project is behind schedule or deadlines can't be missed. "Efficiency" campaigns are typically dreaded because everyone knows they will probably focus on cost-cutting and head-cutting, in an attempt to drive up margins.

At the case companies, by contrast, speed and efficiency were viewed as symbiotic elements that build on each other and provide benefits for all. Bureaucracy is flattened. Competitive advantage is gained. The goal is to *grow* by moving faster than the environment, not just to stay out of trouble by meeting deadlines and profit targets; the company strives to be a *dynamic pace-setter* rather than just a "lean and mean" sweatshop. Moreover, in the cultures of the case companies, this quest invited hearty participation and individual judgment. Employees were given license to "break things" and encouraged to move ahead quickly on the basis of best available information. This is diametrically opposed to the cultural mindset often found at other companies, where people hesitate to upset established routines or take risks, and where decisions are delayed by multiple rounds of approval and sign-off.

In our studies of Google, we learned that *the hesitate-and-delay pattern* had been broken by replacing it with the following, speed-oriented protocol: *Better decisions are to be made, and made as quickly as possible*. Due to this, Larry Page decided in 2014 to slightly change the Google structure in order for employees to achieve faster and better decision-making.[23]

6.5.4 Hiring Is the Most Important Thing We Do

Our assets have legs; they walk home every day.[24] — Andrew Grove, former CEO of Intel

The founders and the employees they choose to hire heavily influence a company's culture. One of our case companies expressed this as "culture is tightly linked to people". What kind of people our case companies were searching for was addressed in Chap. 5, so here we'll just briefly touch on a few key points.

All our case companies expressed the importance of hiring the right people and in most cases the CEO was directly involved in the hiring process as was mentioned earlier in this book. And according to Schmidt and Rosenberg (2014), the most

---

[23] Winkler (2014).
[24] Bahrami (1992), p. 42.

important thing a manager will do at work is hiring people, no matter if the person would be an entry-level engineer or a senior executive.

For this reason, our case companies had prioritized the search and recruitment processes in which the company's employees were expected to invest both time and energy to ensure they got the best possible people or as one of our case companies put it: "here everybody hires".

6.5.5 Product Excellence Is Key

> [The goal is] not 'good enough' products ... [because] then we can't win. — Interviewee at one of our case companies

Everyone knows about Steve Jobs' legendary attention to product quality and detail, but fewer might know that the same factor has been crucial to our six case companies. Google, entering a crowded search-engine market, made initial impact through the strength of its superior search technology and simple, uncluttered user interface. Tesla's strategy of entering the electric vehicle market from the high end could only work if the company produced cars with high-end quality. The social networking companies in our sample (Facebook, LinkedIn, and Twitter) had to constantly upgrade and refine their products to maintain market position, as did the API management firm Apigee.

The importance of focusing on product development was emphasized by John Sculley, Apple's CEO from 1983 to 1993, in remarks he made shortly before leaving the firm:

> As I look back over the last eight and a half years and say, what things would I have done differently, the one that really stands out is that I should've gotten involved in product development a lot sooner than I did. To lead a high-technology company, you really have to lead it through the technology and through the products.[25]

The product is viewed as a solution to user problems, and thus product focus in our case companies naturally leads to a focus on the user. Ideally, the product does such a good job of meeting customers' needs that it becomes *indispensable* to them. For example, Mark Zuckerberg has spoken of Facebook as a "utility"—something that is meant to be an integral part of people's daily lives, like public utilities such as electricity or telephone service.[26]

But a key fact should be kept in mind. In order to pursue such a status, Facebook first had to win market share from other social networking sites, which were launched earlier. A common belief at the case companies was that unless you have outstanding products, you literally can't "stand out" in a competitive market. A subject at one company stated it this way: "We never follow the competition ... That would lead to mediocrity." The culture must be one of daring to do unique things.

---

[25] Bahrami (1992), p. 41.
[26] See for example McCracken (2013).

Product excellence also is tied to recruiting and hiring, as the case companies looked for people who were *passionate* about creating great products. Moreover, to retain these people, they had to be viewed and treated as very high-value employees. A source at one company told us "The most important people are around products," a statement that reflects the kind of view we are talking about.

In a culture of this type, product engineers and developers are the "heroes." Things are arranged to allow them to do their very best work, as opposed to a setup that only calls for routine or good-enough work. As a person in our interviews put it: "You never want engineers to feel they are at an assembly line."

6.5.6 Data-Driven Decision Making and Fast Learning

> It is very important in Google overall to be data driven.[27] — Interviewee at Google

We were told the above during our research on Google. People at other case companies expressed similar views, and it was clear that the goal was to base decisions of all kinds on observable data such as testing results, performance metrics, etc. As one person said, "There is respect for real, statistically right data that can prove the case."

Some interviewees claimed that the focus on data was a result of the company's strong engineering culture. Every decision that can be based on data should be. To the extent that the basis for a decision cannot be quantified, people are expected to compensate by objective reasoning. A company culture with rigorous demands for objectivity is also a secure work environment. There is no nepotism or arbitrariness, and socially speaking, decisions based on data result in a feeling of fairness and accuracy.[28]

Basing decisions on data is also a way to deal with HIPPOs, the Highest Paid Persons in the Organization.[29] These people often influence the decision-making process just because of their rank and position, not necessarily because they have the best input. However, if decisions are made by analyzing data, a company can get around the problem.

Another related practice is to strive for short and fast learning cycles, informed by data from the results. Here, for instance, were descriptions of Google's and Facebook's policies for bringing products to market:

> We start small, launch, see what works, what doesn't, improve, iterate. Launch fast, don't do it perfectly.[30] — Interviewee at Google
>
> Keep shipping [new and different products] ... Get something out, interact with users, learn, improve, and repeat. — Interviewee at Facebook

---

[27] Steiber (2014), p. 53.

[28] Ibid.

[29] Schmidt and Rosenberg (2014).

[30] Steiber (2014), p. 55.

Several of our case companies pursued short learning cycles as a goal in itself. And in general, the companies believed that data-driven decision-making in combination with quick learning cycles is a powerful toolset for long-term competitiveness.

6.5.7 A Flat Organization with Minimal Bureaucracy

> LinkedIn is a bottom-up organization. Individual teams are empowered to set their own strategies and goals, rather than waiting for direction from executive leadership. — Interviewee at LinkedIn

Most large corporations have multiple levels and high degrees of bureaucracy. In Chap. 1 we saw that Gary Hamel and his Moon Shot panel identified this kind of structure as a major obstacle. It stifles speed, adaptability, and innovation. An interviewee at one of our case companies stated this even more dramatically: "Strong hierarchy tends to die." Thus, it is no surprise that all the case companies placed high value on having a flat organization with minimal bureaucracy.

Since layers of bureaucracy can accumulate gradually over time, several of the companies' CEOs had clearly informed employees about their wish to combat the onset of bureaucratic structures and practices. One sent an email on this subject to everyone in the company. Another and early example of bureaucracy-fighting at Google was Larry Page's wish to be able to talk to any engineer whose help he wanted in solving a problem, without going through that engineer's manager.[31] Further, Page instituted an annual "bureaucracy buster" campaign to identify bureaucracy that had entered the organization since the year before.[32]

The ultimate goal is to have an anti-bureaucratic mindset built into the culture, so that people are constantly on the lookout for the warning signs and are proactive about avoiding or eliminating bottlenecks. At one case company we were told that "there is an intolerance for sending up decision-making … that, for us, means that something is broken in the organization, and we need to fix it." Another person described a policy for "clean escalation" of decision-making: if two people disagree about what to do, they "get a manager and solve it there and then."

Structures and procedures can't be eliminated totally, which is why this Commandment calls for "minimal" bureaucracy. Various sources in our research described their company as being *partly* structured or having a structure that's "generally flat but hierarchy does play a role now and then." Still, a basic cultural principle is to favor non-bureaucratic, non-hierarchical approaches wherever possible. At our case companies this involves practices such as trying to push decisions down to a lower level rather than up and encouraging people to pursue what they think is right rather than telling them what to do.

---

[31] Ibid.
[32] Ibid.

6.5.8 Openness and Transparency

> We are extremely transparent and open in our communication ... Ideas come from the collective wisdom of people.[33] — Interviewee at Google

Most people we interviewed during our research on Google said they were surprised by the openness they encountered during their early days at the company. Even high-level executives were available for questions, and practically all information was accessible to employees. This openness was reinforced at the TGIF meetings, which each employee was expected to attend, where the management team and founders discussed matters of interest to the company and answered questions that employees had raised beforehand.

These same elements—a general openness and transparency, achieved by sharing information and having accessible managers and all-hands meetings—were common at all six case companies. The companies also applied open office designs in which the CEOs and executive team members had desks somewhere among their employees.

This openness and transparency are based on *trust*. For instance, when information is shared openly within a company, there has to be confidence that sensitive matters won't be leaked inappropriately to the outside. One case company approached this issue by explicitly telling people what things shouldn't be mentioned elsewhere, and then trusting them to "understand the information's value and keep it inside."

Another dimension of "trust" is trusting people to do their work responsibly without being constantly supervised. Our case companies all had consciously chosen not to apply a lot of policies, instructions, rules, and procedures on how things should be done. Much was left to the individual to choose in a way that looked best for the task. As one executive said, "we have a policy of treating our employees like adults." Another observed that in a company organized and run the way that our case companies are, there really isn't an alternative, anyway: "This is not an organization you can try to control."

All of which leads to the next Commandment on our list.

6.5.9 Leaders, Not Managers

> Lead more, manage less. — one of Jack Welch's principles

The aim of all six case companies was to attract and build leaders rather than managers. At one company the difference was described as follows: a "manager" communicates in one direction, e.g., by giving information, priorities, and instructions. In contrast, a "leader" is excellent at two-way communication, and is more focused on building an excellent team than on his or her own status and power.

---

[33] Ibid, p. 54.

A source at another firm quoted Jack Welch's principle shown above. According to Welch himself, leaders are people who lead with a clear vision. Further,

> they energize, excite and inspire rather than enervate, depress, and control.[34]

On the other hand, *management* in Welch's viewpoint is related to things like close supervision, control, and bureaucracy, and will kill the competitive spirit of a business. Welch also argued that managers deal with status quo rather than change, react rather than create opportunities, enforce organizational rules rather than change them, seek and then follow direction rather than provide a vision to believe in and strategic alignment, and control people by pushing them in the desired direction instead of motivating people by satisfying basic human needs.[35]

Welch's views on leadership correlate well with the view we found when researching our case companies. For example, according to Google, as leaders work in an environment with self-directed and motivated employees, the most important task of leadership is to communicate and clarify the *WHAT* and the *WHY* to their employees.[36] Even if guidance is important, leaders must delegate to their employees *HOW* to perform the work.

Our other case companies agreed that managers were "out" and leaders were in. According to one company, its leaders on all levels shared the firm's strategy, cultural values, and operational priorities. They were well informed and spend time really understanding the business. By doing so, they could ask the right questions, then give employees autonomy in what they do. This way of working demands excellence among the executive team. Its members must ask the right questions and be able to see "patterns" in the data delivered to them and thereby take steps that will help move the organization in the right direction. Another case company provided further insights into the difference between a manager and a leader. According to this company a manager digs into details and stays there, micromanaging people, while a leader digs down, asks the right questions and gets answers, then moves back up to a more holistic level and delegates to the team how to perform the tasks.

And the most holistic level is the one addressed by the final Commandment.

6.5.10 Build an Ecosystem, Not Just a Company

> We live in an ecosystem distinguished by ongoing personal relationships, partnerships, competitors and frequent change. This combination of elements is like our air. — Interviewee at Twitter

The case companies shared a strong common belief in the importance of an ecosystem—the larger system of external relationships and networks, both existing and

---

[34] http://www.1000ventures.com/business_guide/mgmt_new-model_25lessons-welch.html (Accessed 6 Aug 2015).

[35] Ibid.

[36] Steiber (2014).

potential, within which the company operates. According to our previous research on Google, job candidates were asked in interviews not only what they could do for the company but for the ecosystem. Another interviewee at Google told us, "To be aware of how you fit into the ecosystem should be a natural part of your job as a product manager."

By building an ecosystem of win-win relations, a company creates defense mechanisms in the competitive struggle which are harder to overcome than when the company battles alone.

A good example of belief in the power of the ecosystem came when Tesla's CEO Elon Musk announced in 2014 that "Tesla will not initiate patent lawsuits against anyone who, in good faith, wants to use our technology."[37] The reason for this move was to boost the ecosystem for electric cars and thus help Tesla to achieve its mission.

Facebook also demonstrated belief in harnessing the power of an ecosystem. It launched the initiative Internet.org,[38] bringing together technology leaders, nonprofits (NGOs) and local communities to connect the two-thirds of the world's people who did not have Internet access. Another example was Twitter Partner Marketplace[39] in which partners' products and services were presented in order to help businesses thrive on Twitter.

Along with investments in creating ecosystems that are broadly important to the firm and its business model, all companies also worked with external developers as an extension of their product development. Open APIs and regular hackathons were part of normal operations.

Examples like these appear to illustrate an underlying fact: Companies that understand the value of culture know that even the strongest corporate cultures cannot exist in a vacuum. They must thrive by interweaving with, and growing in concert with, their business environments and the societies they serve.

6.6 Recent Developments: The Growing Importance of Culture and the 'Ten Commandments'

While preparing the second edition of this book in 2023, the authors have noticed that their initial 2016 findings on corporate culture appear to be more significant than ever. Researchers, consultants, and business leaders continue to emphasize the value of having a strong culture. And increasingly, the cultural qualities that they identify as being most important are the same as those found among the Ten Commandments outlined above. This suggests that the kind of culture we observed in Silicon Valley is becoming the preferred standard everywhere. Indeed, many observers now urge the adoption of this type of culture for incumbent firms still clinging to old, outmoded cultural forms.

---

[37] Watkins (2014), p. 1.
[38] Facebook (2013).
[39] Twitter (2015).

Several factors are driving the movement toward a new culture. One is the need to be digitally up to date, via digital transformation. Another is the entrance of young Generation Z people into the workforce, and a third is the general desire to be focused on innovation and growth. Here are closer looks at each.

6.6.1 Culture in Digital Transformation

Digital transformation is "an ongoing process of adoption to a significantly changing digital landscape in order to meet the digital expectations of customers, employees and partners."[40] Depending on a company's needs, the transformation may involve making greater use of technologies and trends such as big-data analytics, artificial intelligence, social media, IoT (the internet of things), and more.[41] These technologies can help to produce results that range from highly targeted marketing and seamless customer service to new-product development and more efficient operations. However, for many traditional incumbents, getting the results "is not exclusively a technology-driven challenge." It also "requires deep cultural change."[42]

As noted in a McKinsey & Company survey, an inappropriate culture "is the most significant self-reported barrier to digital effectiveness."[43] Cultural problems at lagging companies include aversion to risk and change, and "siloed mind-sets and behavior"—which do not align with the customer journey, but instead divide tasks into slots that the company can more easily control.[44] Cultural changes that are recommended by various sources include:

- A focus on "self-motivation of employees" who have a "readiness to accept changes."[45]
- "Everyone in the organization must be prepared with an adaptive skill set." The company must have "higher operational transparency" along with a data-driven, "data-sharing mindset" and "a learning-friendly culture."[46]
- "Support from the top" rather than direction from the top: "All leaders need to shift their style from top-down decision-maker to coach." This means moving "from a command-and-control style of leadership to having senior leaders set high-level direction and strategy but giving considerable autonomy to teams charged with execution." Another key step is "removing silos" and creating cross-functional teams able to work in a manner that tracks customer experience. Also, controlled risk-taking should be encouraged, by leveraging digital capa-

---

[40] Teichert (2019).
[41] Ibid.
[42] Nadkarni and Prügl (2021).
[43] Goran et al. (2017).
[44] Ibid.
[45] Verina and Titko (2019).
[46] Nadkarni and Prügl (2021).

bilities to conduct rapid, "small-scale experiments that entail a limited cost in case of failure but can produce highly valuable discoveries."[47]
- Desirable cultural qualities include: collaboration across functions internally, and with external partners as well. Hiring and rewarding entrepreneurial, proactive employees. Building internal and external networks for knowledge and information sharing. An emphasis on constant organizational learning. Support of non-hierarchical discussions, and the democratization of decision processes.[48]
- And last but not least: "A customer-centric organizational culture is more than merely a good thing—it's becoming a matter of survival."[49]

Customer centricity was clearly emphasized by our Silicon Valley case companies in 2016. One of their 10 Commandments was a focus on "Product Excellence," in order to do an outstanding job of serving customers' needs. A customer-centric culture was further reflected in statements like "We actually go out and change … if we are convinced that it was the right thing for users in the long run."

Other parallels to the 10 Commandments should be evident as well. Adaptability to constant change; data-driven decision making and rapid, constant learning; minimal bureaucracy, with authority delegated to individuals and teams at the front lines; openness and transparency; leading instead of micro-managing and building external ecosystems—all these were salient features of Silicon Valley culture in 2016. They are now being encouraged and promoted more widely, to make companies elsewhere fit for the digital age of the twenty-first century.

6.6.2 Culture That Aligns with Generation Z

The Silicon Valley companies called hiring "the most important thing we do." They focused on recruiting people with top technical skills who also would be good cultural fits, since people shape the culture and vice versa. As described in Chap. 5, the ideal cultural candidates were entrepreneurial, adaptive to change, passionate, collaborative, and willing to question the status quo.

It now appears that a new generation entering the workforce has these qualities in abundance. Generation Z consists of people born between the mid-1990s up to about 2010. Roberta Katz, a senior research scholar at Stanford, co-led a multi-year study of Generation Z college students and young working adults in the U.S. and U.K. She summarized the research findings as follows:

> [A] typical Gen Zer is a self-driver who deeply cares about others, strives for a diverse community, is highly collaborative and social, values flexibility, relevance, authenticity, and

---

[47] Bughin (2017).
[48] Teichert (2019).
[49] Goran et al. (2017).

non-hierarchical leadership, and, while dismayed about inherited issues like climate change, has a pragmatic attitude about the work that has to be done to address those issues.[50]

Dr. Katz advised companies to recognize that Generation Z employees may be more likely than older colleagues to question rules and authority. She also pointed out that since these young people grew up with the internet, they became accustomed to understanding—and to wanting to work with—"a world that operates at speed, scale, and scope."[51]

If companies today wish to attract the best and brightest of Generation Z, they must therefore offer a culture which is conducive to the qualities just described. This in turn creates an additional impetus for changing culture in the directions we found in Silicon Valley in 2016.

6.6.3 Culture for Innovation and Growth

The third factor driving cultural change is simply a growing recognition that innovation and growth are keys to success in today's business environment. One sign of this is the widespread interest in the Exponential Organizations (ExO) community, dedicated to learning how companies can have exceptional impact and growth by leveraging "accelerating technologies" in order to "scale as quickly as tech does."[52] Regardless of whether one agrees with all aspects of ExO analysis, it is clear that culture plays a key role in such growth: "the culture of a company—how they operate, make decisions, and what their fears are—sets up the team's mindset … and impacts the company's success."[53]

Case studies of high-growth companies, published on the OpenExO website, also demonstrate this importance. One company profiled in 2022 was Duolingo, the language-learning firm which has grown to have the world's most widely downloaded education app. Although Duolingo was founded and is based in Pittsburgh, a U.S. city far from Silicon Valley, the company exhibits many features of the culture we described in the Valley. For example, Duolingo "launches around 30 new experiments per week and typically runs hundreds of experiments concurrently"—all aimed at enhancing user experience in some way—and "Any team member is empowered to propose and run an experiment by articulating a simple experiment memo."[54]

One final note: Innovation and growth to large scale often requires expanding into global markets. When a company operates in and/or sells into national markets other than its own, a quality called Cultural Intelligence (or CQ, for Cultural Quotient) becomes crucial—namely, the ability to adjust to the culture of a

---

[50] De Witte (2022).
[51] Ibid.
[52] Jeffery (2019).
[53] Nguyen (2023).
[54] Nagpal (2022).

particular foreign country or region. Independent researchers such as David Livermore and his colleagues have begun emphasizing that in order to do this well, the *company's own culture* must be flexible and open, admitting a diversity of viewpoints into decision-making.[55] Thus, we see that in this respect, too, there are increasing imperatives for companies to adopt a culture similar to what our studies revealed in Silicon Valley in 2016.

6.7 Concluding Comments

This chapter has shown why corporate culture is viewed a fundamental success factor in today's business world. It has defined what culture consists of—i.e., a set of guiding beliefs—and described the common core beliefs that animate the cultures of the six case companies in our Silicon Valley studies.

The next chapter will examine in more practical detail how the companies are managed.

References

Bahrami, H. (1992). The emerging flexible organization: Perspectives from Silicon Valley. *California Management Review, 34*(4), 33–52.

Bughin, J. (2017, May 3). *Digital success requires a digital culture*. McKinsey & Company. https://www.mckinsey.com/capabilities/strategy-and-corporate-finance/our-insights/the-strategy-and-corporate-finance-blog/digital-success-requires-a-digital-culture

De Witte, M. (2022, January 3). *Gen Z are not 'coddled.' They are highly collaborative, self-reliant and pragmatic, according to new Stanford-affiliated research*. Stanford News. https://news.stanford.edu/2022/01/03/know-gen-z/

Egigius, H. (1994). *Psykologilexikon (dictionary of psychology)*. Natur & Kultur.

Facebook. (2013, August). Internet.org at Facebook posted https://www.facebook.com/Internetdotorg/info?ref¼page_internal. Accessed 2 Aug 2015.

Goran, J., LaBerge, L., & Srinivasan, R. (2017, July 20). *Culture for a digital age*. McKinsey Quarterly. https://www.mckinsey.com/capabilities/mckinsey-digital/our-insights/culture-for-a-digital-age

Himanen, P., Torvalds, L., & Castells, M. (2001). *The hacker ethic and the spirit of the information age*. Random House.

Jackson, E. (2013, March 26). *The difference between the mindsets of founders and professional managers*. Forbes.com. http://onlinecareertips.com/2013/03/the-difference-between-the-mindsets-of-founders-and-professional-managers/. Accessed 2 Aug 2015.

Jeffery, J. (2019, October 29). *What is an exponential organization?* Entrepreneur. https://www.entrepreneur.com/growing-a-business/what-is-an-exponential-organization/341439

Levy, S. (1984). *Hackers*. O'Reilly Media. Reprinted 2010.

Levy, S. (2011). *In the plex: How Google thinks, works, and shapes our lives*. Simon & Schuster.

Livermore, D., VanDyne, L., & Ang, S. (2021). Organizational CQ: Cultural intelligence (CQ) for 21st century organizations. *Business Horizons, 65*(5), 671–680. https://doi.org/10.1016/j.bushor.2021.11.001

---

[55] Livermore et al. (2021).

McCracken, H. (2013, November 17). *Of course Facebook is a utility!* Time. http://techland.time.com/2013/11/17/of-course-facebook-is-a-utility. Accessed 2 June 2015.

Nadkarni, S., & Prugl, R. (2021). Digital transformation: A review, synthesis and opportunities for future research. *Management Review Quarterly, 71*, 233–341. https://doi.org/10.1007/s11301-020-00185-7

Nagpal, C. (2022, August 28). *Mastering the language of startup success—The Duolingo way.* ExOinsight. https://insight.openexo.com/startup-success-the-duolingo-way/

Nguyen, G. (2023). *The importance of company culture in building an exponential organization.* YouTube video, posted April 2023 at https://www.youtube.com/watch?v=KE0H5jdiewk

Schein, E. (1983). *The role of the founder in the creation of organizational culture (Working Paper #1407-83)*. Sloan School of Management, Massachusetts Institute of Technology.

Schein, E. (1984). Coming to a new awareness of organizational culture. *Sloan Management Review, 25*(2), 3.

Schmidt, E., & Rosenberg, J. (2014). *How Google works*. Grand Central Publishing.

Steiber, A. (2014). *The Google model: Managing continuous innovation in a rapidly changing world*. Springer.

Teichert, R. (2019). Digital transformation maturity: A systematic review of the literature. *Acta Universitatis Agriculturae et Silviculturae Mendelianae Brunensis, 67*(6), 1673–1687. https://doi.org/10.11118/actaun201967061673

Twitter. (2015). The twitter official partner program, posted https://partners.twitter.com/. Accessed 28 July 2015.

Verina, N., & Titko, J. (2019). Digital transformation: Conceptual framework. In *Conference paper: Contemporary Issues in Business, Management and Economics Engineering (CIBMEE) 2019*, Vilnius, Lithuania 9–10 May 2019. https://doi.org/10.3846/cibmee.2019.073

Walters, B. (2004). *The 10 most fascinating people of 2004 (excerpt)*. ABC-TV, excerpt at https://www.youtube.com/watch?v¼0C_DQxpX-Kw. Accessed 2 Aug 2015.

Watkins, W. J. (2014, July 17). *Rethinking patent enforcement: Tesla did what?* Forbes.com. http://www.forbes.com/sites/realspin/2014/07/17/rethinking-patent-enforcement-tesla-did-what/. Accessed 28 July 2015.

Wiberg, L. (1999). *Gränslandet: Ledarskap för medarbetarnas delaktighet och verksamhetens förnyelse* [Borderland: Leadership for employee participation and operations renewal]. Nerenius & Santérus.

Winkler, R. (2014, October 27). *In new structure, Google CEO Page aims for 'Faster, Better Decisions'*. WSJ.com. http://blogs.wsj.com/digits/2014/10/27/in-new-structure-google-ceo-page-aims-for-faster-better-decisions/. Accessed 28 July 2015.

Leading for Entrepreneurship 7

> *Today, entrepreneurial thinking and doing are the most important capabilities companies need from their employees... Entrepreneurial employees possess what eBay CEO John Donahoe calls the founder mind-set [They] drive change, motivate people, and just get stuff done. Indeed, having a founder mind-set doesn't necessarily mean that you are going to start your own company. Many people with such instincts are quite happy to work at companies like eBay or LinkedIn—provided such companies maintain an employment alliance that encourages entrepreneurial behavior.*
>
> Reid Hoffman et al. (2014), pp. 13–14

How did the Silicon Valley companies in our study organize and lead for broad-scale entrepreneurship? Earlier chapters have made the point that the innovativeness and growth of organizations are, to a large extent, based on having many creative employees who are given considerable freedom to develop new ideas and act as entrepreneurs as part of their jobs. One major piece of the puzzle has just been provided in the previous chapter: Culture is of vital importance for socializing individuals to innovate and excel.

Also, at our case companies, the influence of the Silicon Valley context has been considerable. People are encouraged to be entrepreneurial by seeing and experiencing how other companies and people act, within the surrounding community, and by seeing how universities, business angels and venture capital, and other parties all contribute as well to creating new knowledge and bringing it to market.[1]

But given all this, the question remains: What can individual leaders do in order to make their organizations entrepreneurial? The focus here in this chapter is on

---

[1] Steiber and Alänge (2013b).

topics related to leading creative people, while Chap. 8 will delve deeper into the organizational aspects.

This chapter is divided into eight sections, starting with the *Top leaders' roles* in leading for entrepreneurship. Then come two sections that discuss major aspects of leading entrepreneurial employees who need a certain degree of freedom and creative space: first, *Providing direction and expectation level*, and then *Communication and leader behavior*. Next, the particular function of and challenges for *Founder entrepreneurs* are discussed, followed by a review of the *Role of leaders on the middle level*. Then we examine ways to accomplish fast *Decision-making* in an environment, which demands ever shorter lead-times. This is followed by a discussion of *Incentives and motivation* of creative, entrepreneurial individuals and how the habits of good leaders can contribute. Finally, the important issue of *Hiring and developing leaders* is highlighted.

7.1 Top Leaders' Roles

The companies studied all had strong top leaders (including founders) who had created and structured their organizations. These people played a major part in creating their company's culture and they continue to cultivate this culture. Their leadership role consisted of setting visions and communicating goals, being actively involved in what matters for innovation and long term development, monitoring and reviewing what has been accomplished, and making sure that the right creative people were hired, then were offered an environment where they could excel—including a culture that guides and enables initiatives and decision-making on the level of individuals.

Many functions of the top executive identified long ago by Chester Barnard[2] still remain in the new management model, although utilizing "the creativity of many" requires top leaders to refrain from giving strong directions on how something should be done, and instead let their creative individuals come up with new ideas (which in practice may surpass the initial ideas of the executive). For founder/leaders who themselves have shown great technical ability and creativity, it can be challenging not to jump in early and give advice. However, this is an essential part of the social contract with creative individuals. As a leader you have to trust that you've hired people of such a caliber that they are capable of having better ideas than yours. Moreover when people come up with their own ideas, typically in interaction with others, the shared feeling of ownership can increase the odds of turning the ideas into actual innovations.

There is, however, a need for leaders to be technically competent and able to involve themselves with in-depth product discussions. In several of our case

---

[2] Barnard mentioned, for example: developing and maintaining a system of communication through a selection of people and the offering of incentives; securing an informal organization; maintenance of morals, supervision and control; education, training, and formulating and defining purposes and objectives of the organization (Barnard, 1938), pp. 215–234.

companies, founders were still actively involved in innovation and product issues.[3] The primary focus was typically not on making decisions, but on stimulating creative individuals by showing interest and asking informed questions. In the Silicon Valley case companies, top leaders also participated in or led product reviews. They were keen on follow-up and eager to have processes for learning from both successes and failures. At Google, for instance, post-mortem processes ensured that even failed initiatives provided useful output in the form of learning.[4]

What top leaders say and write matters, but most of all they communicate through behavior and through their functions as guides and role models. At Google it is emphasized that strong leaders also are humble, and this has been expressed as a strong value that permeates the organization. Humble leaders can be good listeners, but can still set directions and ask questions.[5]

7.2 Providing Direction and Expectation Level

Internal entrepreneurs need some kind of direction in order to channel their creativity towards what is viewed as strategically worthwhile by the organization. This direction must be communicated very clearly to each and every one, although still not written in stone in a way that would limit creativity.

The companies in our study all used strong overarching visions/missions as foundations for their reasons to exist. These visions/missions also helped attract creative individuals to join their ranks. The visions and missions expressed remarkably challenging tasks for the employees but they remained open in terms of how the challenge would be overcome, in order not to restrict creativity. Another note: our case companies are all positioned to utilize the Internet for ongoing innovation. Internet-based solutions will be part of the innovation arsenal for most organizations in the future.

Here are the mission statements of each of our case companies, as downloaded from their websites in May 2015.

Apigee's Mission:	"To deliver products that make every business a digital business." (Later further specified with the statement: "Apigee helps businesses use APIs to securely share data and services across a myriad devices and channels.")
Facebook's Mission:	"To give people the power to share and make the world more open and connected. People use Facebook to stay connected with friends and family, to discover what's going on in the world, and to share and express what matters to them".
Google's Mission:	"To organize the world's information and make it universally accessible and useful."

---

[3] Focus on product excellence is one of the key cultural attributes described in Chap. 6.
[4] Steiber (2014), p. 73.
[5] Steiber (2014), pp. 65–66.

LinkedIn's Mission:	"Connect the world's professionals to make them more productive and successful."
Tesla's Mission:	"To accelerate the advent of sustainable transport by bringing compelling mass market electric cars to market as soon as possible."
Twitter's Mission:	"To give everyone the power to create and share ideas and information instantly, without barriers."

In these statements, not only did the companies express a direction, they also set very high expectation levels. They expected their employees to join in and work towards extremely ambitious goals, which was one of the ways in which the companies aimed to be different from "traditional" firms. Employees knew that innovation was part of the job, and that while some of it could be incremental, they should also contribute to developing ideas that are transformative and/or highly scalable. At Google this was communicated internally through the precept "Think Big" (later replaced by CEO Larry Page's directive to "Think 10X").

> The obvious benefit of thinking big is that it gives smart creatives much more freedom. It removes constraints and spurs creativity. thinking big is actually a very powerful tool for attracting and retaining smart creatives.[6]

Corresponding imperatives at LinkedIn were "Dream Big," "Get Shit Done" and "Know How to Have Fun." CEO Jeff Weiner even doubled the ante set by Page at Google, when he defined "Dream Big" as expanding your thinking 20X.[7] Here is Weiner's account of what inspired him to formulate the three mantras just mentioned—and why he thinks they all go together:

> It all started in a meeting where a talented team was presenting their plan but their objectives were still way off what I would have expected them to be targeting Without hesitation, I challenged the team to increase their long-term goal by roughly 20x. Regardless of whether or not they could hit the target (which I think they can), the point was to get them thinking much bigger, without constraints, and to start by asking the question, "What would it take…?" When well reasoned, that kind of vision can be highly inspirational, change the way teams solve for a specific opportunity or challenge, and ultimately, transform the trajectory of a company. During this particular meeting, I ended up writing down two simple words to capture this quality: "Dream big," with the intention of cascading the theme more broadly. Almost immediately after seeing those words in writing, I realized the message was incomplete Asking people to dream big without delivering on the vision was not only an incomplete sentiment, it could carry the unintended consequence of producing pie-in-the-sky thinking without anything to show for it. If a goal is truly visionary, it's going to be confronted by doubters, skeptics, and those threatened by its realization. … Some of the most capable people they just "get sh*t done." It then occurred to me that I've known a number of people who embodied the ability to dream big and get sh*t done, but who also proved very difficult to work with. I've reached a point in my career where I want to be surrounded by people who not only share a vision, but a genuine commitment to upholding their company's culture and values. They are team players, don't take themselves too

---

[6] Schmidt and Rosenberg (2014), pp. 217–219.
[7] Weiner (2014). https://www.linkedin.com/pulse/20140824235337-22330283-the-three-qualities-of-people-i-most-enjoy-working-with

seriously, and "know how to have fun." And with that, I added a third circle to the Venn diagram.[8]

Shared values are integral parts of the cultural belief system in a company. They provide strong guidance, not least through peer accountability, which is why in some cases they are formally stated and oft repeated. For example, everyone has heard of Google's "Don't be evil." Chairman and former CEO Eric Schmidt (along with CEO advisor Jonathan Rosenberg) explained its role as follows:

> "Don't be evil" is mainly another way to empower employees Googlers do regularly check their moral compass when making decisions. When Toyota invented its famous kanban system any employee on the assembly line could pull the cord to stop production if he noticed a quality problem. The same philosophy lies behind "Don't be evil," a cultural lodestar that shines over all management layers, product plans, and office politics.[9]

The companies studied were all in a sense startups, and as mentioned in Chap. 5, the founders and early employees had been the primary actors who contributed to shaping the companies' cultures. To keep innovative cultures alive, it is a major task of top leaders to consciously cultivate and maintain them. Some of our case companies had created elaborate and systematic processes for hiring, developing and firing employees in order to sustain their company culture.[10] Others also considered culture of extreme importance but had different approaches to maintaining it. For example, an interviewee at one case company said that in accordance with its high-trusting culture and tradition of delegation, it has left hiring and firing to the employees' discretion.

7.3 Communication and Leader Behavior

Organizations have long been viewed as "systems of consciously coordinated activities ... of two or more persons"[11] in which survival is built upon the employees' willingness to cooperate, the ability to communicate, and the existence and acceptance of common purpose. Therefore, the issue of communicating purpose to employees has long been seen as central. Traditionally, the top leader communicated goals to the next management level, which in turn translated these to goals for the next level, and so forth. In Japanese-inspired policy deployment the top leaders' goals were also iterated through a "catch-ball" process with the next level[12] and then through a similar communication process all the way down to the shop floor, where each individual ideally would understand how his/her personal goals connect to the company's priorities.[13]

---

[8] Ibid.
[9] Schmidt and Rosenberg (2014), p. 65.
[10] Steiber (2014).
[11] Barnard (1938), p. viii.
[12] Shiba et al. (1993).
[13] Alänge (1994).

In the Silicon Valley companies studied, this way of systematically breaking down company goals had been at least partly replaced by an extreme transparency and direct communication by the top leader with everyone in the company. From its start, Google's founders used Friday afternoons to speak openly to all employees about the issues at hand and challenges to come for the company.[14] After the IPO in 2004, what could be communicated was somewhat restricted because of stock market regulations, but the intention from top leadership was still to make everyone aware of the actual situation and what were considered priorities for Google.[15] Every employee was trusted and had access to all information presented at the Board meetings, except for parts restricted by regulation. The written information was sent out through a company-wide email immediately after each Board meeting.[16] Similarly, Elon Musk made very open and often public statements on the next moves and priorities of Tesla, which reached the employees not only through direct internal routes, such as emails, but also through different forms of social media.[17] Other communication was only for internal use:

> Elon sent an internal email to everybody in our organization about the importance of having minimal bureaucracy. Paraphrasing, he said: By far the most common way of communicating is chain of command which means you always flow communication through your manager. This is dumb. Chain of command serves to enhance the power of the manager but it fails to serve the company. Anybody can and should email or talk to anyone else according to what they think is the fastest way to solve a problem to the benefit of the company… — Interviewee at Tesla

In this direct way Tesla's CEO heavily influenced the organization's set of beliefs. But Musk also influenced these through behavior, such as putting a majority of his time into developing the company and personally being willing to take big risks, and by being directly involved in hiring of people. In addition, he was very accessible for employees at his corner desk of Tesla's facilities, setting the stage for a very open company where only two persons had personal offices, the heads of HR and Legal.

At Google each individual also had personal strategic goals to attain. They were called OKRs—Objectives and Key Results, defined to be easily measurable for follow-up—and on the individual level they connected to Google's Think Big imperative.[18] OKRs should be stretch goals that are hard to achieve, but still

---

[14] Steiber (2014).

[15] Steiber and Alänge (2013a).

[16] Schmidt and Rosenberg (2014), pp. 175–176.

[17] For example, Musk's presentation of the Tesla Powerwall was posted on YouTube in May 2015 and had over 2.6 million views in 3 months (Musk, 2015). https://www.youtube.com/watch?v¼yKORsrlN-2k

The video drew much attention—for example, Carmine Gallo in *Forbes* commented that it is designed like a TED talk which, in 18 min, "offers leaders a blueprint for how to launch a product." (Gallo, 2015). http://www.forbes.com/sites/carminegallo/2015/05/04/teslas-elon-musk-lights-up-social-media-with-a-ted-style-keynote/

[18] Steiber (2014).

7.3 Communication and Leader Behavior

realistic; if all OKRs were to be attained, then that would show they were not aggressive enough. The OKRs of each person at Google, including the CEO's, were posted on the corporate intranet and accessible by all employees—which meant that there was total transparency concerning both the company's (CEO's) quarterly priorities and each individual's quarterly priorities.[19] After the CEO had posted his OKRs he hosted a company-wide meeting to review them together with product and business leaders, who commented on what these OKRs meant for their teams. They also publicly reviewed their own (and their teams') results in relation to last quarter's OKRs and discussed why they succeeded or failed.[20] Contrary to policy deployment, the OKRs are not comprehensive as "they are reserved for areas that need specific focus and objectives that won't be reached without some extra oomph. Business-as-usual stuff doesn't need OKRs."[21]

What are the requirements that communication must meet in order to be perceived as valid? Employees need to perceive it as genuine and timely, both regarding facts and regarding the beliefs upon which the company strategies are built. Furthermore, a general culture of openness and transparency can contribute to the perception that communication is trustworthy and that there are no hidden agendas. Finally, leaders' visibility and behavior matters, as employees read the behavior to figure out what really matters, regardless of what has been said or written.[22]

> [T]his is the leader's ... task: walking the talk of the mission statement. the organization must actually support employees' ability to achieve meaningful goals. In the best companies, where employees are engaged and performance shines, leaders at all levels respect employees and consistently strive to give them the autonomy, help, resources, and time they need to do great work.[23]

Our Silicon Valley case companies excelled in these areas, with top leaders who communicated openly and directly to their employees at the same time that they visibly participated in, and put a focus on, what was considered of vital interest: innovation and new business models. In one of the companies an interviewee expressed this to us as follows:

> Leaders have to be open to ideas, be flexible and agile, keep a higher level of transparency, sharing the WAY, and be far more open with information, fighting confidentiality.

And, here is another example of how a top leader (and founder) set the focus on innovation and speed through his own behavior, as described by a case company interviewee:

---

[19] Schmidt and Rosenberg (2014), p. 177.
[20] Ibid, p. 178.
[21] Ibid, p. 222.
[22] Grove (1996).
[23] Amabile and Kramer (2012). https://hbr.org/2012/12/to-give-your-employees-meaning

[The company is organized] in an orbit around the CEO and he has ideas flying around him all the time. [Also,] Writing code … is part of core behavior … People want to build stuff that is so awesome … so they can talk to the CEO about it.

The companies naturally were using their own products in practice. For example, at Facebook the company was run on Facebook, organized in small groups; LinkedIn was using its platform for professionals, including for its Alumni network; Google naturally used Search and other products.

7.4 Founder Entrepreneurs

As mentioned, in all companies we studied, the founders still played an active role in either executive or board positions. Looking back into history, the role of founders has always been significant for companies' development. However, the "old truth" was that the entrepreneur was absolutely vital for the startup while a professional manager was needed for continued growth. Apple played by this axiom when Steve Jobs recruited an experienced large-company top executive, John Sculley, to succeed him as CEO in 1983. Jobs remained as chairman of the board, but in 1985 he was forced out of Apple. Then in 1997, a dwindling Apple brought Jobs back as an entrepreneurial savior, resulting in one of the most impressive revitalizations of a going concern that has ever been seen. The question now is if the old axiom is obsolete—maybe entrepreneurs are needed all along the development curve, in order for companies to stay competitive in fast-moving markets.

Looking back, IBM's second CEO, Thomas Watson Jr., had created the foundation for a long-term commercial success story based on computer science and mainframe computers. However, when the business context changed, partly as an effect of IBM's own contributions to popularizing the personal computer, IBM found itself obsolete and on the verge of bankruptcy. The new CEO Lou Gerstner had to change almost everything, including the company's detailed dress code, in order to restructure IBM into a service organization and an open-innovation company pioneering intellectual property trading as a new business area. Thus, although Watson Jr. and his father (the founding CEO) had been very influential and laid the foundation for a whole industry, a new entrepreneurial CEO was needed in the top position in order to make a radical change of the business model. In other cases, the visions and directions formulated by founders and early leaders can live through decades provided they are general enough and reflect the spirit of the company. George W. Merck, who was CEO of the US-based Merck & Co. from 1925 to 1950, set a primary focus on providing medicine for the people, not on profits, and for decades this worked as a strong motivating factor for creative employees at Merck.[24]

> We try never to forget that medicine is for the people. It is not for the profits. The profits follow, and if we have remembered that, they have never failed to appear.[25]

---

[24] Our own interview data from Merck in 1988.
[25] George W. Merck in 1950, quoted in Collins and Porras 1994 (2002), p. 48.

This quote has a direct parallel in the Google founders urging employees to create new products and services that were of value for users, and not to bother about the business model initially, as expressed in the Founders' IPO Letter in 2004: "Serving our end users is at the heart of what we do and remains our number one priority."[26] In their book *How Google Works*, Eric Schmidt and Jonathan Rosenberg added that the full sentence should read "focus on the user and all else will follow."[27] And they continued "This means that … we trust that our smart creative will figure out how to make money from it. It could take a while, so sticking it out requires a lot of confidence. But it is usually worth it." For example, when Paul Buchheit was developing Gmail as a 20%-time project, he wanted to find a way to generate revenue but was told "to just concentrate on making Gmail great. We'll worry about revenue later."[28] Schmidt and Rosenberg commented: "But Gmail was Paul's baby, and he ignored us. Gmail launched a few months later. Its ads did not generate much revenue, but the technology was later refined to improve our AdSense product, … a multibillion-dollar business."[29]

The Merck quote above refers to the "noble goal" of developing medicines to cure people and it served as a strong motivator for innovation at Merck. Such ambitions, beyond making users/customers happy and thus making profits, can both attract people to the company (as pointed out in Chap. 5) and provide intrinsic motivation to excel. For example, Tesla's ambition to contribute to a sustainable society is one such noble goal and so is Google's broad vision of making the world's information accessible and useful, in combination with the founders' famous "Don't be evil" mandate.

7.5 The Role of Leaders on the Middle Levels

While many traditional activities remain for the top leaders, middle management at our case companies had a role quite different than in a traditional company. A common thread at all the companies was the desire to have few layers between the CEO and floor level. This means that mid-level leaders had more direct reports, which in some companies was expressed in heuristics such as Google's "Rule of 7"[30] mandating that each leader should have at least seven direct reports. A flat hierarchy in combination with meritocratic direction means that hierarchical position has another meaning. The basic idea of making many creative individuals excel has even more implications on this level of management. The focus becomes on facilitating and creating the opportunities for subordinates to take initiatives, and to work on developing and testing their own ideas—sometimes, in relationships they have developed with colleagues who report to other leaders. For technically savvy leaders on the

---

[26] Page and Brin (2004). https://investor.google.com/corporate/2004/ipo-founders-letter.html
[27] Schmidt and Rosenberg (2014), p. 214.
[28] Ibid, p. 228.
[29] Ibid.
[30] Steiber (2014), p. 69.

middle management level, restraining the urge to provide early direction can be very challenging, as this used to be one way that competent middle managers were appreciated.

A mid-level leader at a case company explained this challenging role to us as follows:

> You give people sort of limited resources and let them try something and as a manager you get out of the way. I like to make sure that we are trying and we are testing; I don't have to see what they see. Someone said "I have a great idea and I have a team that believes deeply in this concept and I want to try it" … I said "let's go." I am supportive, even if I don't see what they see. Because if I start to put my judgment on top, I will become a layer, I will inhibit that innovation—my job is to support that innovation…the main thing, I am there to support them. I know them, I trust them, I have worked with them. I said: "I don't know what you see, I don't see what you see… [but] as long as it is on strategy, it is on brand…if you guys believe in this, and this is your bet, I will be behind you."

We've noted that employees in the case companies were typically urged to think big, in terms of scaling of product ideas for global markets. However, one interviewee emphasized that in coaching people to innovate, part of the mid-level leader's role could be helping some people who are thinking *too* big, by breaking their idea down into smaller, manageable pieces that can be taken forward step-by-step.

7.6 Decision-Making

Our case companies all needed rapid decision-making in order to shorten lead times for innovation. The way this was done differed to some extent, as the companies were of different size and were structured in different ways.

During early idea phases, Google had utilized its 20% rule empowering creative individuals to develop their own ideas. Regarding engineers, a manager could only delay the start of such independent work if he/she believed that it could jeopardize an important delivery within the regular work assignment. Individuals presented their idea to other engineers who, if they believed it was promising, could decide to support the development with their own 20% work time. This meant that independent of managers, Google engineers could decide by an internal crowd-decision-making process to proceed developing an idea at least towards a working prototype. The role of the manager was then to support the work regardless of whether he/she could see the potential or not. This included providing the engineers access to IT-based test systems for rapid, scalable testing.

At Facebook the process was typically a bit different. Founder Mark Zuckerberg was generally available on a weekly basis to listen to new ideas from engineers. Also, in frequent 24-h Hackathons aiming at producing new code, the result could be prototypes that were demonstrated to a leadership group including Zuckerberg. This group could then make rapid decisions on continued development of the prototypes:

Hackathons are a big tradition at Facebook. They serve as the foundation for some great (and not so great) ideas. It gives our employees the opportunity to try out new ideas and collaborate with other people in a fun environment.[31]

Here at Facebook, we believe that every engineer possesses amazing ideas and creativity. Hackathons are a longstanding tradition at Facebook where our engineers stay up all night to create a working product or prototype from scratch. Remember—done is better than perfect. The winning team will get the chance to compete against teams from other Hackathons both domestically and internationally at the Hackathon Finals and be judged by our executives.[32] — held at Facebook HQ in Menlo Park, California in November!

There are, however, various other ways to speed decision-making. They include involving users and customers either openly, in voting procedures, or by launching products for users, who through their user behavior provide feedback for the developers. At Internet-based companies such as Google, Facebook and Twitter the latter alternative is used frequently. For example, in a matter of days Google could test two different product concepts on millions of users and receive accurate numerical data showing which concept was preferred, "based on how real users behave."[33]

7.7 Incentives and Motivation

Interviewees at our case companies affirmed that creative, entrepreneurial individuals were motivated by intrinsic incentives. This is supported by research done elsewhere, including the work of the noted research team Teresa Amabile and Steven Kramer, who found that the strongest motivating factor for knowledge workers is making progress in meaningful work. They suggest that managers can positively influence employees' well-being, motivation and creative output if they know how to catalyze and nourish progress and are aware of what actions can be negative.

> Through exhaustive analysis ... of knowledge workers, we discovered the progress principle: Of all the things that can boost emotions, motivation, and perceptions during a workday, the single most important is making progress in meaningful work. And the more frequently people experience that sense of progress, the more likely they are to be creatively productive in the long run.[34]

Catalysts are actions that support work, such as setting clear goals, allowing autonomy, providing sufficient resources and time, etc. These have an impact both on actual progress and on peoples' motivation to do a great job. Nourishers are acts of interpersonal support such as respect and recognition, encouragement, emotional comfort, and opportunities for affiliation.[35] Catalysts and nourishers can alter the meaningfulness of work and signal to people that their work and they themselves

---

[31] Facebook (2015a). https://www.facebook.com/hackathon
[32] Facebook (2015b). https://www.facebook.com/events/828648753872660/
[33] Steiber and Alänge (2013a).
[34] Amabile and Kramer (2011), p. 72.
[35] Ibid, p. 76.

are important to the organization, thus amplifying the operation of the progress principle.

The Silicon Valley case companies worked very much according to this progress principle through the kinds of management actions that Amabile and Kramer view as "common sense" and "common decency."[36] For example, Google's eight good habits of great leaders[37] had both catalyst and nourishing functions:

Being a good coach includes giving specific and constructive feedback, holding regular meetings with each employee, and developing solutions to problems in a way that utilizes each employee's strengths.

Empowering your team and not micromanaging means balancing between giving freedom to employees and being accessible for support. The leader should also assign challenging tasks to support the employees' willingness to take on big problems.

Expressing interest in employees' success and well-being entails showing interest in one's employees by getting to know them as people, not just as employees. A leader must ensure that new employees feel welcome, and if they wish to change projects, the leader should make it easier for them to do so.

Being productive and results-oriented means focusing on what one wants the group to accomplish and on how every employee should contribute to the goal. A leader should support the employees by prioritizing the tasks at hand and by making decisions that will eliminate obstacles.

Being a good communicator and listen to your team involves being aware that communication is a two-way street that involves both listening and sharing. A good leader should arrange meetings for all the employees, be clear about the group's objectives, stimulate dialog, listen to questions, and perceive what is bothering the employees.

Helping your employees with career development entails actively supporting the employees in their career development and helping to broaden their skills and education.

Having a clear vision and strategy for the team means keeping the group focused on goals and strategies, as well as getting them to discuss and advance the group's vision and goals.

Having key technical skills so you can help advise the team means acquiring the technical expertise necessary to provide good advice to one's group. This also means rolling up your sleeves and working side by side with your group when this is needed.

By being aware of good leader's habits, communicating them and following up regularly to provide feedback on each leader's behavior, Google could develop its leaders and assure that they were up to the required standards.[38]

---

[36] Ibid, p. 77.
[37] Quoted in Steiber (2014), pp. 63–64.
[38] Steiber (2014).

7.8 Hiring and Developing Leaders

The hiring and development of leaders is very important as they have a strong influence on others. For example, unethical behavior by people in leadership positions can be very detrimental to the culture of an organization. Some case companies had installed procedures by which candidates for promotion to leadership were evaluated not only by their supervisors, but also from the perspective of peers and subordinates. Google had a process where at least five peers had to agree on a person's promotion to a leadership position. The evaluation was backed up by data from the yearly employee surveys that measured leadership abilities.[39]

The classical question of whether a person can be developed into a leader or is born a natural leader has no simple answer, as both views can be true. Google's promotion process might have led to a selection of natural leaders, but at the same time the company had shown it believed that individuals can become better leaders through socialization, role modeling, feedback processes and training. For example, former Intuit CEO Bill Campbell, the coach that the central Google leaders shared as an advisor with Apple's Steve Jobs, considered that leadership is possible to learn and there are many examples provided by the biographies of Jobs[40] and the Google leaders.[41] Thus, the HR department put considerable resources into evaluating leaders, promoting desired leadership traits and supporting leadership development. The moral-compass (Andon[42]) function of Google's "Don't Be Evil" also assisted leaders in their decision-making, eliciting comments such as "This is not Googley" from their subordinates.[43] However, one of the most essential mechanisms was the initial hiring process, where Google tried to weed out unethical behavior by testing and inquiring for ethics—as the view was that it is very hard to change a person's ethics.[44]

Some of the case companies viewed ethics as an integral part of their culture and cared deeply about maintaining ethical practices. As at Google, this included carefully screening candidates for hiring because unethical behavior could negatively affect company culture, especially if unethical individuals assumed leadership roles. However, management also had a responsibility for ethics after people had become employees. In Schmidt and Rosenberg's book the issue is discussed in a poetic way, referring to ethical people as "knights" and the unethical as "knaves."

> There is no room for knaves. And generally, in our experience, once a knave, always a knave. Fortunately, employee behavior is socially normative. In a healthy culture of knight-

---

[39] Ibid, pp. 67–68.

[40] Isaacson (2011).

[41] Schmidt and Rosenberg (2014).

[42] Originating in the Toyota Production System, *andon* is the way line workers can stop the production by pulling a cord, in order to make everyone focus on finding the root cause of a problem before more waste is produced.

[43] Schmidt and Rosenberg (2014).

[44] Steiber and Alänge (2013a).

ish values, the knights will call out the knaves for their poor behavior until they either shape up or leave.

As a manager, if you detect a knave in your midst it's best to reduce his responsibility and appoint a knight to assume it. And for more egregious offenses, you need to get rid of the knave, quickly. Smart creatives may have a lot of good traits, but they aren't saints, so it's important to watch your knave quotient.[45]

The authors also made a point about distinguishing "knaves" from "divas," who can be very valuable to organizations even though their ego-driven personalities do not fit standard social norms.

Knaves are not to be confused with divas. Knavish behavior is a product of low integrity; diva-ish behavior is one of high exceptionalism…As long as their contributions match their outlandish egos, divas should be tolerated and even protected…Remember that Steve Jobs was one of the greatest business divas the world has ever known![46]

7.9 Recent Findings

In line with the findings from our case companies in 2016, several researchers have published articles that emphasize the importance of entrepreneurial leadership for companies' development.[47] The recent publications have authors from America, Africa, Asia, and Europe. This appears to indicate that the value of entrepreneurial leadership for stimulating innovation, through initiatives by employees, has become recognized globally.[48]

Systematic literature reviews and analyses, by Christian Harrison et al. and by Catherine M. Clark et al., showed that entrepreneurial leadership is still a comparatively new research area, but that it is an important factor in enhancing organizations' performance in turbulent and competitive environments.[49] The reviews found multiple behaviors and attributes correlated with being an entrepreneurial leader, such as vision, effective communication, risk-taking, and creativity.[50]

Interestingly—and perhaps not surprisingly—other research has indicated that founder-leaders are more likely to be entrepreneurial than non-founder leaders.[51] Further, firms led by a founder CEO have a greater tendency to pursue growth-oriented strategies than firms led by a professional CEO.[52]

---

[45] Schmidt and Rosenberg (2014), pp. 49–51.
[46] Ibid.
[47] See for example Akbari et al. (2021) and Iqbal et al. (2022).
[48] For example: Paudel (2019), Bagheri and Harrison (2020), Li et al. (2020), Bagheri et al. (2022), Hussain et al. (2023) and Shiferaw et al. (2023).
[49] Harrison et al. (2016) and Clark et al. (2019)
[50] Ibid.
[51] Renko et al. (2015).
[52] Abebe et al. (2020).

Samundra Paudel also found that entrepreneurial leadership has a significant positive effect on both organizational innovations and business performance.[53] This positive relationship has been observed especially in companies led by founder-CEOs, which differ systematically from successor-CEO firms. Founder-CEO firms in the aggregate had higher firm valuation and stronger stock-market performance than non-founder CEO firms.[54]

There have been relatively few articles on how entrepreneurial leadership could be taught.[55] Not much has been done in terms of university education for use within companies, and in a 2023 article, Martin Lackéus proposed a unifying concept called "work-learn balance," which could contribute to creating a shared view between the two worlds—industry and the university—and a better understanding of entrepreneurial leadership.[56] Some schools, including Chalmers University of Technology, have initiated courses that prepare students for entrepreneurial leadership by having them spend part of their time working directly with large companies to introduce an entrepreneurial approach.[57] For existing executives of large firms, there are also organizations that offer various programs in learning to lead for innovation, e.g., Plug and Play.[58]

7.10 Concluding Comments

At our Silicon Valley case companies and other entrepreneurial firms, the assumption is that creative individuals can excel in developing innovations and make them succeed in practice, *if* they are given the right conditions to develop and test their ideas. This assumption puts high demands on leaders at all levels to provide both the required guidance and enough freedom and space for people to use their creativity. Leaders need to master a form of soft guidance through visions, culture and their own behavior, combining this with firm goals and clear expectations that can be tracked on the basis of hard data.

While there are areas in which leaders need to make decisions, the ambition is to speed up innovation processes by directly involving creative employees in new forms of decision-making. An important role of leaders is to support individuals and teams, and to provide the right conditions for innovation and entrepreneurship. The increasing demands on leaders make the recruitment and further development of leaders absolutely essential.

A major challenge is that leaders need to be able to simultaneously handle both the present (exploitation) and the future (exploration). An additional complexity is that they need to work in an open environment where innovation increasingly takes

---

[53] Paudel (2019).
[54] Fahlenbrach (2009).
[55] E.g., Roomi and Harrison (2011).
[56] Lackéus (2023).
[57] See for example Chalmers (2023).
[58] Plug and Play (n.d.).

place in interaction with others. These organizational issues of ambidexterity and open innovation will be discussed in the next chapter.

References

Abebe, M. A., Li, P., Acharya, K., & Daspit, J. J. (2020). The founder chief executive officer: A review of current insights and directions for future research. *Corporate Governance: An International Review, 28*(6), 406–436.

Akbari, M., Bagheri, A., Imani, S., & Asadnezhad, M. (2021). Does entrepreneurial leadership encourage innovation work behavior? The mediating role of creative self-efficacy and support for innovation. *European Journal of Innovation Management, 24*(1), 1–22.

Alänge, S. (1994). The new paradigm for industrial practices: Total quality management in 1994 (*CIM Working Papers*, WP 1994–01).

Amabile, T. M., & Kramer, S. J. (2011). The power of small wins. *Harvard Business Review, 89*(5), 1–12.

Amabile, T. M., & Kramer, S. J. (2012, December 19). To give your employees meaning, start with mission. *Harvard Business Review*. https://hbr.org/2012/12/to-give-your-employees-meaning. Accessed 31 July 2015.

Bagheri, A., & Harrison, C. (2020). Entrepreneurial leadership measurement: A multi-dimensional construct. *Journal of Small Business and Enterprise Development, 27*(4), 659–679.

Bagheri, A., Akbari, M., & Artang, A. (2022). How does entrepreneurial leadership affect innovation work behavior? The mediating role of individual and team creativity self-efficacy. *European Journal of Innovation Management, 25*(1), 1–18.

Barnard, C. I. (1938). *The functions of the executive*. Harvard University Press.

Chalmers University of Technology. (2023). *Entrepreneurship and business design*. MSc. University web page https://www.chalmers.se/en/education/find-masters-programme/entrepreneurship-and-business-design-msc/ Accessed 27 July 2023.

Clark, C. M., Harrison, C., & Gibb, S. (2019). Developing a conceptual framework of entrepreneurial leadership: A systematic literature review and thematic analysis. *International Review of Entrepreneurship, 17*(3), 347–384. https://www.senatehall.com/entrepreneurship?article=639

Collins, J., & Porras, J. I. (1994). *Built to last: Successful habits of visionary companies*. HarperCollins.

Facebook. (2015a). *Hackathon page on Facebook*. https://www.facebook.com/hackathon. Accessed 31 July 2015.

Facebook. (2015b). *Facebook Sao Paolo Hackathon page on Facebook*. https://www.facebook.com/events/828648753872660/. Accessed 31 July 2015.

Fahlenbrach, R. (2009). Founder-CEOs, investment decisions, and stock market performance. *Journal of Financial and Quantitative Analysis, 44*(2), 439–466.

Gallo, C. (2015, May 4). *Tesla's Elon Musk lights up social media with a TED style keynote*. Forbes.com. http://www.forbes.com/sites/carminegallo/2015/05/04/teslas-elon-musk-lights-up-social-media-with-a-ted-style-keynote/. Accessed 29 July 2015.

Grove, A. S. (1996). *Only the paranoid survive: How to exploit the crisis point that challenge every company and career*. Currency Doubleday.

Harrison, C., Paul, S., & Burnard, K. (2016). Entrepreneurial leadership: A systematic literature review. *International Review of Entrepreneurship, 14*(2), 235–264. http://www.senatehall.com/entrepreneurship?article=544

Hoffman, R., Casnocha, B., & Yeh, C. (2014). *The Alliance: Managing talent in the networked age*. Harvard Business Review Press.

Hussain, G., Samreen, F., Riaz, A., Ismail, W. K. W., & Sultan, M. (2023). A cross-level relationship between entrepreneurial leadership and followers' entrepreneurial intentions through entrepreneurial self-efficacy and identification with the leader under moderating role of cultural values. *Current Psychology*. https://doi.org/10.1007/s12144-023-04935-0

Iqbal, A., Nazir, T., & Ahmad, M. S. (2022). Entrepreneurial leadership and employee innovative behavior: An examination through multiple theoretical lenses. *European Journal of Innovation Management, 25*(1), 173–190.

Isaacson, W. (2011). *Steve Jobs*. Simon & Schuster.

Lackéus, M. (2023). Work-learn balance—A new concept that could help bridge the divide between education and working life? *Industry and Higher Education, 0*(0), 1–14.

Li, C., Makhdoom, H. U. R., & Asim, S. (2020). Impact of entrepreneurial leadership on innovative work behavior: Examining mediation and moderation mechanisms. *Psychology Research and Behavior Management, 13*, 105–118.

Musk, E. (2015, May 1). *Tesla powerwall keynote*. Posted on YouTube. https://www.youtube.com/watch?v¼yKORsrlN-2k. Accessed 29 July 2015.

Page, L., & Brin, S. (2004). *An 'owner's manual' for Google's shareholders*. Posted in Google/Investor Relations. https://investor.google.com/corporate/2004/ipo-founders-letter.html. Accessed 31 July 2015.

Paudel, S. (2019). Entrepreneurial leadership and business performance: Effect of organizational innovation and environmental dynamism. *South Asian Journal of Business Studies, 8*(3), 348–369.

Plug and Play. (n.d.). *About Plug and Play: We are building the world's leading innovation platform*. Organization website. https://www.plugandplaytechcenter.com/about/. Accessed 27 July 2023.

Renko, M., El Tarabishy, A., Carsrud, A. L., & Brännback, M. (2015). Understanding and measuring entrepreneurial leadership style. *Journal of Small Business Management, 53*(1), 54–74.

Roomi, M. A., & Harrison, P. (2011). Entrepreneurial leadership: What is it and how should it be taught? *International Review of Entrepreneurship, 9*(3), 1–48.

Schmidt, E., & Rosenberg, J. (2014). *How Google works*. Grand Central Publishing.

Shiba, S., Graham, A., & Walden, D. (1993). *A new American TQM: Four practical revolutions in management*. Productivity Press/The Center for Quality Management.

Shiferaw, R. M., Birbirsa, Z. A., & Werke, S. Z. (2023). Entrepreneurial leadership, learning organization and organizational culture relationship: A systematic literature review. *Journal of Innovation and Entrepreneurship, 12*(38), 1–20.

Steiber, A. (2014). *The Google model: Managing continuous innovation in a rapidly changing world*. Springer.

Steiber, A., & Alänge, S. (2013a). A corporate system for continuous innovation: The case of Google Inc. *European Journal of Innovation Management, 16*(2), 243–264.

Steiber, A., & Alänge, S. (2013b). The formation and growth of Google Inc.: A firm-level Triple Helix perspective. *Social Science Information, 52*(4), 575–604.

Weiner, J. (2014, August 24). *The three qualities of people I most enjoy working with*. Posted on LinkedIn. https://www.linkedin.com/pulse/20140824235337-22330283-the-three-qualities-of-people-i-most-enjoy-working-with

8. The Entrepreneurial Organization Is Dynamic and Ambidextrous

> *Developments in the global economy have placed a premium on the ability of companies to become entrepreneurial and agile at home and abroad, requiring in turn that management formulate and follow good strategies and organize to allow and promote flexibility, learning, and, of course, innovation. This is the price of survival and growth in much of today's global economy. However, economic theory, if not management theory, is decades behind in recognizing these new realities.*
>
> David Teece (2014), p. 348

The past few chapters have delved deeply into the human aspects of the new management model: We've looked at the "special breed of people" it requires, the importance and desired attributes of the culture that is created, and the qualities that leaders must exhibit. Now we shift the focus to key organizational and strategic issues. In order to remain entrepreneurial beyond the startup stage, an organization has to be designed and managed for that purpose. As we've seen earlier, it must have dynamic capabilities—the ability to sense and seize new opportunities while transforming itself accordingly—and it must be ambidextrous, able to exploit current business and explore new possibilities at the same time.

Since these vital qualities are related we'll address them together, and the chapter does this from several angles. We are going to look at steps taken in both our Silicon Valley case companies and companies elsewhere, and we will combine the insights of leading management researchers with observations and interviews of people on the front lines, within the companies.

The first section here presents a brief discussion of dynamic capabilities; then come descriptions of various approaches to ambidexterity and to open innovation, which in concert are two important organizational explanations of our case companies' dynamic capabilities. These are treated in much more detail, as they lead us directly into examining how sizable, existing companies are organized and managed to pursue *ongoing innovation*.

8.1 Dynamic Capabilities

The Silicon Valley companies in our study were chosen because of their explicit ambition to remain dynamic and keep on innovating. As Google cofounder Larry Page put it:

> I don't think we're going to run out of important things to do, compared with the resources that we have. There are many, many problems in the world that need solving.[1]

The case companies were all relatively young when the first edition was written in 2015, and while the companies were in different stages of growth, they all aimed to preserve some of the startup characteristics that made them innovative. Google at that time was a 17-year-old firm and the others—LinkedIn, Tesla, Facebook, Twitter and Apigee—were between 9 and 13 years old. Yet within those fairly short time frames they had grown dramatically. Google at the start of year had more than 50,000 employees and was still expanding; the rest except for Apigee had staffs ranging from several thousand to over 10,000 employees and were likewise not finished growing. Privately-held Apigee—a highly focused specialty firm serving businesses, not mass consumer markets—had only about 400 employees but was penetrating global markets.[2]

What the case companies had done was impressive, given that organizations typically lose their innovativeness over time, as new procedures and rules aimed at strengthening key business processes seem to stifle innovation. Dorothy Leonard-Barton (1992) has observed that after some time, due to changes in the environment—e.g., new technology, new customer groups, new suppliers and business models—a firm's core capabilities become core rigidities. This adds an important temporal dimension, which emphasizes the need to continually improve and innovate.

---

[1] Lashinsky (2012). http://fortune.com/2012/01/19/larry-page-google-should-be-like-a-family/ (accessed 6 July 2015).

[2] Employment figures (as of 31 December 2014) are from the annual reports 2015 for Facebook, Google, LinkedIn, Tesla, and Twitter—plus through www.bloomberg.com for Apigee (accessed 1 August 2015). The companies had been growing rapidly, so the numbers will not be accurate when you read this—but they will provide a picture of their relative size and founding year:

No. of empl. 31 Dec 2014	Start year	No. of empl. 31 Dec 2014	Start year		
Apigee	409	2004	Facebook	9199	2004
Twitter	3638	2006	Tesla	10,161	2003
LinkedIn	6897	2002	Google	53,600	1998

8.1 Dynamic Capabilities

As we saw in Chap. 2, Teece and Pisano (1994) refer to the source of sustained competitive advantage as dynamic capabilities, where the term "dynamic" refers to the shifting character of the environment. The term "capabilities" emphasizes the key role of strategic management in adapting, integrating, and re-configuring internal and external organizational skills, resources and functional competencies toward the changing environment. Thus, Teece et al. (1997) defined dynamic capabilities as "the firm's ability to integrate, build, and reconfigure internal and external competences to address rapidly changing environments." For applied purposes Teece (2014) disaggregated dynamic capabilities into: (1) identification, development, co-development, and assessment of technological opportunities in relationship to customer needs (sensing); (2) mobilization of resources to address needs and opportunities, and to capture value from doing so (seizing); and (3) continued renewal (transforming).

It is in this context that there is a need for entrepreneurs, which Schumpeter (1942) expressed as:

> The function of entrepreneurs is to reform or revolutionize the pattern of production by exploiting an invention or, more generally, an untried technological possibility for producing a new commodity or producing an old one in a new way, by opening up a new source of supply of materials or a new outlet for products, by reorganizing an industry and so on.[3]

The concept of dynamic capabilities is about being able to thrive when the context is changing and new opportunities need to be identified and acted upon. However, in order to survive and develop for the future, a company also needs to manage the present simultaneously. The ability to focus on both time perspectives at the same time has been called ambidexterity.

8.1.1 Ambidexterity in Theory

Companies constantly face the challenge of being excellent in satisfying today's customers while working on products and services for tomorrow—ones which could even be a direct threat to today's. March (1991) expressed this as being able to pursue both exploitation (of current business) and exploration (for the future).[4] Tushman and O'Reilly (1997) argued that managers need to build ambidextrous organizations, which they described as

---

[3] Schumpeter (1942), p. 132.
[4] The question of how to pursue both exploitation and exploration had, however, been on the agendas of both researchers (Ala¨nge, 1987) and practitioners even before March (1991) stated his well-quoted dichotomy. Long before, Schumpeter had dwelled upon the issue of statics and dynamics, referring to the difference between continuous adjustments in small steps and the carrying out of new combinations, which he called innovation (Schumpeter, 1912, 1934).

organizations that celebrate stability and incremental change as well as experimentation and discontinuous change simultaneously.[5]

In the age of the internet and cheap information processing, rates of change have accelerated and in many industries the time has been reduced for exploitation of existing products and services. This forces companies to increase their focus on exploration and development of both new offerings and new business models. IT and the internet have also opened up new models of collaboration with entities and individuals outside the firm. This has led to increased testing of new collaborative approaches to innovation, contributing to a greater variation in the new ideas that are being generated.

In accordance with an article by Benner and Tushman (2015), we see two major challenges for the entrepreneurial firm. The first is to deal with the "traditional" view of ambidexterity, of being able to juggle between exploitation and exploration, and the second is to address the issue of where innovation should be located—inside or outside of company borders.

> … because of fundamental changes in innovation, i.e. the dramatic reduction of communication and information processing costs and the increasing modularization of products and services triggered by digitalization and internet, the fundamental mechanisms and locus of innovation have shifted over the past decade. The intrusion of community or peer innovation shifts the locus of exploratory and exploitative innovation from the firm … to the community (and associated open logic).[6]

In line with Teece (2014), Benner and Tushman made a strong argument for the need to critically scrutinize established research knowledge of innovation, and they claim a need for empirical studies as there have been major changes in technology and organizing which means that the "nature of innovation has shifted":

> This shift has profound implications for research and theory on innovation and organizations. Many of our core organizing assumptions and associated research and theory may be outdated. If the nature of innovation has shifted, then our research and theory on innovation must shift back to more inductive, or problem centered work.[7]

8.1.2 The Challenge of Ambidexterity

The question of how to make large incumbent firms more innovative has been on the agenda for many years, among practitioners and academics alike, but it is still a question open to both inquiry and practical experimentation. Below we will describe how our Silicon Valley case companies had dealt with the issue of simultaneously pursuing exploration and exploitation, taking into account both internal and external

---

[5] Tushman and O'Reilly (1997), p. 14.
[6] Benner and Tushman (2015), pp. 11–12.
[7] Benner and Tushman (2015), p. 12.

organizing. We will also briefly discuss the approaches observed in these companies with reference to some of the suggestions brought forward in literature on how to deal with ambidexterity.

There were various ways that our Silicon Valley case companies had organized to cope with the ambidexterity challenge. First, these companies were innovating inside their present operations and had developed work practices built on bottom-up approaches, in order to create variation. A second, classical way of being ambidextrous was to create a separate unit responsible for innovations beyond the present core. A third and further step was to introduce various forms of open innovation, involving contributions from external parties that included communities of users and makers. For all these ways of organizing for ambidexterity, the behavior of top executives was important, as the time they spent on an issue reflected their focus—which could be either on organizing to deliver the present products/services efficiently, or on ensuring continual innovation.

We will start with a discussion of how our case companies innovated *inside* their present operations.

8.2 Innovation by Many, Inside Present Operations

What was special among the Silicon Valley case companies was that they had designed their organizations to be ambidextrous in regular operations. They had done so in response to the speed of their industries, which created a demand for very frequent innovation cycles. The foundation for this way of working was laid by the steps described in earlier chapters: hiring creative, entrepreneurial people; building a culture that values innovation, and having leaders who support it. On top of this foundation came the strategic and organizational steps used by the companies to stimulate, direct, and coordinate internal innovation.

8.2.1 Top Executive Focus

A starting point is that top executives, in their own behavior, show the importance of ambidexterity. The specific way this was done differed among the companies studied. At Tesla, CEO Elon Musk put a lot of his time into developing the firm. At Facebook, former Google VP Sheryl Sandberg ran the ongoing operations as COO while products and technology were the domain of founder CEO Mark Zuckerberg, who constantly supported innovation by being present and involved in decision-making related to *new* products and services. Through this division of areas of responsibility, Facebook created a base for both exploration and exploitation wherein people on each side had the ambition of excelling in what they did.[8] According to the authors' own research, Google's founders chose in a similar way to put a focus on innovation by assuming technology- and product-oriented roles,

---

[8] Sheryl Sandberg held the position of COO until August 2022 when she resigned and moved on.

maintaining the freedom to delve into new areas without getting overwhelmed by all the important issues that belong to daily operations. This freedom was reinforced by the founders not using a calendar on which meetings with them could be booked in advance. (The exceptions were their weekly leadership meetings with then-CEO Eric Schmidt and the Friday discussions with all Google employees).

This focus on products and technology required the founders and top executives to have excellent technical knowledge and business understanding, which was the case among the companies researched. As noted in Chap. 6, the founders and CEOs typically had technical backgrounds in computer science, with considerable personal experience in coding. The ability of top leaders to simultaneously engage in both incremental and radical innovation, focusing not only on exploitation but also on exploration, has been described as a capacity to "juggle" different organizational architectures and cultures, thereby building and managing ambidextrous companies.[9]

8.2.2 The 'Semi-Structured' State

Another characteristic of the case companies was that they described themselves as semi-structured. They were wary of becoming too process-oriented and too rigid. However, looking into different areas of the companies, there were areas where process management was of more importance, e.g., distribution and sales. A source at one company also commented that "We are semi-structured but more and more standardized when some best practices turn into structure".

This is in line with Brown and Eisenhardt's (1997, 1998) finding that successful and continuous multi-product innovation combines limited structure ("semi-structures"), in terms of clear managerial responsibilities and project priorities, with extensive communication to manage current projects and allow for freedom and improvisation in the actual development process. This semi-structured state is a "dissipative equilibrium" that requires constant managerial attention to avoid slipping into either pure chaos or pure structure, i.e., to balance at the "edge of chaos." This core concept indicates that self-organization occurs when there is some structure but not too much.

8.2.3 Small Teams

The organizational solution practiced was the use of small teams of creative individuals to generate and implement new ideas. The teams tended to be highly autonomous and self-driven, and to move fast. A 2011 *Forbes* article on innovation at Google quoted CEO Eric Schmidt as saying[10]:

> We don't have a two year plan. We have a next week and a next quarter plan. Most of our successful products were built by small teams reacting quickly.

---

[9] Tushman and O'Reilly (1997), p. 37.
[10] http://onforb.es/qHi7ON (accessed 26 July 2015).

8.2 Innovation by Many, Inside Present Operations

And one of our interviewees at another case company described this way of working as follows:

> In a command-and-control structure … you put the best people in manager positions and the system relies on these people. They command and control. The problem is that the system tolerates incompetence [as everyone else does not need to be as good]. The system also gets bottlenecks in the best people, e.g., for decision making. Further this system can't scale. What instead was learned from Amazon and startups is that you ONLY should have the best people. You use small teams, and they solve their own problems without a lot of checks conducted by managers. This model is the new model—small teams with autonomy.
>
> No titles are used and no organization chart. The small teams need to be leveraged by using open source, cloud services [IT solutions] and move fast. … They have the mantra "Autonomy-Accountability-Alignment." Autonomy: small teams that make decisions. Accountability: They are accountable for a set of business problems to solve, and Alignment: The small teams are loosely coupled so there is not a conflict and chaotic picture [presented] towards customers or overall strategy.

As can be seen, the interviewee believed that with small teams it is possible to *scale*, while this is harder in the traditional way of organizing. Also, the small-team model is a bottom-up approach to solving problems and has the potential to generate a broader variation of new ideas, through the involvement of many internal problem-solvers.

8.2.4 Transparency and Openness

The approach of having creative individuals work in autonomous small teams is dependent on the individuals being aware of their company's priorities. Thus, another characteristic that the companies shared was that they were extremely transparent. The previous chapter described how Google's founders shared what they perceived as challenges for the company and were open to questions from any employees. Moreover, all employees had access to basically the same written material as the Google board of directors.[11] LinkedIn was another very transparent company, sharing what was most essential with all employees. As at Google, this was not viewed as a problem. One interviewee said:

> At LinkedIn, we have a policy of "treating our employees like adults." We are as open as we can be at company meetings with details of the business, and on the occasions when something is private, our CEO simply asks people not to speak about it outside the company.

8.2.5 Heuristics or 'Simple Rules'

Important tools for building ambidexterity are heuristics or simple rules that emphasize the needs for doing regular work while also doing something beyond the regular, and that build both aspects into the social contract between the company and its

---

[11] Schmidt and Rosenberg (2014), pp. 175–176.

creative individuals. Google's 70-20-10 rule introduced by Eric Schmidt[12] was an example of this, stating that 70% of one's work should be focused on today's core activities, 20% on things that are new and emerging but related, and 10% in totally new areas that have a high risk of failure but could be of major benefit for future development. Such a rule helps assure that in times of budget cuts there will always be some resources and attention devoted to forward-looking ideas. According to our interviewees, LinkedIn used a similar 70-20-10 rule indicating that 70% of its people's work should be core, 20% strategic and 10% venture.[13] Google also used its time-allocation rule to further stimulate the bottom-up process of selecting new areas to explore, and generating ideas within those areas. Through the opportunity for others to join the initial idea provider, adding their 20% time, Google created an internal crowd decision-making process for early-stage innovation, wherein Googlers developed initial prototypes in small groups.

Garud et al. (2011) explored practices at 3M Corporation, a company that has been able to sustain innovation for over a century while serving as inspiration for many other companies, including Google. Since ideas that emerge by serendipity can easily be lost amidst daily routines, 3M created mechanisms to keep those ideas alive. One was the well-known "15 % exploration time" option that individuals at 3M could use to develop an idea. While simple rules of this kind may sound very straightforward, and are easily communicated to outsiders, in fact 3M's innovation practices were far more complex. They included fostering ongoing interactions and relations between employees, and reinforced the *culture* of innovation through "innovation narratives." Garud et al. (2011) proposed a perspective that considers the interplay of many aspects associated with innovation, in "interwoven complexity arrangements". They concluded their analysis by saying:

> In sum, the complexity arrangements at 3M activated multiple agentic orientations simultaneously. Agency was shaped by all of the practices in place at 3M—by the myriad products, artifacts and actors, by the relational processes that were spawned, by the temporal dynamics that were implicated in any innovation journey, and by the mindful applications of guidelines. Narratives of innovation helped endogenize these practices in such a way that innovation complexity was harnessed in a productive way. Thereby, creativity and serendipity became part and parcel of engaged and informed work, during which employees experimented … and in the process generated new insights.[14]

Sull and Eisenhardt (2015) provided further examples of how the use of simple rules can speed up decision-making when many empowered and creative individuals independently can contribute to their organizations' strategic goals. One interesting example is how Netflix was able to limit bureaucratic procedures by instead relying on simple rules and trust in their own employees' personal abilities and judgment:

---

[12] http://money.cnn.com/magazines/business2/business2_archive/2005/12/01/8364616/index.htm (accessed 27 July 2015).

[13] Companies such as Coca-Cola were also using 70-20-10 rules for innovation. Other companies used other variants of simple rules to focus on innovation, such as 3M's Thirty Percent Rule stipulating that 30% of each division's revenues must come from products introduced in the last 4 years.

[14] Garud et al. (2011), pp. 31–32.

Many companies rely on thick policy manuals to control people who might abuse their discretion. But these bad apples represent a tiny fraction of all employees. Netflix determined that 97 % of their employees were trustworthy. Nearly all of the company's time writing, monitoring, and enforcing detailed personnel policies was directed at the remaining 3 percent. Rather than continue to produce binders of detailed regulations, Netflix executives concentrated on not hiring people who would cause problems, and removing them quickly when hiring mistakes were made. This change allowed the company to replace thick manuals with simple rules. For example, the policies for expenses, travel, gifts and conducting personal business at work, were reduced to four rules: 1) Expense what you would not otherwise spend; 2) Travel as if it were your own money; 3) Disclose nontrivial gifts from vendors; and 4) Do personal stuff at work when it is inefficient not to.[15]

8.2.6 Intrinsic Incentives in Meaningful Work

As pointed out in Chap. 7, creative and entrepreneurial individuals are motivated by intrinsic incentives—e.g., by the very opportunity to create something new—and the strongest motivating factor is making progress in meaningful work.[16] Schumpeter pointed to this phenomenon decades ago when he wrote that the entrepreneur is motivated by "the joy of creating, of getting things done, or simply of exercising one's energy and ingenuity" and "seeks out difficulties, changes in order to change, delights in ventures."[17]

The case companies followed the "progress principle" described in Chap. 7 through management actions that could be viewed as catalysts—e.g. setting clear goals, allowing autonomy and providing sufficient resources and time—while they also utilized acts of interpersonal support (nourishing) such as respect and recognition, encouragement, emotional comfort, and opportunities for affiliation. Catalysts and nourishers can alter the meaningfulness of work and signal to people that their work and they, themselves, are important to the organization, thus simplifying the operation of the progress principle.[18] Although work in itself typically was both challenging and motivating in our Silicon Valley case companies, the existence of 20% time and the 70-20-10 principle provided additional mechanisms for creating a focus on, and progress in, work that people perceived as meaningful.

> The thing that really has stuck with me from when I was at Stanford is that when you're a grad student, you can work on whatever you want. And the projects that were really good got a lot of people really wanting to work on them. We've taken that learning to Google, and it's been really, really helpful. If you're changing the world, you're working on important things. You're excited to get up in the morning. That's the main thing. You want to be working on meaningful, impactful projects, and that's the thing there is really a shortage of in the world.[19] — Larry Page, Google

---

[15] Sull and Eisenhardt (2015), p. 227.
[16] Amabile and Kramer (2011).
[17] Schumpeter (1934), pp. 93–94.
[18] Amabile and Kramer (2011).
[19] Lashinsky (2012). http://fortune.com/2012/01/19/larry-page-google-should-be-like-a-family/ (Accessed 6 July 2015).

In the companies we studied, several interviewees commented on the importance of recognition by top leaders. However, the opportunity of pitching new ideas and being appreciated by peers was also emphasized by some of them. In the engineering culture of Silicon Valley it wins status if peers step in and contribute with their own time and effort to the continued development of one's idea.

8.2.7 Rapid Learning Processes

The demands for speed and innovation also create a need for rapid learning processes. This was a characteristic shared by all companies studied. And this was the way that they were able to turbocharge their organizations for continual innovation. Through its Fish and Dog Food programs, Google ran a number of tests on internal users before testing a new product externally.[20]

Eric Reis's concepts of validated learning and minimum viable product[21] were followed, wherein the basic idea is to get an early-stage product or service out to customers for feedback that enables learning for further development.

> Create a product, ship it, see how it does, design and implement improvements, and push it back out. *Ship and iterate.* The companies that are the fastest at this process will win.[22]

Ries himself (2011) learned the hard way, by making mistakes and finding out what worked while starting a new company in Silicon Valley. He also had the opportunity to learn from serial entrepreneur Steve Blank and took inspiration from Toyota and the lean manufacturing movement. The result was his book *The Lean Startup,* which presents five principles, with the first two arguing for the importance of entrepreneurship: (1) Entrepreneurs are everywhere, and (2) Entrepreneurship is management. The third and fourth principles have to do with the rapid learning processes used by successful startups: (3) Validated learning, and (4) Build-Measure-Learn. The fifth principle is (5) Innovation accounting, indicating the need of measuring progress, setting milestones, and prioritizing work. Referring to the principles of rapid learning, Ries commented that

> The logic of validated learning and the minimum viable product says that we should get a product into customers' hands as soon as possible and that extra work we do beyond what is required to learn from customers is waste. On the other hand, the Build-Measure-Learn feedback loop is a continuous process. We don't stop after one minimum viable product but use what we have learned to get to work immediately on the next iteration.[23]

The argument he brings forward is that large incumbent firms also need to embrace these principles in order to learn fast and innovate rapidly. This is in accordance

---

[20] Steiber (2014), p. 73.
[21] Ries (2011).
[22] Schmidt and Rosenberg (2014), p. 234.
[23] Ries (2011), p. 228.

with Brown and Eisenhardt's (1997, 1998) finding that successful multi-product innovation is based on continuous experimentation into the future. One of their core concepts—that of working at the *"edge of time"*—indicates that change requires thinking simultaneously about multiple time horizons: past, current, and future. The critical management issue is how to manage all time frames without being trapped in any one. The "edge of time" approach includes two building blocks: first, *regeneration,* which looks into how managers can utilize the past to gain advantages. The second is *experimentation,* which shows how managers can experiment with a wide variety of low-cost probes to gain insight and strategic flexibility. Here, options and learning are central components, and constant but thin management is seen as a virtue.

8.2.8 Big Data on User Behavior

A good way of obtaining user information is through data mining, and all of our case companies were or could become database giants on the internet. It was possible for them to analyze user data which, in a very short time, could provide excellent information for decision-making about concepts tested in real-world experiments. At Google, such user data could be available within 24–48 h.[24]

In a world where multitudes of new products and services are launched, every one cannot be a market success. Thus there is also a need to close down those that turn out less successfully. This too can be facilitated by user/customer data, as was noted by Eric Schmidt and Jonathan Rosenberg in their book about Google:

> Ship and iterate doesn't always work. After launching, some products will get better and gather momentum while others will wither. The problem is, by the time a product has gone to the market there has been a significant amount of resources and emotion invested in it, which can get in the way of good decisions. Forgetting sunk costs is a tough lesson to heed, so in a ship-and-iterate model, leadership's job must be to feed the winners and starve the losers, regardless of prior investment. To decide which efforts are winners and which are losers, use data. This has always been the case, but the difference is how quickly data is available and how much of it there is.[25]

Next, we will discuss the second alternative that companies generally have, innovation by creating separate units.

8.3 Innovation by Separate Innovation Units

The classical way to deal with ambidexterity has been to create an innovation unit that can be separated from the demands of ongoing operations in core areas. To some extent this was also practiced among our case companies—especially when innovative new startups had been acquired.

---

[24] Steiber and Alänge (2013a).
[25] Schmidt and Rosenberg (2014), p. 235.

8.3.1 Acquisitions

An acquired product or technology can be totally integrated if it is close to the acquiring firm's core business. Or, it can be kept within a separate unit or company if it is something new outside the core that needs its own development space. As we wrote in a 2013 article:

> A considerable number of new products introduced by Google come from smaller companies acquired by Google, e.g. Android and YouTube. The reason for acquiring a company could be the innovation itself, or the fact that Google sees an advantage in further developing the idea or product into something with a higher potential that might be linked to existing Google products. The acquisition can also be based on the fact that the entrepreneurs/engineers behind the company have proved they have the unique competence that Google needs and, hence, the company formation could be viewed as another filtering process to identify and access competence. Finally, Google also acts directly as a venture capitalist through Google Ventures and is also actively involved in spin-offs of internally generated ideas.[26]

Chesbrough (2002) commented that this type of investment can be difficult for large firms.

> Large companies have long sensed the potential value of investing in external startups. More often than not, though, they just can't seem to get it right.[27]

However, the acquisition of smaller firms is an important source of innovation, regardless of whether the company is acquired in order to develop a new business area, or to be linked to an existing business, or is simply being acquired because of its competencies.[28] Since it is not always easy to profit from purchasing early start-ups, even if their potential is high, some large companies only consider acquiring small firms with proven markets—a trend very similar to the movement of venture capital away from early-stage investment.

8.3.2 Corporate Ventures

Some of our case companies had corporate venture units investing in startups that might be important for the company in the future and/or provide a good return on investment. Google Ventures had, for example, backed more than 300 companies according to its website in 2015.[29] The unit's strategy had been to invest in ambitious companies in every field, but with a special focus on machine learning and life science.

---

[26] Steiber and Alänge (2013b), p. 589.
[27] Chesbrough (2002), p. 90.
[28] Steiber and Alänge (2013b).
[29] www.gv.com (accessed 3 August 2015).

8.3 Innovation by Separate Innovation Units

In order to manage innovation, large corporations have also long developed various units that serve a *boundary-spanning role*.[30] These boundary-spanning units act both as filters and facilitators.[31] Examples include corporate venture units, new businesses that are viewed either as potential spin-offs/spin-outs or as entities which, if successful on their own, can be brought back to a business unit within the large firm. However, Hill and Birkinshaw (2014) commented that:

> Corporate venture … suffer[s] from a high failure rate…CV units endure by developing an ambidextrous orientation themselves—they build new capabilities for the parent firm while simultaneously leveraging its existing strengths. …[and by] nurturing a supportive relational context…with three different sets of actors—parent firm executives, business unit managers, and …the venture capital community.
>
> Although some CV units may engage with additional partners (such as entrepreneurial young firms, university scientists, suppliers, or consumers) …these three sets of actors represent the principal network of resource holders…[32]

The argument that Hill and Birkinshaw bring forward is that in order to serve as a boundary-spanning unit for the large firm, the corporate venture unit itself must be ambidextrous:

> Such boundary-spanning units … typically have ostensibly exploratory charters and provide linkages to various external actors. And …they have to integrate their activities with those of technical core units. … [This] requires a level of ambidexterity on the part of the boundary-spanning unit itself. … [I]n fostering ambidexterity senior managers have to learn to overcome cognitive contradictions and to build appropriate coordination mechanisms to generate an appropriate mix of exploration and exploitation. In addition, they need to attend to the processes through which resources are acquired, combined, and transformed to generate ambidextrous outcomes.[33]

An example of a boundary-spanning unit that aimed to build ambidextrous competencies was [and still is] General Electric Appliances' offspring FirstBuild. This is an independent innovation unit designed like a startup, with access to communities for crowdsourcing, and to emerging markets to test new products on a limited scale. In addition, it has access to resources from the "mother ship" GEA—which positions FirstBuild as a startup with access to large company resources for scaling, situated within regular GEA business units.[34]

8.3.3 Small Firm-Large Firm Ventures

The strength of small high-tech firms is in their ability to rapidly develop new ideas and test them on customers, while their weakness is related to their limited ability

---

[30] Thompson (1967).
[31] Aldrich and Herker (1977).
[32] Hill and Birkinshaw (2014), p. 1905.
[33] Ibid, p. 1921.
[34] Alänge and Steiber (2015).

to scale up operations for a high-volume market. Large firms typically show the opposite areas of strength and weakness. That has led some authors to suggest different ways of cooperation between creative startups and well-established large firms.[35] Rothwell and Dodgson (1991) commented:

> Not only do large and small firms separately play an important role in technological innovation, but they often play interactive and complementary roles.[36]

As early as 1982, Rothwell and Zegveld[37] observed that:

> The most popular form of venture management … is joint small firm-large firm ventures. Here the small firm generally supplies the dynamism, vigour, commitment and technology [i.e. supplies the entrepreneurial function] while the large firm supplies access to capital and to a comprehensive network of distributors, sales and after-sales servicing.

However, the authors also noted that

> Because of the very different behavioural characteristics of large and small firms, such a relationship can be fraught with problems.

Tesla, in its ambitious endeavor to move the transportation industries toward more sustainable solutions,[38] had—as a relatively small startup at the time—teamed with considerably larger players in both the automobile industry (Mercedes and Toyota) and in battery technology (Panasonic). These large firms had also invested in Tesla, and both Mercedes and Toyota were utilizing technology developed by Tesla for their new electric cars. The cooperation with Panasonic was even more substantial, including investments in a new battery factory, which would allow the partners to substantially decrease the manufacturing costs per unit by virtue of very high-volume production in their new Gigafactory.[39]

8.3.4 Spin-Ins and Incubation

There are companies that have built strategies seeking to combine the market strength of large corporations with the nimbleness and creativity of small firms, but they are not numerous. One company that has served as a role model is Cisco Systems:

> Clearly, the decision to pursue spin-ins and incubation simultaneously helped Cisco establish a leadership position in disruptive innovation … But what is the best approach? The answer depends on what your organization is trying to accomplish. Cisco … has gained from each. But it chooses between them based on specific conditions. When a new idea has

---

[35] Mansfield (1968) and Pavitt (1984).
[36] Rothwell and Dodgson (1991), p. 125.
[37] Rothwell and Zegveld (1982), p. 111.
[38] Lee and Jay (2015).
[39] http://www.teslamotors.com/blog/panasonic-and-tesla-sign-agreement-gigafactory (Accessed 27 July 2015).

significant synergy with existing products or go-to-market strategies, Cisco will incubate the idea internally. Alternatively, the company often looks outside its walls when it wants to pursue something that is very different or unfamiliar.[40]

Google, being the largest of our case companies, had in 2011 developed a scaleable platform for incubation called Google for Entrepreneurs. A small global team supported entrepreneurs in 125 countries over the internet, through partners and through current or planned campuses in London, Madrid, Tel Aviv, Sao Paolo and Seoul. The purpose was to support the development of new companies by partnering "with startup communities and building campuses, where entrepreneurs can learn, connect, and create companies that will change the world." Simultaneously, Google had the opportunity to disseminate platforms and products, such as Google Apps, the Google Cloud Platform, and Google Developer Tools.[41]

Let's now turn to the third and final way of creating an ambidextrous organization, through various approaches to open innovation.

8.4 Open Innovation Approaches

Although our Silicon Valley case companies were technology-based startups grown large and were known to be organized for continual innovation, their internal resources were clearly not enough. Thus, we found a general awareness of open innovation among our interviewees, which was expressed in a remarkably similar way across the companies studied. All said, in essentially the same words: "There are more smart people outside than inside our organization." The companies' industries demand such a speed and intensity of innovation that input from external sources is seen as a necessity.

In addition to investing in acquisitions and corporate ventures, there are other ways to obtain external innovation input, which require less initial investment. The traditional way is to hire competent people from universities and from other firms, which still was extremely important for the companies studied. However, there are many other possibilities as well, including research cooperation and/or joint funding, supplier innovation, open platforms and crowdsourcing. The use of external open platforms also provided a foundation for strategies focused on cultivating ecosystems, wherein the firm could only control external resources to a limited extent. Thus, a major part of innovation activity took place in various forms of interactions with external actors, such as universities, suppliers, developer partners, customers and users.

---

[40] Sidhu (2010), pp. 31–32.
[41] https://www.googleforentrepreneurs.com/campuses/ (Accessed 3 August 2015).

8.4.1 University Interaction

The Silicon Valley companies had access to Stanford University and the University of California, Berkeley in their vicinity, but research cooperation went beyond working with these nearby partners (which also were important as sources of graduates for hiring as employees). Collaborations—and recruiting efforts—did extend to leading research universities in other parts of the world. The previously cited *Forbes* article in 2011 quoted Google's then-CEO Eric Schmidt as follows:

> If people have been working at a company too long they're inculcated in a development process that is relatively predictable.... Real innovation is hard to do when you have a process culture with six sigma [i.e., extremely low-defect manufacturing]. Risk management is around the process, keeping it the same. That is one reason why Google hires so many grad students and professors—things like tenure aside, they're used to more turmoil in their ideas about how the world works.[42]

In addition to hiring from universities, the case companies developed various cooperation programs focused on research and innovation. Google had both a more traditional open-call research fund, where anyone could apply for research grants, and a program in which promising research/innovation areas were identified internally and accomplished researchers were then invited to be part of a joint project.[43]

8.4.2 Suppliers as Innovators

Close interaction with industrial suppliers is nothing new, but even here the rapid development cycles put new demands on traditional relationships. Tesla had assumed the role of technology supplier to incumbents such as Mercedes and Toyota, in order to fulfill its vision of renewing the industry towards sustainable transportation. As noted earlier, Tesla also had made its patents available for others to use. This could have led to the development of a shared technology platform within battery technology for electric cars and other applications. Suppliers to the case companies could also be part of innovation processes, such as in the case of Panasonic contributing battery technology to Tesla (although this cooperation also resulted in a joint production venture, the Gigafactory, mentioned above).

8.4.3 Crowdsourcing from Users and Communities

The case companies tested various ways of collecting data or ideas directly from users and other external contributors. Facebook was regularly arranging short-duration hackathons to solve defined problems rapidly. A first prototype was

---

[42] Hardy (2011). http://onforb.es/qHi7ON (accessed 27 July 2015).
[43] Steiber and Alänge (2013b).

available in 24 h and was given a go-ahead for further development quickly. Other companies also arranged hackathons and other kind of tournaments or competitions in order to stimulate idea generation and problem solving. In these cases, there is a need for transparent rules of ownership of intellectual property.

Increasingly, companies are looking for ways of connecting to external idea providers and external users that can contribute to evaluating product/service concepts. Boudreau and Lakhani (2013) researched the crowdsourcing concept from various perspectives:

> Crowdsourcing generally takes one of four distinct forms—contest, collaborative community, complementor, or labor market—each best suited to a specific kind of challenge.[44]

A *contest* is a classical way of searching for solutions to complex or novel problems through large-scale and diverse independent experimentation. The problem must be generalized, and according to Boudreau and Lakhani the best uses are for "highly challenging technical, analytical, and scientific problems; design problems; creative or aesthetic projects." Through *collaborative communities*, many contributions can be aggregated into a value-creating whole. The challenge is that crowds lack shared culture and cohesiveness, which makes it harder to control and makes IP hard to protect. Boudreau and Lakhani therefore suggest that the best uses of this form are for "customer support communities; wikis; open collaboration projects for information and software products with complementary assets in the firm; [and] FAQs".

Complementors can be encouraged to come up with innovative solutions to users' problems with a firm's core product. There is a challenge in providing access to the functions and information in the core product while protecting firm assets. According to Boudreau and Lakhani the best uses are for "open operational, product or marketing data initiatives; content mashups; apps". Finally, the purpose of *labor markets* is to efficiently and flexibly match talent to discrete tasks. The challenge is identifying which problems to farm out and how to manage this, and the best uses are for well-established categories of work, human computation, and repeated tasks.

The Silicon Valley companies in our study used various approaches for idea generation. They were all strong on internal processes, although not always in a traditional way. Their approaches were not only based on what the R&D organization could accomplish, but also on what creative individuals could do, regardless of position in the company (see the previous section on internal processes). However, several of our interviewees from various case companies made identical comments along the lines of: "Although we know our internal strengths, we are aware that there is even more competence outside of our organizations, which we need to tap into to keep being in the innovative forefront." Thus, the companies utilized different forms of crowdsourcing to obtain an inflow of ideas with greater variation, and they also utilized crowds for idea selection. However, idea selection was frequently based on big data on user behavior, rather than on specific inquires to customers/users concerning what new things they might value.

---

[44] Boudreau and Lakhani (2013), p. 63.

8.4.4 External Development Platforms

A development platform is a way of contributing to innovation without directly managing the creative input. In line with Gawer and Cusumano (2014) we define external (industry) platforms as: *"products, services, or technologies that act as a foundation upon which external innovators, organized as an innovative business ecosystem, can develop their own complementary products, technologies, or services."* Apple's application platform for iPhones was relatively tightly controlled by Apple, while Google's Android platform represented an approach that was more open in character. Social networking sites, such as at our case companies Facebook, LinkedIn, and Twitter, are also external development platforms. Other companies have even built facilities with office space for developers who want to work on their platforms while having direct access to the platform owners' competence and resources (e.g. AT&T Foundry), while others have been created as virtual meeting places accessible from all over the world in combination with physical space in selected cities (e.g. Google and Microsoft).

> Google's products [e.g. platforms, APIs] by definition created numerous linkages within the industry helix, e.g. to industrial players viewed either as customers, suppliers or developer partners to Google. Google has also been involved in various open-source initiatives and contributed in various ways to the development of the Internet.[45]

These types of external platforms are dependent on network effects,[46] which means that as there are more users of the platform, the more attractive it is for other companies to join and develop their products on the platform, and the more applications that are available, the more attractive it becomes for users—and vice versa. Therefore, scaling (with rapid global growth) has been a major concern for all of the case companies, including Tesla with its battery-charging infrastructure.

8.4.5 Cultivating Ecosystems

Relying on external technology and innovations also puts new demands on large firms to develop the ability to manage and utilize resources that the company does not fully control. This, in turn, leads towards an understanding of the need to cultivate ecosystems[47] that can provide a massive contribution of innovative capability but also means sharing wealth with others, based on the assumption that the whole cake will grow considerably larger.

> Reduced information costs enable organizations to engage communities of developers, professionals, and users for core innovative activities, frequently through platforms, ecosystems, and incorporating user innovation.[48]

---

[45] Steiber and Alänge (2013b), p. 589.
[46] Gawer and Cusumano (2014).
[47] Steiber and Alänge (2013b).
[48] Altman et al. (2015), p. 353.

For example, in April 2015, Apigee announced that its partner ecosystem was expanding. The CEO explained the importance of developing an ecosystem as follows:

> Our mission is to make every business a digital business, and our growing ecosystem of partners is helping us. Businesses across industries are looking for modern, API-centric platforms to drive new digital channels and deliver new customer experiences. We look forward to continuing to work with our partners such as SAP, along with recognized systems integrators, to scale and accelerate our global reach.[49]

In a corresponding way, Facebook, Google, LinkedIn and Twitter are platform companies that could have more than one platform in parallel, such as Google's Android, YouTube and Adwords. When it comes to platforms, the importance of network effects has been understood at least since the telecommunication industry emerged in the late nineteenth century. Today, this has been expressed in terms of "scaling," which implies growing something very fast and globally.

> The ecosystem matters a lot. The most successful leaders in the Internet Century will be the ones who understand how to create and quickly grow platforms. A platform is, fundamentally, a set of products and services that bring together groups of users and providers to form multisided markets.[50]

8.5 Concluding Comments in 2016

All of the Silicon Valley case companies could be said to have dynamic capabilities, enabled by not only the entrepreneurial people and an innovative culture (as we discussed in Chaps. 5 and 6), but also by the organizational components discussed in this chapter: internal ambidextrous and learning organizations, separate innovation units, and open innovation and external platforms. A factor of major importance is a top leadership which itself has ambidextrous abilities, being able to keep a steady focus on innovation and the future without ignoring the importance of today's operations. The demand on top leadership is to enable and create the degree of structure and values needed for small teams and entrepreneurial individuals to excel in increasingly open-innovation environments.

As a basic idea is to utilize the creativity of many to the benefit of the organization, the work itself has to be meaningful and provide intrinsic motivation. Guiding direction is provided by a combination of vision/mission, values, and beliefs, which, based on experiences, have been transformed into simple rules. And of course, another important element is supportive leaders who know both how to stimulate individuals by insightful questions and to assist individuals to set personal goals that are regularly reviewed (as was discussed in Chap. 7). Absolutely essential is a focus on continual learning where new ideas can be rapidly tested in the real world, with users and customers, providing feedback based on firm data about actual user/customer behavior.

---

[49] http://apigee.com/about/press-releases?page¼1 (Accessed 1 August 2015).
[50] Schmidt and Rosenberg (2014), pp. 78–79.

Sometimes innovation is best developed in a separate unit apart from regular operations. The Silicon Valley companies, which excelled at involving everyone in developing new ideas inside present operations, still utilized various forms of separate units, such as acquisitions that sometimes were left as autonomous entities, new ventures with partners, and incubation of promising ideas.

All case companies agreed on the necessity of working in an open environment. This was uniformly expressed in words such as "even if we have excellent people inside our organization, there is still much more competence out there"—so all companies made serious efforts to network, crowdsource ideas and cooperate with external partners. In this sense open innovation was a natural and integrated way in which the case companies innovated with user input and together with external partners, including startups, suppliers and universities or research institutes. The understanding that companies develop together with other actors in ecosystems, sometimes based on common technological platforms, contributed to our case companies not only viewing themselves as being participants but also as active orchestrators and developers of their ecosystems.

8.6 Recent Developments

This section documents the growth of our case companies since the book's first edition in 2016 and notes some significant trends in the organization of firms.

8.6.1 Employment in Case Companies

Although a definitive cause-and-effect relationship cannot be proved, the benefits of having dynamic capabilities and ambidexterity may perhaps be reflected in the continued growth of the case companies. Out of the six companies, five kept growing dramatically after our first edition, while the smallest—Apigee—had a successful exit via acquisition. Growth is measured here by number of employees.

During 2015, as we were compiling the first edition, Google had about 61,000 employees. By the end of December 2016 the count grew to 72,053, and later, even though Google/Alphabet conducted significant layoffs from 2022 into early 2023, the total number in June 2023 was still 181,798. Tesla grew from 17,782 in December 2016 to 99,290 in 2023, i.e., about 5.5x as many. Facebook had 17,048 in December 2016 and grew to 86,482 in December 2022, but with subsequent layoffs the number was 65,964 in May 2023. LinkedIn reported 9601 employees as of June 2016 and grew to about 19,000 by April 2023. Twitter had 3583 employees in December 2016 and grew to over 7500 early in 2022, and then massive cuts began after Elon Musk led a purchase of the company in October 2022. Various reports placed the April 2023 headcount at about 1500. The sixth case company, Apigee, had 412 employees in August 2016, shortly before its acquisition by Google was announced in September of that year. Google completed the acquisition 2 months later and has absorbed Apigee into its cloud operations.

8.6.2 Evolving Organizational Trends

The organizational landscape has continued to undergo significant transformations driven by technological advancements, changing market dynamics, and the need for increased agility and innovation. Here we focus on the emergence of four concepts: the Agile Organization, Decentralized Autonomous Organization, Ecosystem Organization, and Exponential Organization. The concepts are described briefly below, along with their implications in shaping the future of organizations.

Agile Organizations embrace flexibility, adaptability, and collaboration as core principles. Derived from agile software development practices, these organizations emphasize iterative and incremental approaches to project management and decision-making. In a 2023 book, Linda Holbeche examines how agility enables organizations to respond effectively to changing market demands: Agile organizations foster cross-functional teams, quick feedback loops, and a customer-centric mindset, enabling them to deliver value rapidly and continuously improve their processes.[51] The agile movement has grown popular overall, and is supported by numerous consultancies and related organizations that offer official certification in the approach.[52]

The Decentralized Autonomous Organization (DAO) is an innovative concept that commonly leverages new technologies such as blockchain and smart contracts to enable decentralized decision-making and governance. Scholars Robbie Morrison et al., Wulf A. Kaal, and Kumar Saurabh et al. highlight the potential of this concept for enhancing open innovation processes and fostering collaboration. According to the authors, this form eliminates the need for centralized authorities, enabling stakeholders to participate in decision-making through e.g., voting mechanisms. By leveraging blockchain's transparency and immutability, the form also offers greater trust and accountability.[53]

Ecosystem Organizations recognize the interdependencies and collaborations among various entities, including firms, customers, suppliers, and even competitors. In a 2023 paper, Nicolai J. Foss et al. explored the concept and implications of ecosystem organizations from a dynamic capability perspective. (David Teece was a co-author of this paper.) Ecosystem organizations harness the power of networks and partnerships to create and capture value collectively. By fostering collaboration, sharing resources, and leveraging complementary capabilities, the organizations can achieve competitive advantages in dynamic market environments.[54]

Exponential Organizations are characterized by their ability to achieve rapid and scalable growth by leveraging emerging technologies, platforms, and business models. The 2014 book *Exponential Organizations: Why New Organizations Are Ten Times Better, Faster, and Cheaper than Yours*, by Salim Ismail et al., delved into the

---

[51] Holbeche (2023).
[52] See for example Scrum Alliance (2023).
[53] Morrison et al. (2020), Kaal (2021), and Saurabh et al. (2023).
[54] Foss et al. (2023).

strategies and attributes of such organizations. Exponential organizations employ technologies such as artificial intelligence, cloud computing, and the Internet of Things to disrupt traditional markets. They focus on scaling rapidly by leveraging external resources, co-creating value with their communities, and leveraging platforms to achieve exponential impact.[55] This approach has gained traction internationally. As of 2023, Ismail had co-founded and was chairing a web-based "OpenExO" community for help with applying the methods,[56] and also released an updated edition of the 2014 book.[57]

8.6.3 Conclusions

We are witnessing transformative trends in the organization of firms to adapt to the changing business landscape. The trends fit well with the characteristics of the Silicon Valley companies described in this chapter. The conclusion is therefore that these characteristics are still highly valid for organizations in 2023. By embracing these organizational characteristics, commonly enabled by digital technology, firms can enhance their agility, innovation, and capacity to create sustainable value in the digital and sustainable age. The evolution from tall organizations to decentralized, agile, and collaborative organizations therefore seem inevitable in a fast-changing world.

References

Alänge, S. (1987). *Acquisition of capabilities through international technology transfer*. PhD dissertation, Chalmers University of Technology, Gothenburg.

Alänge, S., & Steiber, A. (2015). *The best of both worlds: Combining the strengths of small start-ups with a large corporation's advantages*. Draft.

Aldrich, H., & Herker, D. (1977). Boundary spanning roles and organization structure. *Academy of Management Review, 2*(2), 217–230.

Altman, J. E., Nagle, F., & Tushman, M. L. (2015). Innovating without information constraints: Organizations, communities, and innovation when information costs approach zero. In C. E. Shalley, M. A. Hitt, & J. Zhou (Eds.), *The Oxford handbook of creativity, innovation, and entrepreneurship* (pp. 353–378). Oxford University Press.

Amabile, T., & Kramer, S. J. (2011). The power of small wins. *Harvard Business Review, 89*(5), 70–80.

Benner, M. J., & Tushman, M. L. (2015). Reflections on the 2013 decade award: 'Exploitation, exploration, and process management: The productivity dilemma revisited' ten years later. *Academy of Management Review, amr-2015*, 1–36.

Boudreau, K. J., & Lakhani, K. R. (2013). Using the crowd as an innovation partner. *Harvard Business Review, 91*(4), 60–69.

---

[55] Ismail et al. (2014).

[56] OpenExO (2023).

[57] Ismail et al. (2023).

References

Brown, S. L., & Eisenhardt, K. M. (1997). The art of continuous change: Linking complexity theory and time-paced evolution in relentlessly shifting organizations. *Administrative Science Quarterly, 42*(1), 1–34.

Brown, S. L., & Eisenhardt, K. M. (1998). *Competing on the edge: Strategy as structured chaos.* Harvard Business School Press.

Chesbrough, H. (2002). Making sense of corporate venture capital. *Harvard Business Review, 80*(3), 90–99.

Foss, N. J., Schmidt, J., & Teece, D. J. (2023). Ecosystem leadership as a dynamic capability. *Long Range Planning, 56*(1), 102270. https://doi.org/10.1016/j.lrp.2022.102270

Garud, R., Gehman, J., & Kumaraswamy, A. (2011). Complexity arrangements for sustained innovation: Lessons from 3M corporation. *Organization Studies, 32*(6), 737–767.

Gawer, A., & Cusumano, M. A. (2014). Industry platforms and ecosystem innovation. *The Journal of Product Innovation Management, 31*(3), 417–433.

Hardy, Q. (2011, July 16). *Google's innovation—And everyone's?* Forbes.com. http://onforb.es/qHi7ON. Accessed 27 July 2015.

Hill, S. A., & Birkinshaw, J. (2014). Ambidexterity and survival in corporate venture units. *Journal of Management, 40*(7), 1899–1931.

Holbeche, L. (2023). *The agile organization: How to build an engaged, innovative and resilient business.* Kogan Page.

Ismail, S., Malone, M. S., & Van Geest, Y. (2014). *Exponential organizations: Why new organizations are ten times better, faster, and cheaper than yours.* Diversion Books.

Ismail, S., Diamandis, P. H., Malone, M. S., & Kurzweil, K. (2023). *Exponential organizations 2.0: The new playbook for 10x growth and impact.* Ethos Collective.

Kaal, W. A. (2021). *A decentralized autonomous organization (DAO) of DAOs.* Available at SSRN 3799320. https://papers.ssrn.com/sol3/papers.cfm?abstract_id=3799320

Lashinsky, A. (2012, January 19). *Larry Page: Google should be like a family.* Fortune. http://fortune.com/2012/01/19/larry-page-google-should-be-like-a-family/. Accessed 6 Aug 2015.

Lee, M., & Jay, J. (2015). Strategic responses to hybrid social ventures. *California Management Review, 57*(3), 126–147.

Leonard-Barton, D. (1992). Core capabilities and core rigidities: A paradox in managing new product development. *Strategic Management Journal, 13*, 111–125.

Mansfield, E. (1968). *The economics of technological change.* W.W. Norton & Co.

March, J. G. (1991). Exploration and exploitation in organizational learning. *Organization Science, 2*, 71–87.

Morrison, R., Mazey, N. C., & Wingreen, S. C. (2020). The DAO controversy: The case for a new species of corporate governance? *Policy and Practice Reviews, 3*. https://doi.org/10.3389/fbloc.2020.00025

OpenExO. (2023). *Our team: Meet the faces behind OpenExO Inc.* Organization website: https://web.openexo.com/team/

Pavitt, K. (1984). Sectoral patterns of technical change: Towards a taxonomy and a theory. *Research Policy, 13*, 343–373.

Ries, E. (2011). *The lean startup: How constant innovation creates radically successful businesses.* Portfolio Penguin.

Rothwell, R., & Dodgson, M. (1991). External linkages and innovation in small and medium-sized enterprises. *R&D Management, 21*(2), 125–138.

Rothwell, R., & Zegveld, W. (1982). *Innovation and the small and medium sized firm.* Frances Pinter.

Saurabh, K., Rani, N., & Upadhyay, P. (2023). Towards blockchain led decentralized autonomous organization (DAO) business model innovations. *Benchmarking: An International Journal, 30*(2), 475–502. https://doi.org/10.1108/BIJ-10-2021-0606

Schmidt, E., & Rosenberg, J. (2014). *How Google works.* Grand Central Publishing.

Schumpeter, J. A. (1912). *Theorie der wirtschaftlichen Entwicklung.* Duncker & Humblot.

Schumpeter, J. A. (1934). *The theory of economic development: An inquiry into profits, capital, credit, interest, and the business cycle.* Harvard University Press.

Schumpeter, J. A. (1942). *Capitalism, socialism and democracy*. George Allen & Unwin (1976 edition).

Scrum Alliance. (2023). *You want certification. You need community. We give you both.* Organization website: https://www.scrumalliance.org/

Sidhu, I. (2010). *Doing both: How Cisco captures today's profit and drives tomorrow's growth*. FT Press.

Steiber, A. (2014). *The Google model: Managing continuous innovation in a rapidly changing world*. Springer.

Steiber, A., & Alä̈nge, S. (2013a). A corporate system for continuous innovation: The case of Google Inc. *European Journal of Innovation Management, 16*(2), 243–264.

Steiber, A., & Alä̈nge, S. (2013b). The formation and growth of Google Inc.: A firm-level Triple Helix perspective. *Social Science Information, 52*(4), 575–604.

Sull, D., & Eisenhardt, K. M. (2015). *Simple rules: How to thrive in a complex world*. John Murray.

Teece, D. (2014). The foundations of enterprise performance: Dynamic and ordinary capabilities in an (economic) theory of firms. *The Academy of Management Perspectives, 28*(4), 328–352.

Teece, D., & Pisano, G. (1994). The dynamic capabilities of firms: An introduction. *Industrial and Corporate Change, 3*(3), 537–556.

Teece, D., Pisano, G., & Shuen, A. (1997). Dynamic capabilities and strategic management. *Strategic Management Journal, 18*(7), 509–533.

Thompson, J. D. (1967). *Organizations in action: Social science bases of administrative theory*. McGraw-Hill.

Tushman, M. L., & O'Reilly, C. A., III. (1997). *Winning through innovation: A practical guide to leading organizational change and renewal*. Harvard Business School Press.

The Silicon Valley Model 9

The purpose of this chapter is to describe a new management model for ongoing innovation, characterized by being dynamic, ambidextrous, and open in nature. This new breed of management model has been developed specifically to fit well in a rapidly changing world.

To recap what was said earlier in the book: This "new" model has been emerging gradually over recent years. We observed and analyzed it in use at our six case companies in Silicon Valley—although elements of it are also used in leading companies elsewhere, around the world.

The model is not simple. It has many elements: underlying concepts, beliefs, and practices that can be found in common across our case companies, despite differences of execution and detail. Preceding chapters have identified various sets of these elements, and we will conduct the task of synthesis in this chapter by reviewing them.

We will start, however, with a brief introduction to some interesting research on organizational design. Then we will summarize what we have learned in previous chapters of this book and end by presenting a conceptual Silicon Valley Model.

9.1 The Evolution of a New Breed of Organizations

In order to sort out if our case companies represented a new breed of large corporations, managed in a different way than "traditional firms," we first turned to some findings by Henry Mintzberg, an internationally renowned academic and author on strategy, business and management.

In 1980, Mintzberg presented a synthesis of previous research on organization design in the highly regarded journal *Management Science*.[1] He described five very different organizational models: The Simple Structure, The Machine Bureaucracy,

---

[1] Mintzberg (1980).

The Professional Bureaucracy, The Divisional Form, and The Adhocracy. He found that a normal growth pattern for an organization is to move from a simple structure to one characterized by more bureaucracy.

The simple structure is typical of smaller organizations. There is usually minimal structure, with coordination of tasks done mainly through direct supervision by top management. As the company grows it changes and becomes more complex. Jobs become more specialized and in some cases also more formalized, as in larger firms. Coordination of tasks in these large companies is usually done through increased standardization of work processes (e.g. for production), of skills (e.g. in consultancy firms or more service-oriented firms), or of output (e.g. in firms with different divisions controlled by standardization of output, such as sales figures). The increased standardization of work, skills, or output also allows the company to use larger internal units.

Decision-making power in these organizations is handled differently. In a large firm with both specialized and formalized jobs, power tends to stay at the top and among middle managers. In organizations like consultancy firms with less formalized jobs, the power tends to be decentralized to the professionals to a higher degree, and for organizations that use the divisional form as their main structure, the power tends to be at the division heads.

However, there is one common factor for these larger organizations—they all act in fairly stable environments. In addition, *the more the organization coordinates through standardization of work processes and keeps power in the top layer, the less complex the environment can be.* So, if you have a company or organization that operates in a stable and non-complex environment, then this kind of organizational design and logic is something for you. However, most organizations do not live in such an environment any longer, which is why a need has emerged for a new type of logic and design.

9.1.1 The New Model's Roots in 'Adhocracy'

According to Mintzberg, researchers started to identify a new form of organization after World War II. This new form was used by younger organizations of varying sizes. It was used more in dynamic and complex environments and was often associated with highly sophisticated and automated technical systems. This new organizational form was called "Adhocracy." The concept was put forward by Warren Bennis in his 1968 book *The Temporary Society*,[2] then popularized in 1970 by Alvin Toffler in *Future Shock*. It has since become often used in management theory, with further development by academics such as Mintzberg. For Mintzberg, an Adhocracy is a complex and dynamic organizational form[3] and it is different from bureaucracy. Like Toffler, Mintzberg considers *bureaucracy a thing of the past, and Adhocracy*

---

[2] Bennis and Slater (1968), pp. 53–77.
[3] Mintzberg (1989).

9.1 The Evolution of a New Breed of Organizations

one of the future.[4] When done well, Adhocracy can be very good at problem solving and innovations and thrives in a diverse environment. However, it seems to require the above-mentioned sophisticated technical systems in order to develop and thrive.[5]

The Adhocracy form reminds one very much of the new experimental organizational forms that we referred to in Chap. 3, which were observed by the researcher Homa Bahrami in Silicon Valley in the early 1990s. She also emphasized the importance of information technology in the development of this new form.

So, what are the characteristics of an Adhocracy? Mintzberg described it as having:

- A highly flexible and organic structure
- Little formalization of behavior, and job specialization not necessarily based on formal training
- Employees grouped in functional units but deployed in small, market-based teams
- Cooperation by relying on liaison devices to encourage mutual adjustment within and among the small teams
- Selective decentralization and power-shift to specialized teams (i.e., with power delegated to these teams or to certain places in the organization for local decision-making)
- High cost of communication (which is why information technology is necessary)
- A culture emphasizing non-bureaucratic work

As is clear from these points, the management approaches we observed in Silicon Valley seem to match the description of Adhocracy very well, although the concept has been further developed. What we call the Silicon Valley Model could therefore be viewed as the result of a long evolution—an "organizational trajectory" that started sometime after World War II and in 2016 was represented, in perhaps its most evolved form, in companies like Google, Facebook and our other case companies. In this context, it is interesting to acknowledge Mintzberg's and Toffler's beliefs that the bureaucracy model belongs to the past and the Adhocracy model belongs to the future, i.e. it is here to stay and is not a phenomenon that is specific to a certain industry or region.

To sum up: The Silicon Valley Model could be based on what in earlier research was called the Adhocracy model. Since this model seems to require sophisticated technology and automation, it therefore might reflect a development trajectory that has run in parallel with and benefited from the development of the information technologies, and later the Internet and social media technologies.

We believe that the Silicon Valley Model can be viewed as a proven, scalable version of the Adhocracy model. This means that the model works not only in young, small firms but also in large global companies such as Google, with over 50,000 employees in 2015 and activities all over the world.

So, let us assume that our case companies' model was built on an organizational model that evolved over the past 60 years and that in 2016 was far more advanced

---

[4] Travica (1999).
[5] Ibid.

than the Adhocracy model described in 1980 by Mintzberg.[6] How can this model be conceptualized and described? One way is to summarize what we have learnt so far about our case companies and then "package" these findings into a synthesis that will represent the Silicon Valley Model.

9.2 The Silicon Valley Model: 'A Startup in a Large Suit'

In fast-changing VUCA environments that are typical of nearly every industry today, the best companies are *entrepreneurial*. They are adept at, or even paranoid[7] about creating, recognizing, and seizing business opportunities. They're constantly carrying out initiatives to launch new product offerings, or to grow and improve existing ones; they are always looking to enter new markets or improve their position in existing ones. These entrepreneurial companies can also pivot quickly in the sense of changing or adapting their business or revenue models and they are *proactive*. When they make changes of any kind, they tend to be ahead of the curve instead of reacting to moves by competitors. Often, they'll change what is already working if they think they can make it better. Because they take forward-looking risks, rather than running the larger risks of path dependency and stagnation, their ambition is to avoid becoming blindsided by change or being forced into emergency measures to rescue the company.

To use Peter Drucker's definition of an entrepreneur, these firms "always search for change, respond to it, and exploit it as an opportunity." In many ways they retain and express the dynamic qualities of their founders; they continue to be as innovative as they were in the startup phase despite having grown much larger. For this reason, we call them "startups in large suits."

Now let's review what makes them able to behave as they do. Below are key elements of the new management model, as we have described them in the book so far.

9.2.1 Major Elements of the Silicon Valley Model

- First of all, the case companies had ambitious, compelling VISIONS and socially significant missions. The visions and missions attract people who want to make an impact in the world, challenging them to think big and out of the box.
- The second element was a strong, visionary and entrepreneurial TOP LEADERSHIP. Top leaders had the "founder's mindset," cultivating an entrepreneurial culture within the organization. They had an innovation- and growth-oriented focus, along with deep knowledge of the industry, business model,

---

[6] Mintzberg (1980).

[7] Former Intel CEO Andy Grove wrote a book called *Only the Paranoid Survive* (Grove, 1996). This motto of his emphasizes the responsibility of a leader to be on watch constantly for technological changes and competitors' actions—especially at strategic inflections points that may signal either new opportunities, or the beginning of the end if left unattended.

9.2 The Silicon Valley Model: 'A Startup in a Large Suit' 163

operations, and key technologies. This enabled them to ask the right questions, and they were personally involved in recruiting ever-higher standards of new employees. Goals like speed, innovation and adaptability ranked high on the executive agenda.

- Third was a belief that the right PEOPLE are essential—people who are entrepreneurial, who constantly question the status quo, and are passionate, adaptable and collaborative. All our case companies focused on hiring, retaining, and fully investing in and utilizing this kind of people. Both parties—the firm and the employee—were expected to invest a lot in the relationship, even if it might be short-term. The case companies trusted their employees and therefore cultivated an environment that was transparent and open. On-the-job training was preferred to classroom training and people were given freedom and challenging tasks from the start. They were expected to continually innovate and contribute to the firm. Due to the importance of both operational efficiency and entrepreneurship, people in the Silicon Valley Model had to be multidimensional, with a clear core of an entrepreneurial mindset and experience. The focus on adaptability and entrepreneurship as core competencies made the organizations more able to be innovative in parallel with operating the current business. It also made the companies more dynamic and flexible according to what was going on in the technology and the market space.
- Fourth, the CULTURE was strong and was used as a governance mechanism, to allow "soft" control and coordination of work without creating unnecessary bureaucracy. It allowed both clarity in direction and a lot of flexibility for employees. Our six case companies had cultures built around a set of beliefs that emphasized being different, speed, adaptability, the importance of the "right people," and having "leaders" rather than managers to coach these people. Further, the beliefs were strong regarding the importance of product excellence; being data-driven and learning fast; having a flat, open and transparent organization; and finally building an ecosystem, not only a company.
- LEADERS on all levels were ambassadors for the firm's culture. Acting as team coaches rather than managers, they communicated vision and direction but left how to execute a task to members of the team. Leaders coached and facilitated their teams to excellence, practiced two-way communication, and worked with the team if necessary. They knew their business and technologies and could ask the right questions, leaving the team to find answers and solutions.
- The ORGANIZATION combined the organizational logic of optimizing daily operations (exploitation)—according to a conventional planning-and-control approach—with innovation (exploration), which requires greater freedom, flexibility, and a more open attitude toward experimentation. This *Ambidexterity*, along with *Open Innovation* provided some of the main explanations behind the Silicon Valley Model's *Dynamic Capabilities*. The internal organizational structures were non-bureaucratic, loose and transparent, which made these companies flexible and suited for a dynamic world. Another contributor to flexibility was the use of flat and semi-structured organizations in which employees belonged to functional areas but worked in small, often product-oriented teams. The case

companies used standard mechanisms for idea generation and for developing ideas into innovations that were tested, usually at scale, with real-time data. These mechanisms were combined with bottom-up processes for key functions like strategy development. Further, as the firms were practicing open innovation, they networked with their surroundings to gain resources and ideas, both in a more classical way and in new forms. Finally, the Silicon Valley Model companies did more than tap into external innovation systems. They *actively created and cultivated their ecosystems*, rather than just being participants.
- The COORDINATION of people and tasks was done through a bold, engaging vision and mission, a shared set of beliefs and, as we learned in Chap. 8, through simple (or heuristic) rules. Complementing these soft mechanisms were clear performance and evaluation systems focused on key priorities—down to an individual level. Coordination was *not* done through formalization of job descriptions, which created a higher degree of flexibility and therefore of adaptability in the Silicon Valley Model.
- AUTOMATED INFORMATION PROCESSES. Organizations following the Silicon Valley Model embedded IT, big data analytics and social media as strategic parts of their operations. One reason was obviously to "eat their own dog food",[8] that is, to operate with and use their own products and services. However, perhaps a more important reason was the cost of communication, which was high in this type of firm. Social media and IT can support automation of information processes and therefore allow a lower cost of communication. In fact, keeping costs down when scaling the business is critical for this kind of "data intensive" firm.[9]

Regarding social media, Google, Facebook, LinkedIn and Twitter used their own tools and platforms for internal communication. For example, at Facebook each product team, subgroup, and project team could create its own Facebook group, which allowed the members to focus their interactions within the most pertinent audience.[10] The importance of social media such as Facebook, Twitter, and Google+ was expected to increase.[11]

The brief summary of the elements above can be visualized in a conceptual model. As with all such models, ours is not meant to cover every detail of what we discovered. Rather, we will try to present a good but simplified synthesis of the reality we saw at our case companies.

---

[8] A quote from one of our interviewees at Google in 2010.

[9] Google was forced to maniacally control costs because it learned that "anything that scales with demand is a disaster if you are not cheap about it".... As a service grows more popular, its costs must grow in a "sub-linear" fashion.... Another technique Google employed was to automate everything possible: "We're doing too much of the machines' work for them." All quotes are from Jackson (2013).

[10] Gabbard (2012).

[11] Wadee (2013).

9.3 A Conceptual Model, Visualized

It is extremely challenging to visualize this kind of complex, sophisticated, organic organizational form in a model. A typical "organization chart" won't do the job since the very structure of the firm is dynamic and fluid—it can be changed to fit an ever-changing environment. Also, many elements of the model cannot be placed into separate, stand-alone compartments: "culture" permeates the organization, "people" are everywhere within it, and so forth.

The best we can do is return to the systems approach described in Chap. 2. There it was said that an organization should be viewed as a system with many interdependent elements. Thinking of it in those terms, the Silicon Valley Model could be visualized as a management system in which the elements gravitate around central strategic intentions, as shown in Fig. 9.1.

In this rendering of the Silicon Valley Model, you can see that the main elements—as we've just described them—are interconnected. Moreover, keep in mind that the whole management system is dynamic and therefore embeds *Dynamic Capabilities*. All of the elements work together, revolving or "cycling" around the central intentions of growth and innovation—with adjustments and additions constantly being made in order to bring in new ideas and people, and to bring forth new

Fig. 9.1 The Silicon Valley Model

products or services. This keeps the organization rolling along through the ever-shifting currents of change.

In order to bring out the distinctive features of this new model we can simply ask: How does it differ from what is usually done? The next section offers a point- by-point comparison.

9.4 Differences Between a Traditional Management Model and the Silicon Valley Model

Let's compare the core elements of the Silicon Valley Model to those of a more traditional large-firm model: the Machine Bureaucracy described by Mintzberg in his 1980 synthesis of research on organizational design.[12] Table 9.1 shows a simplified comparison, which we can then discuss further.

If we start with *top leadership*, the top executives in the Silicon Valley Model had a strategic intent to pursue innovation and growth and their focus was primarily

Table 9.1 Characteristics of the Traditional model versus the Silicon Valley Model

Element	Traditional model	Silicon Valley model
Strategic intent of top leaders	Cost and profitability	Innovation and growth
Main focus of top leadership	Internal	External
People	Valued for operational competencies.	Valued for entrepreneurship as a core competence.
Culture	Emphasizes efficiency, low risk, control, and quality.	Emphasizes uniqueness, risk taking, adaptability, speed and fast learning.
Leaders	*Managers.* Set direction and priorities. Instruct what should be done and in many cases how it should be done. Follow up, check and control.	*Coaches and facilitators.* Together with the teams, set direction and priorities but leave the HOW to the team members. Facilitate and coach the team in reaching goals.
Organization	Bureaucratic, highly structured, hierarchical. Use of larger work units. Vertically distributed decision power. Mostly focused on internal innovation.	Organic, semi-structured, flat. Use of small teams. Selective decentralization. Temporarily, decision power can be centralized to the top. Focused on both internal and external innovations.
Coordination mechanisms	Through standardization of work processes, job descriptions and skills.	Through compelling vision, shared values, simple rules, and key priorities.
Automated information processes	Lower degree. Cost of communication is lower.	Higher degree. Cost of communication is high.

---

[12] Mintzberg (1980).

external, rather than internal.[13] In addition, the top leadership had a founder's mindset, cultivating the entrepreneurial culture within the organization. In the more traditional bureaucratic model, the strategic intent is mostly on cost and profit and the focus tends to be more internal. The top leadership in this kind of organization rarely has the founder's mindset but rather the "business" or "financial" mindset. Already here we see some reasons why the Silicon Valley Model more naturally becomes ambidextrous.

Turning next to *people*, the Silicon Valley Model requires people who are adaptive, passionate, question the status quo, and are collaborative. But the core competence in the Silicon Valley Model is entrepreneurship. This doesn't mean that operational efficiency of the business is unimportant, but it is not the overriding, dominating goal. However, as noted earlier, due to the importance of both entrepreneurship and operating efficiency in the Silicon Valley Model, people must be multi-dimensional around their entrepreneurial core. In the traditional large firm, entrepreneurship as a core employee competence is quite rare. Instead, operational competence is emphasized, searched for, and rewarded. This in turn can impair the company's ability to be ambidextrous and responsive.

The *culture* of the Silicon Valley Model is emphasized as important and is very strong. It places high value on qualities such as uniqueness, risk taking, adaptability, speed and fast learning. In comparison, the traditional large bureaucratic firm could also have a strong culture but a culture that emphasizes efficiency, low risk, control, and quality, which possibly impedes experimentation and more radical innovation.

Further, *leadership* in the Silicon Valley Model is primarily characterized by coaching and facilitating teams to excellence. Leaders set directions (usually together with the team) and communicate priorities but leave the execution of tasks to the team members. The daily leader will need to juggle between operations and innovation and needs to support his/her team if problems occur. In the traditional model, not only do daily leaders set direction and priorities, they also often instruct and inform team members what should be done, how and by whom. Then they follow up and control output.

The (semi) structured Silicon Valley Model is characterized by a *flat, non-bureaucratic and loose (organic) organization*. There is limited standardization of work processes and jobs. This make the firms extremely flexible, as do the use of small teams that are quite independent. Decision-making power in the Silicon Valley Model is selectively decentralized to local decision makers and teams. Temporarily, the decision-making power can be centralized to the very top. This happens for instance when the firm need to transform itself quickly in order to reap benefits of new opportunities or react to competitors' actions. Due to the semi-structured and flexible organization together with a high focus on both internal and external innovations, the Silicon Valley Model allows ambidexterity. The traditional bureaucratic organization, in contrast, has a formal and stable structure, usually with large internal units. The large size of the units is partly made possible by the standardization

---

[13] However, the top leadership in several of our cases divided the responsibility for an internal efficiency-oriented focus and an external, more future-oriented focus between different individuals.

of work processes and job descriptions. In the traditional firm model, the power is usually vertically distributed, with top executives and middle layers have higher power than lower levels. Due to the traditional organization's more formal, top-down and stable structure together with less focus on external innovations, this type of organization usually has a lower degree of ambidexterity. To be noted, in recent decades, the "stability" of structure in organizations might even have increased through process orientation and the focus on minimizing variation, which in many cases has been the goal of the quality movement.

The *coordination* of people and tasks in the Silicon Valley Model is done through soft mechanisms complemented with clear performance and evaluation systems focused on key priorities, rather than through formal standardization of job descriptions and processes. In the traditional bureaucratic model, coordination relies heavily on standardizing work roles and processes, rules, and procedures of all types.

Finally, the cost of communication is high in the Silicon Valley Model. This new model requires openness, transparency and frequent networking across people and teams. This is one reason why information and communication processes are, and need to be, highly automated with the help of IT. The traditional model has a lower communication cost, as much of the information travels along vertical lines and in many cases is "locked in" to certain groups and classified as confidential. This way of distributing information is almost a necessity if the organization doesn't use automated information processes to deal with an increased, real-time, rapid flow of information.

We have now conceptualized the Silicon Valley Model and compared it to a traditional bureaucratic model, with the latter described mainly according to the work of Mintzberg.[14] The comparison vividly shows that *the new model is the polar opposite of the old in every major respect*. We will now scrutinize the Silicon Valley Model in comparison to the Six Basic Principles for a Changing World that were introduced in Chap. 2, analyzing to what extent the Model fulfills these principles.

9.5 The Silicon Valley Model and the Six Basic Principles for a Changing World

It is of interest to see how the Silicon Valley Model aligns with the six principles described in Chap. 2. As mentioned, the six principles are distilled from a great body of management research on what makes a firm competitive for the long term in rapidly changing environments. Research has found these principles being used in many industries—and so, if the Silicon Valley Model supports the principles, this could suggest that the Model also is fit for wide use.

Throughout the book (and especially in Chap. 8) we've seen indications that the Silicon Valley Model is fulfilling criteria such as dynamic capabilities by e.g., being ambidextrous and having a high focus on open innovation. But let's review the principles again, in light of all that we now have learned about the Silicon Valley Model.

---

[14] Mintzberg (1980).

9.5 The Silicon Valley Model and the Six Basic Principles for a Changing World

Principle 1: *Dynamic capabilities.* The Silicon Valley Model clearly embeds Dynamic Capabilities. In fact, companies using the Silicon Valley Model were adept or even paranoid at creating, recognizing, and seizing business opportunities in a continuous quest for further high growth. Their choice of people, culture, and their way of organizing and leading their business allowed the firms to be highly dynamic.

Principle 2: *A continually changing organization.* The case companies were based on the very belief that everything will change. Therefore, every aspect of the organization was designed and geared not only to "react" to change but to initiate it, proactively, by constantly generating new ideas and seizing new opportunities. This quality of being change-oriented extended from the culture and from the kinds of people recruited—people who are eager and able to do something new—into the various organizational structures and mechanisms we've described, which encouraged bottom-up flows of idea generation and development. We would thus claim that the Silicon Valley Model very strongly supports a continually changing endeavor.

Principle 3. *A people-centric approach.* Not only in this chapter, but throughout the book, we've seen repeatedly that the case companies had a central emphasis on attracting, retaining, and nurturing the "right people" for the kinds of work they did. We've learned the core qualities of these people: they were entrepreneurial and passionate; they questioned the status quo; they were adaptable and collaborative. The companies actively encouraged these qualities and also put great effort into coaching and evaluating people, without micromanaging how they do their work. Therefore, the Silicon Valley Model is based on a very people-centric approach.

Principle 4. *An ambidextrous organization.* The firms following the Silicon Valley Model were, as we have seen, by nature ambidextrous. Their products and services were in daily use by huge numbers of people worldwide, which meant that current operations *had to* be tuned to deliver the goods efficiently—and to scale up efficiently, in order to meet growing demand—while innovation proceeded constantly as well.

Principle 5. *An open organization that networks with its surroundings.* A company can be more or less open to integration with its surroundings. Our companies following the Silicon Valley Model were effective at tapping into both internal and external innovation systems. And, as noted, the companies actively sought to build and sustain a larger ecosystem rather than just being part of it. The Silicon Valley Model could therefore be viewed as highly open and networking.

Principle 6. *A systems approach* to work differs from the conventional linear way of working. Companies using the Silicon Valley Model believed strongly in the importance of qualities like speed, adaptability and constant innovation. By embedding these beliefs in their culture and in everything they did, such as selection of people, desired leadership style, and choice of structures and processes, they truly followed the principle of the systems approach. In short, they had designed a "management system" consisting of interlinked and interdependent elements such as vision/mission, top management, people, culture, etc. that all were geared towards the strategic intents of growth and innovation.

9.6 Summing Up Key Points …

This chapter has presented the Silicon Valley Model as a "Management System" in which eight core elements gravitate around a central strategic intention of Growth and Innovation.

We have compared the Silicon Valley Model to a traditional bureaucratic model, with the latter described mainly according to the work of Mintzberg (1980). The comparison vividly shows that the new model is the polar opposite of the old in every major respect.

Finally, we have seen that the Silicon Valley Model follows all six basic principles that were presented in Chap. 2. The six principles are distilled from a great body of management research on what makes a firm competitive for the long term in rapidly changing environments, which is why this could mean that the Silicon Valley Model also is fit for wide use.

In both this chapter and earlier, in Chap. 3, we have also introduced findings from other researchers that indicate that the Silicon Valley Model could be a result of an evolution affected by the development of information technologies, the internet and social media. We also saw in Chap. 1 that the increase of knowledge workers (or "smart creatives" as Schmidt and Rosenberg called them),[15] together with an increased need for entrepreneurship overall due to a VUCA world, may well have influenced this "organizational trajectory." Further, Chap. 3 showed that the norms of the Valley region also have played an important role in the development of the Silicon Valley Management model.

9.7 Recent Developments and Further Thoughts

Research since the book's first edition in 2016 continues to confirm the value of the type of model presented here. For example, a study of high-growth startups in Canada focused on identifying the characteristics needed to navigate today's VUCA business settings:

> The study found [that] decentralized decision-making mechanisms and non-hierarchical structure … promoted business agility and transparent communication and increased collaboration among team members. In addition, transparent communication, reward systems, and employee learning and knowledge sharing promoted creativity and innovation. Flexible organizational structure and cultural values that foster innovation, teamwork, and knowledge sharing were noted to increase business growth addressing VUCA challenges effectively.[16]

---

[15] Schmidt and Rosenberg (2014).
[16] Konyu-Fogel (2022).

9.7 Recent Developments and Further Thoughts

At the same time, there also continues to be a great deal of experimentation with new kinds of management and organization structures.

> In private as well as public organizations, we have seen changing organizational forms, a growing amount of importance placed on social networks, and many different experiments with flat organizations (absent hierarchy).[17]

One could say that the field of organizational design is undergoing a renaissance. In Chap. 10, the Recent Developments section will present several brief case studies of long-established companies and business units adopting new management models. All appear to be variations on the Silicon Valley Model — using the same underlying principles but applying them in different ways, some of which borrow concepts from a range of new schools of thought.

The reasons for this surge of interest seem clear. Given the turbulence of the modern business climate, researchers and practitioners are increasingly drawn to designing organizations for a future that will require them to be adaptive, fast, and effective in response to opportunities and challenges in global and local markets. Also, some research indicates that the younger generations have a dislike for rigid authority, and the movement of these generations into the workforce has helped to spur interest in creating work environments that people will find attractive and fulfilling.[18]

9.7.1 The Evolution of Adhocracy

Looking farther back, we find the adhocracy model still relevant. As early as 2010, in a paper titled "Revisiting Adhocracy," the scholar Timothy E. Dolan foresaw the model both persisting and evolving into new shapes. Two key trends he noted at that time were "a comprehensive shift in organizational orientation from standardized function to project work," and a "shift of routine bureaucratic functions to automated systems that free personnel from such an orientation and towards a professional focus."[19] The conclusion of the paper is worth quoting from, as follows.

> "New Adhocracy" is a result of the acceleration of history aided and abetted by enhanced data processing and communications technologies. Certainly, a standing cadre of specialists physically located on an organization's property is no longer required. Maintaining them in a highly standardized organizational form (bureaucracy) is likewise of marginal utility in an age of volatile environmental change. ... It is not just a matter of having a larger organizational toolbox, but of having the right tools for the right contexts. ... Adhocracy is increasingly the normative form for endeavors in a constant state of becoming and not compatible with institutionalization. However, the next wave; the new adhocracy; describes a radically altered set of relationships between institutional operational cores, with an eliminated or flattened middle line, and a highly fragmented support staff and techno-structure often

---

[17] Burton et al. (2020).
[18] Ibid.
[19] Dolan (2010).

[consisting of] contracted individuals and entities not otherwise formally affiliated with a particular organization.[20]

In fact, the use of outside contracting and independent freelancers has grown significantly. Although the extent of these practices is hard to measure with precision, due to their fluid and varied nature, two separate studies in the United States showed close convergence recently. One survey found that during 2022, 39% of the U.S. workforce performed freelance work either part-time or full-time,[21] while a multi-factor study set the figure at 36%, up from 27% in 2016.[22] Companies from all industries hired these people, with the terms and duration of the engagements varying greatly; the individuals ranged from local laborers and service workers to professionals working remotely at their computers.[23]

Information technologies have played multiple roles in this growth. Contracting as needed, either with individuals or external teams, is now global via the internet. Numerous web-based services exist for finding the requisite talent, and much of the work itself is IT-related.[24] The overall result is an increased decentralization of firms, with a corresponding need for management systems that are nimble enough to manage dispersed and constantly changing pools of workers.

9.7.2 The Next Evolutionary Step?

Aside from contracting, most companies still need sizable staffs of regular employees. And a general trend worth watching on this front is greater delegation of authority. Already, in the Silicon Valley Model and similar approaches, we see a movement away from top-down bureaucracy with rigid structures and procedures. The new normal in these cases is for teams and individuals to have considerable autonomy and freedom to self-manage, within certain guidelines. There is also usually the allowance for product ideas and new strategies to percolate from the bottom up, instead of being decided only at the top levels. The next evolutionary step might therefore be the emergence of entire organizations that are self-managed — on such a scale that hundreds or even many thousands of employees, interactively and collectively, take charge of situational decision-making and shape the strategic directions of the enterprise.

Ideally this would make the organization more innovative and responsive, by tapping the abilities of everyone more fully, and by enabling new insights to be shared and acted upon. If management layers and bureaucratic hurdles can be reduced, cost-efficiency should improve as well.[25] Some say the time is now right

---

[20] Ibid.
[21] Segal (2022) and Davis (2022).
[22] McKinsey & Company (2022).
[23] Ibid.
[24] Segal (2022).
[25] Martela (2019).

for experiments along these lines, in part because "sophisticated IT systems have made it possible to coordinate the actions of thousands of people in real-time, making self-management more possible than in previous eras."[26] And indeed, recent research has documented many cases of self-managing organizations (SMOs), defined as those that have radically and systematically decentralized authority to the degree of almost abolishing middle management and supervisor-subordinate relationships.[27] Companies often highlighted in SMO case studies include Buurtzorg Nederland, W.L. Gore, Haier, Morning Star, Valve, and Zappos.[28]

SMO models can present challenges of their own. For example, the online retailer Zappos and the publishing-platform company Medium both tried a formalized system of self-management called Holacracy. Each encountered difficulties in adapting to the system, and also perceived shortcomings such as insufficient focus on customers.[29] However, Zappos responded by phasing out elements that didn't work for the company, while phasing in other self-management concepts,[30] and Medium dropped the system but announced a revised approach emphasizing distributed authority, transparency, and nimbleness.[31]

Both companies have changed further since these decisions were made. They may be making additional changes as you read. The bottom line is that in the quest for new ways to manage companies, evolution and experimentation continue. The next chapter, our final one, will explore the wider applicability of the Silicon Valley Model—beyond the Valley and beyond the internet and IT industries.

References

Bennis, W., & Slater, P. (1968). *The temporary society*. Harper & Row.
Burton, R., Håkonsson, D. D., Larsen, E. R., & Obel, B. (2020). New trends in organization design. *Journal of Organization Design, 9*, 10. https://doi.org/10.1186/s41469-020-00072-1
Davis, K. (2022, March 21). Why so many people are freelancing. *Fast Company*. https://www.fastcompany.com/90732237/why-are-so-many-people-freelancing
Dolan, T. E. (2010). Revisiting adhocracy: From rhetorical revisionism to smart mobs. *Journal of Futures Studies, 15*(2), 33–50. https://jfsdigital.org/wp-content/uploads/2014/01/152-A03.pdf
Doyle, A. (2016, March 4). Management and organization at Medium. Executive blog post on Medium. https://blog.medium.com/management-and-organization-at-medium-2228cc9d93e9#.dbliza3ee
Gabbard, J. (2012, April 24). Answer to "What tools does Facebook use for internal communication and project management?" on Quora. http://www.quora.com/What-tools-does-Facebook-use-for-internal-communication-and-project-management. Accessed 31 July 2015.
Groth, A. (2020, January 29). Zappos has quietly backed away from holacracy. Quartz. https://qz.com/work/1776841/zappos-has-quietly-backed-away-from-holacracy

---

[26] Ibid.
[27] Lee and Edmondson (2017).
[28] See for example Martela (2019).
[29] Groth (2020).
[30] Ibid.
[31] Doyle (2016).

Grove, A. S. (1996). *Only the paranoid survive: How to exploit the crisis points that challenge every company and career*. Currency Doubleday.
Jackson, J. (2013, November 27). Here's how Google and Amazon scale up their huge IT operations. *Computerworld*. http://www.computerworld.com/article/2486298/data-center/here-s-how-google-and-amazon-scale-up-their-huge-it-operations.html. Accessed 31 July 2015.
Konyu-Fogel, G. (2022). Organizational design in a volatile, uncertain, complex, and ambiguous (VUCA) world: A multi-case study of high-growth emerging startups in Canada. Conference paper: Association of International Business Research and Practice, 2022 MBAA International, Chicago. https://www.researchgate.net/publication/360614527_Organizational_Design_in_a_Volatile_Uncertain_Complex_and_Ambiguous_VUCA_World_A_Multi-Case_Study_of_High-Growth_Emerging_Startups_in_Canada
Lee, M. Y., & Edmondson, A. C. (2017). Self-managing organizations: Exploring the limits of less-hierarchical organizing. *Research in Organizational Behavior, 37*(2017), 35–58. https://doi.org/10.1016/j.riob.2017.10.002
Martela, F. (2019). What makes self-managing organizations novel? Comparing how Weberian bureaucracy, Mintzberg's adhocracy, and self-organizing solve six fundamental problems of organizing. *Journal of Organization Design, 8*, 23. https://doi.org/10.1186/s41469-019-0062-9
McKinsey & Company. (2022, August 23). Freelance, side hustles, and gigs: Many more Americans have become independent workers. McKinsey website article. https://www.mckinsey.com/featured-insights/sustainable-inclusive-growth/future-of-america/freelance-side-hustles-and-gigs-many-more-americans-have-become-independent-workers
Mintzberg, H. (1980). Structure in 5's: A synthesis of the research on organization design. *Management Science, 26*(3), 322–341.
Mintzberg, H. (1989). *Mintzberg on management: Inside our strange world of organizations*. Free Press.
Schmidt, E., & Rosenberg, J. (2014). *How google works*. Grand Central Publishing.
Segal, E. (2022, December 13). How and why the freelance workforce is setting new records. Forbes.com. https://www.forbes.com/sites/edwardsegal/2022/12/13/how-and-why-the-freelance-workforce-is-setting-new-records/?sh=5200e65b4b1
Toffler, A. (1970). *Future shock*. Bantam.
Travica, B. (1999). *New organizational designs: Information aspects*. Ablex Publishing Corp.
Wadee, Z. (2013, January 25). Facebook your boss: Using social media in internal communications. *TheGuardian.com*. http://www.theguardian.com/careers/careers-blog/facebook-employers-encourage-social-media. Accessed 27 July 2015.

Implications Beyond Silicon Valley   10

Executives in many industries may be skeptical about new management models from Silicon Valley firms. A common objection is: "These are mostly software companies. How would their lessons apply to the packaged-food industry, or chemicals, or …?"

Problems of translation must be considered, but good models have proved to be highly adaptable. Variations of the management concepts TQM (Total Quality Management) and Lean Production, which draw heavily on the experiences of Toyota in Japan, are for example now used in industries vastly different from auto making.

What reasons are there to believe that the model identified in Silicon Valley can have broader application outside the area and in other industries? One reason is that the model's various characteristics can be found in organizations elsewhere and in industries outside the IT/internet world. As just pointed out in Chap. 9, the Silicon Valley Model has many features identical to the "Adhocracy" model,[1] which was first identified decades ago. This led us in Chap. 9 to conclude that the practices we identified, in the case companies we investigated, could be viewed as the latest step in the development trajectory of Management of the Firm.

The characteristics of the companies researched have been presented as different building blocks in previous chapters. In Chap. 9 those findings are synthesized in the form of a conceptual model of the Silicon Valley Model. To recap the model briefly, its first five elements are: a socially significant and challenging vision, a visionary, entrepreneurial and growth-oriented top leadership, a resource of and belief in entrepreneurial people, a culture that can guide and motivate these individuals, and leaders who support them. The last three elements are: an organization with employees working in small teams in an organic, flat and open environment, in steady interaction with the surrounding ecosystem; coordination of work primarily

---

[1] Mintzberg (1980).

through a strong vision/mission, culture and simple rules but also through clear performance and evaluation systems; and automated communication processes with the support of information technologies. Together they form the Silicon Valley Model, which is a management system of interlinked and interdependent elements.

The question now is: Can this system of elements also be applied in organizations outside Silicon Valley and in other industries?

- First, we will analyze the extent to which companies outside the Valley have utilized *individual elements* of the Silicon Valley Model.
- Then we will investigate whether there are companies in other industries and geographical locations using the *entire system* of interlinked elements that constitute the Silicon Valley Model.
- Finally, we'll investigate and discuss whether the model could be utilized in *parts* of an organization, to provide increased ambidextrous and dynamic capability.

10.1 The Use of Elements of the Silicon Valley Model in Other Companies

This analysis follows the logic of the eight elements of the conceptual model presented in Chap. 9, except that we have divided the "organization" element into two parts—"ambidexterity" and "open innovation"—and present them under two separate headings. The elements analyzed below are therefore: vision; top leadership; people; culture; leaders; ambidexterity; open innovation; coordination; and IT platforms.

10.1.1 An Inspiring and Socially Significant Vision

There is no reason that organizations need to be located in Silicon Valley to develop big, compelling VISIONS and socially significant missions. As mentioned in Chap. 7, Merck's vision of developing medicines beneficial to humankind served such a function since the early 1950s and helped stimulate people to excel in innovation, resulting in a company that was the most admired in the US.

Another more recent example of a vision that fulfilled the criteria of being inspiring, challenging and socially significant was GE's vision for its health business, "healthymagination," expressed as follows:

> We're committed to continuously developing and investing in innovations that deliver high-quality, more affordable healthcare to more people around the world.[2] —Sue Siegel, CEO, GE Ventures & healthymagination

---

[2] General Electric Company (2015b) http://www.ge.com/globalimpact2013/#/healthymagination

10.1 The Use of Elements of the Silicon Valley Model in Other Companies

And Siegel continues:

> It's a lofty mission that requires a collaborative team to drive innovation. In 2013, healthymagination activated a new approach to driving innovation through: Corporate Venture Capital—Investing and partnering with startups to accelerate growth and commercialize innovative ideas; Incubations—Driving GE growth by testing and developing market-shaping business platforms; Collaboration—Expanding healthymagination's work to team up with key industry partners on significant global health challenges; and Walking the Talk—Through GE's Human Resources team, deepening the Company's internal culture of health and helping export that to our external communities.

Thus, the first element seems quite amenable to use in other industries and geographical areas.

10.1.2 Visionary, Entrepreneurial and Growth-Oriented Top Leadership

Second, we found that the Silicon Valley case companies had strong, visionary, entrepreneurial and growth-oriented TOP LEADERSHIP with the "founder's mindset"—a mindset of cultivating the entrepreneurial culture, and one focused on innovation and external growth-orientation. There are successful companies in other industries and locations that have kept the founder's mindset for a very long period of time, such as IKEA, where the founder and former CEO Ingvar Kamprad's vision has motivated many co-workers to excel.[3] These leadership qualities can be even more accentuated in the case of established firms that want to develop dynamic capabilities and focus on innovation. Procter & Gamble's launch of its "Connect+Develop" initiative in 2000 was a good example, showing the importance of a top leadership committed to innovation. The new CEO A.G. Lafley took a public stand and launched a new and open approach to innovation, whereby 50% of P&G's innovation should come from outside the company.[4] However, one major obstacle is that large incumbent firms, which have existed for many years, typically also tend to have a history of working according to a big-firm mentality. This is a mindset that's very different from startups and also from the Silicon Valley companies in our study, which in 2016 were relatively young companies that had strived to keep a startup identity.

> … to create a better everyday life for the many people

Further, it is not enough for top leaders only to communicate visions. Entrepreneurial leadership also includes "getting things done" and leading people to use their creativity in fruitful ways. Thus, the identified need for deep knowledge of the industry, business model, operations, and of key technologies, enabling leaders to ask

---
[3] IKEA (2015) http://www.ikea.com/ms/en_IE/about_ikea/the_ikea_way/our_business_idea/index.html
[4] Birkinshaw (2010).

employees the right questions, could also be a characteristic of great CEOs in other industries and places. The former Scania CEO Leif Östling, who was at the helm of a very successful large truck manufacturer for over 20 years, has been described as having exactly these qualities.[5] Moreover issues like innovation and flexibility, in terms of both products and labor, have definitely been of importance on Scania's executive agenda.

10.1.3 Belief and Investment in Entrepreneurial People

The belief that PEOPLE can make a difference—especially if they are entrepreneurial, passionate, constantly questioning the status quo, adaptable and collaborative— is perhaps easier to express than to live by. In our research we were amazed by the extent to which our case companies focused on hiring, developing, and creating opportunities for creative people to excel. This could be at least partly an effect of the very competitive labor market in Silicon Valley, where people easily move between employers. It has also led to the development of employment contracts with specified durations of 2–3 years (the tour of duty), in order to meet both the individual's need for development and the company's need for 100% creative effort over a predictable span of time.

This type of contract is not common in most other geographical areas. It does have some similarity to longer-term consultancy contracts, which, at least in some countries, have been a standard procedure for many years—although in that usage, the contract has been with a firm of consultants. Our case companies also used more traditional rotation of employees in order to provide new challenges and inspiration, while simultaneously developing their competence and understanding of the company. Here a parallel exists, as special programs for rotating new "learning" engineers can be found in many companies outside the Valley.[6] Also, policies requiring (and helping) employees to change positions regularly, such as Google's suggestions of looking for a new internal job every 18 months, can be found in other parts of the world.[7]

The case companies all were transparent and open with information, reflecting high trust in their employees, who were expected to be entrepreneurial, innovative and contribute to the firm. Although this is not common in all large firms, a similar situation can be found at companies in a variety of industries, for example at W.L. Gore and 3M. In the Silicon Valley case companies even new employees were given freedom and challenging tasks from the start of their employment. Once

---

[5] Alänge and Steiber (2009).

[6] E.g. ABB and Lantmännen.

[7] For example, in Nokia there was "a strong pressure from top management for systematic job-rotation at all leadership levels (every 2–3 years). This rotation appeared to be a powerful way to increase employee's competence and knowledge of the company, and it also prepared employees for change and prevented the emergence of hidden agendas and political inertia" (Alänge & Miconnet, 2001), pp. 8–9.

again, a similar approach has been in place elsewhere, for example at Nokia in Finland[8] and at Morning Star (see Chap. 2), where no one had a boss.

10.1.4 A Culture That Guides and Motivates Entrepreneurial People

The CULTURE of the case companies was strong and used as a governance mechanism to provide "soft" control that didn't create unnecessary bureaucracy. It allowed both clarity in direction and a lot of flexibility for employees. Our six case companies had cultures built around beliefs such as "we are not an ordinary company," and "things change constantly and you have to be adaptable," "speed matters," "hiring is the most important thing you can do," and "product excellence is key." The cultures also value "data-driven decision making with fast learning cycles," a "flat organization with minimal bureaucracy," "openness and transparency," and having "leaders, not managers," and they strived to "build an ecosystem, not just a company." This set of beliefs was remarkably similar for both the IT/internet companies and the electrical vehicle firm in our study, but they are not common for large corporations in general. However, it is still possible to find companies pursuing a similar set of beliefs outside Silicon Valley, such as 3M, W.L. Gore, IKEA[9] and Nokia at the end of 1990s.[10]

10.1.5 Leaders Who Support Entrepreneurial People

In our case companies LEADERS on all levels behaved according to company culture, communicated vision and direction but left how to perform a task to members of the team. They coached their teams to excellence, practiced two-way communication and worked with the teams if necessary. The leaders knew their business and technologies and could ask the right questions, which elicit good answers. W.L. Gore is an example of a company outside Silicon Valley and in another industry that is well-known for practicing this kind of leadership, where the associates in small teams are supported to excel and use their own creativity to the benefit of the company. The same situation exists at Morning Star, where the employees are given freedom and responsibility to make decisions, to self-organize and to negotiate responsibilities with their peers. Also at IKEA, co-workers are expected to take

---

[8] Ibid.

[9] CEO Anders Dahlvig described IKEA culture as "Things like informality, cost consciousness, and a very humble and 'down to earth' approach. Also letting people have responsibilities" (Kling & Goteman, 2003), p. 35.

[10] "what is probably most striking to outside observers is Nokia's flat hierarchy. Nokia's management style emphasizes individual initiative, controlled improvisation, achievement, pragmatism, and decisions are taken 'where the knowledge is'" (Alänge & Miconnet, 2001), p. 7.

initiatives and be entrepreneurial, interacting with others in order to mobilize internal support for their new ideas.

Early-stage decision-making (about new ideas and innovations) in our case companies was thus based on leaders' trust in the capacity of entrepreneurial people in small teams to decide well on their own. In addition, early decision-making can benefit from the wisdom of both internal crowds and external crowds (which, in our case companies, was typically measured in terms of user behavior). This form of decision-making is also practiced by companies in other industries and other geographical areas. In addition to using conventional communication platforms for crowd-input of ideas, they also use internet platforms in early-stage decision-making of this type; one organization that does so is GEA's FirstBuild unit.

10.1.6 An Ambidextrous Organization

The case companies showed an ability to be AMBIDEXTROUS through the way they organized their regular operations. They combined the organizational logics of optimizing daily operations, according to more of a planning-and-control approach (exploitation), with innovation (exploration), which requires greater freedom, flexibility, and a more open attitude toward experimentation. The key ingredients for ambidexterity in the case companies were the entrepreneurial and adaptive people, the culture, and leaders who facilitated employees working in small teams in non-bureaucratic structures. Their internal structures were adaptive, loose and extremely transparent, which made these firms flexible and fit for a dynamic world. Part of the explanation for this flexibility was the use of flat and semi-structured organizations where employees belonged to functional areas but worked in small teams.

Flat, semi-structured organization can however also be found in other industries, for example at IKEA, where the culture and flexible organization motivate co-workers to be creative.[11] W.L. Gore has used an even more extreme way of creating a flat team-based organization for innovation by everyone, through a title-free approach in which all associates (employees) are linked for person-to-person communication with no intermediaries, and associates step forward to lead when they have the expertise to do so.[12] The result is that anyone can interact with anyone else in Gore's "lattice" structure, under the assumption that serendipity will lead to new product and business opportunities. Similar lines of thinking also lie behind our case companies' way of organizing to facilitate the sharing of ideas and create opportunities for serendipity events. What can be challenging in a more traditional US context is to establish a low formalization of jobs, as the standard is to use clearly defined job descriptions. On the other hand, low formalization of jobs is common in many Scandinavian companies, such as IKEA, which indicates that some ways of organizing may depend on local traditions and culture.

---

[11] Totrakarntrakul and Lang (2008).
[12] Manz et al. (2009), pp. 240–241.

Mechanisms for idea generation and for rapid development of concepts that are tested on users, usually based on real-time big data analysis, were standard procedures within the case companies. The mechanisms used in our Silicon Valley companies were however not unique. In some cases, they even originated in other industries and geographical locations. For example, Google's well-known 20% time for working on one's own ideas is a variant of what 3M practiced for a very long time with its 15% time policy, which led to products like Post-its. And W.L. Gore has provided its employees with 10% free time to innovate.

So, while many of the ways of organizing for ambidexterity have been practiced outside Silicon Valley, it remains a major challenge for most large companies. The opportunity is also a major one, though, as ambidexterity combined with open innovation can greatly facilitate the development of needed dynamic capabilities.

10.1.7 Open Innovation

Open innovation, whereby the firms network and interact with their surroundings, is a key ingredient of the Silicon Valley Model. Our case companies had various ways of interacting with external actors, including ways that demanded big investment—such as acquisitions—to interaction through tournaments and hackathons, where the investment at least initially could be much less. Crowd processes were used primarily for idea generation, although big data on user behavior were routinely collected and analyzed.

Organizations elsewhere, such as FirstBuild and Local Motors have used another way of crowdsourcing and crowd-decision-making, through a totally transparent development process where both internal and external individuals can volunteer and vote on the internet for different design solutions that have been generated through internet/maker-facility hackathons.[13] As mentioned above, the Connect+Develop approach by P&G used a similar way of opening up for external ideas. However, the notion of opening up for external ideas has been on business agendas for a much longer time. DuPont is an example of an incumbent that since 1909 has had a strategy of, when needed, turning to the outside world for new product ideas and new industry segments.[14]

The Silicon Valley Model companies were not only effective in tapping into the external innovation system, but also actively cultivated their ecosystems, rather than just being participants. The idea of cultivating ecosystems for growth has come into focus in Silicon Valley, especially after the success of Apple's and Google's ecosystems of app developers emerged. This has led to an increasing interest in research on external or industry-wide platforms and ecosystems.[15] Also, large European technology firms, such as Janssen (part of Johnson & Johnson) in Belgium and Philips in Holland, have turned to open innovation in order to speed up development

---

[13] Alänge and Steiber (2015).
[14] Hounshell and Kenly Smith (1988).
[15] Gawer and Cusumano (2014).

and become more dynamic. In 2003 Philips opened its large corporate development site in Eindhoven for external small and large firms to co-locate and form an open innovation ecosystem.[16] Janssen Pharmaceutica (Belgium) launched its open innovation initiative in 2009, supported by a top management statement very similar to expressions from our case companies: "While Janssen has thousands of bright scientists, there are millions of brilliant scientists and engineers outside—so whatever you do, make sure you connect with the outside world."[17] One example of this is Janssen Labs Flanders[18] (Belgium), which along with Janssen Labs San Diego (USA) is a life science incubator developing an innovation ecosystem where independent emerging companies are being co-located with their own staffs.[19] The basic idea of industries developing together is however a lot older, e.g., in industrial districts[20] and development blocks,[21] and it can be utilized in any industry where there are linkages between companies.

Also, many companies worldwide now practice open innovation on a case-by-case basis by using innovation contests or, alternatively, third-party websites that serve as "innovation marketplaces." In these contests or on these websites, the company can post a technical problem or need that it has, essentially issuing an open call for solutions.[22] There are challenges to benefiting from competencies and resources that you cannot directly control, as is the case with external developer platforms, but at the same time open innovation offers major opportunities, which perhaps are just starting to be explored.

10.1.8 Coordination

The Silicon Valley Model is based on entrepreneurial individuals working in small self-managed teams, along with intricate ways of *coordinating* work through a combination of soft guidance and hard data measurement and follow-up. The ambitious visions/missions in combination with a company culture expressing a clear set of beliefs, often supplemented by simple rules,[23] provide the general direction that allows for creative inputs from teams and individuals. The general

---

[16] Philips Research (2015) http://www.hightechcampus.com/about_the_campus/#article/ecosystem/
[17] Interview with Janssen Pharmaceutica (Belgium) in 2014.
[18] Will be operational in 2015.
[19] Johnson&Johnson(2014).https://www.jnj.com/news/all/Janssen-Labs-Expanding-and-Accelerating-Coast-to-Coast–Unveils-Plan-to-Enhance-the-Innovation-Ecosystem-with-New-Incubator-in-South-San-Francisco-and-Awards-One-Year-of-Lab-Space-to-Three-Innovative-Healthcare-Companies-in-Boston
[20] Marshall (1892).
[21] Dahmén (1950).
[22] Web platforms such as InnoCentive [now Wazoku Crowd] and Innoget are examples of general-purpose innovation markets, where needs and solutions in many different categories can be posted, and there are also such websites for particular industries or technical fields.
[23] See Chap. 8 for examples of the use of simple rules in our case companies.

guidance is complemented by top leadership's explicit company focus areas, combined with quarterly goals that are followed up through clear performance and evaluation systems, based on hard data on all levels, including leadership, team and individuals. In order to coordinate activities, transparency internally is needed so everyone can have real-time access to relevant information, both through available data systems and through a culture that allows for communicating with anyone inside the organization.

The use of explicit visions/missions, shared culture and simple rules is also something that can be found in other companies and other types of organizations.[24] Further, the clear performance and evaluation system used by our case companies was introduced through the business network, by a board member/venture capitalist who knew about the approach from Intel.[25] Thus, the coordination element seems to be in use in other industries and other geographical areas as well.

10.1.9 Information and Communication Technologies: Do the Silicon Valley Companies Have a Unique Edge?

In the Silicon Valley case companies, communication technologies and social media platforms were utilized in daily work in more or less *automated processes*. In addition, many employees, as part of their work, were developing new applications and services. These technologies and platforms facilitated sharing of insights, ideas and solutions, and they also provided opportunities for asking questions to internal and external crowds. Since technologies of this kind are at the heart of what the case companies do (and a large share of their employees have computer science backgrounds), they probably have an advantage in introducing technology-based communication. However, except in cases where IT illiteracy hampers the use of them, it is clear that all kinds of companies can benefit from using new communication technologies, even if they lack the competence in developing new tools themselves. The IT/platform competence of our case companies might provide some first-mover advantage in managing by the Silicon Valley Model, but it does not prevent companies in other industries from moving towards similar ways of managing and utilizing new communication technology as a means.

Indeed, companies in more traditional industrial areas have been rapidly building software and internet competencies, as they foresee that a large share of future innovations will involve software/internet based platforms. For many companies not only does the interaction between *people* provide a major means of innovation, but also the platforms on which "things speak to things" offer tremendous potential for innovation. One example came from GE. While GE's ecomagination program utilized communication platforms to crowdsource ideas that could provide environmentally friendly innovations and create relationships to new suppliers, GE also saw a large innovation potential in the industrial internet:

---

[24] Sull and Eisenhardt (2015).
[25] Schmidt and Rosenberg (2014), 220–221.

The integration of efficient hardware with Internet-enabled software is THE NEW FRONTIER in natural resource productivity. We call this Digital Resource Productivity ... the combination of ecomagination solutions with Industrial Internet software innovations.[26] — Brandon Owens, director of ecomagination Strategy & Analytics at GE

10.2 Can the Whole System of Interlinked Elements Be Used Outside Silicon Valley?

We've now seen that many companies in other industries and places have used individual elements of the Silicon Valley Model. However, what was distinctive about our case companies was that they used all of the elements together, as interlinked and interdependent parts of a comprehensive new *management system*. It is this system, as a whole, that truly constitutes the Silicon Valley Model. And in order to consider the prospects for wider use of the whole model, three questions should be addressed.

- We have called our case companies "startups in large suits" because they retained the entrepreneurial qualities of their startup stages. In one sense, this could be a *result* of using the Silicon Valley Model, and to some extent it may also be a prerequisite for using it—i.e., the fact that these companies had a startup culture and a "founder's mindset" *to begin with* could've helped them to develop and implement the whole model successfully. So, the first question is: To what extent can a startup culture be kept (or re-created) in large, older companies that may have developed many bureaucratic features over the years?
- Second: Are there companies outside Silicon Valley now using all elements of the model together, as a system?
- And third: Could the Silicon Valley Model, as a whole, be used in selected departments or segments of a large incumbent in order to improve its responsiveness, speed, and ability to innovate?

10.2.1 Startup Culture in Mature Companies

The Silicon Valley Model emphasizes the importance of entrepreneurship on all levels of the organization, from top leadership through the rest. The case companies have been able to do this, but then again, they were all relatively young companies and still had founders among the top leadership or on their boards. What are the prospects for firms that don't have these characteristics, and might need to re-acquire the startup culture and mindset?

---

[26] General Electric Company (2015a). See also Owens (2014).

10.2 Can the Whole System of Interlinked Elements Be Used Outside Silicon Valley?

There have been several attempts to revitalize existing firms by building on the experiences of startups, such as implementation of the Lean Startup methodology.[27]

So, while the need has been identified and there have been many efforts along the line of taking inspiration from startups, it can still be difficult to accomplish. For example, GE had some success in applying Lean Startup practices in regular R&D departments but also encountered various large-firm rigidities. This made GE try a different way to emulate a startup situation, rapidly testing new product concepts and obtaining feedback from customers, through the FirstBuild approach.[28]

Such evidence suggests that incumbents wishing to foster a startup mentality may need to do more than introduce specific tools or selected elements; they may need to look into the issue from a systems perspective. A parallel can be drawn here to the fact that Western companies achieved very limited results by trying to import individual parts of the Japanese quality approach, such as quality circles, until they realized that quality had to be viewed and practiced as a system (TQM) to gain impact.[29]

10.2.2 A System of Interconnected Elements

So, the next question becomes: can the Silicon Valley Model, with all of its necessary elements, be applied as a complete management system in other industries or geographical areas?

A systems approach to work differs from the conventional linear way of working. The case companies were guided by overarching beliefs or principles that impacted everything they did—people, leadership, structure, incentives, hiring, and interaction with the surrounding world. These basic beliefs were ingrained and made explicit in value formulations that described the companies' cultures. The beliefs typically included a focus on speed, the importance of flexibility and adaptability, a focus on user/customer experiences through product excellence, and above all an emphasis on innovation and growth. Hence, starting out from challenging visions/missions and guided by these overarching principles, all the other elements need to be synchronized to contribute to the same direction. This is the challenge for leaders who, with the founder's touch, want to develop and sustain truly dynamic capabilities, allowing their companies to be excellent both in the present and in developing their futures.

The Silicon Valley Model is developed based on the case companies' way of organizing to be entrepreneurial and dynamic. And we can identify other larger firms that work according to similar principles. Both 3M, a role model for decades, and W.L. Gore, a startup from the 1950s, show the characteristics of having a systems approach to staying innovative and dynamic. An interesting observation is that

---

[27] Ries (2011).
[28] Alänge and Steiber (2015).
[29] Alänge (1992).

3M experienced a few years of diminishing innovation performance after introducing a highly process-oriented, Six Sigma-driven management model.

Later, a new CEO changed focus to once again reestablish 3M's systems approach to innovation and turned the trend around.[30]

However, 3M and W.L. Gore are *two* examples of rather nimble companies. Many large incumbents are not so nimble and may not be inclined to undertake a major overhaul of how they think, manage, and operate. Turning such companies in a totally new direction could be very difficult, and certainly it is not something that one could expect to be done quickly or in a single stroke.

In short, we are suggesting that the biggest obstacle to wider adoption of the Silicon Valley Model is *not* that the model itself doesn't translate to other industries or locations. There are strong indications that it can be applied in these other situations quite well. The biggest obstacle would appear to be the institutional inertia that exists in many large firms—the effect of having used a polar-opposite model (the traditional bureaucratic model) for so long that it has become deeply embedded, and hard to dislodge.

This leads to the question of whether it could be possible to benefit from the Silicon Valley Model in certain areas or units of an organization.

10.3 Use of the Model in an Innovation Unit Within a Large Company

Large bureaucratic incumbents are, in one sense, finely tuned machines that use highly efficient processes to reach large markets. Not only is it difficult to radically change a firm of this kind, it might not even be a sensible idea from a business perspective. But the need for developing dynamic capabilities to seize new opportunities is definitely there, if the organization is to have a future at all. And the challenge of ambidexterity—i.e., building a strong "exploration" function to go along with efficient exploitation—can be solved in different ways. One, as we've seen, is to create separate units with the task of focusing on exploration, and for such units the Silicon Valley Model can be valuable. In some cases, examined above, large companies have tried to become more innovative by connecting to smaller companies through innovation platforms, such as GE's CEO-driven ecomagination initiative that opened up existing business units for new ideas and for new relationships beyond their regular suppliers. But as we also have seen, it can be hard to do something dramatically new inside existing R&D or business-unit organizations, which is why GE Appliances (GEA) took the further step of launching a totally independent unit, FirstBuild, where new ways of innovating could be organized based on a startup logic that, in some ways, goes even further than what was identified in the Silicon Valley Model.[31]

---

[30] Garud et al. (2011).
[31] Alänge and Steiber (2015).

An initiative of this type can be a useful first step toward adopting the new model. It is also possible that some of the model's elements can be utilized on a project level in large organizations—again, perhaps, as a way of building initial inside experiences for future application on a broader basis within the company.

Several companies outside Silicon Valley have experimented with various kinds of innovation units based on a different logic than regular operations. The farmer-owned agricultural cooperative Lantmännen in Sweden develops new ideas both internally and in open innovation collaborations, such as with researchers at universities, inventors and startup entrepreneurs. In order to transform potential ideas to actual product innovations and new business concepts, Lantmännen established an internal innovation/business concept generation unit, The Greenhouse.[32] This unit has the ambition of educating employees and simultaneously developing promising innovation concepts—either for renewing internal business units, or for further development in an external business incubator.[33] Similar units can be found in many other large corporations—one well-known example in Silicon Valley is at Cisco Systems.[34] The reason for developing this kind of unit is to let creative employees work according to another, more dynamic logic which encourages them to innovate and further develop their entrepreneurial capabilities. In this context, the Silicon Valley Model could provide inspiration.

10.4 Recent Developments: Further Dissemination of the Silicon Valley Model

Since the book's first edition, there has been much more evidence of companies outside Silicon Valley adopting similar management principles. Further research by co-author Dr. Annika Steiber uncovered multiple large-scale cases that were already in progress, while new experiments were launched at divisions of global firms across a range of industries — from financial services to power tools. All have shown significant signs of success. The pre-existing cases were found at major Chinese, European, and American companies with track records of spectacular high growth. In the new experiments, a shift to Silicon Valley-style management has enabled traditional businesses to respond to changing market conditions and improve their performance.

Here are selected brief case studies of each. This update section also describes an emerging trend that is motivating still more firms to move toward management principles aligned with the Silicon Valley Model.

---

[32] Lundberg (2015).
[33] Interview with Lantmännen, November 2014.
[34] Sidhu (2010), pp. 25–30.

10.4.1 New Models in China

Starting in 2016, Dr. Steiber conducted in-depth studies of six firms that had played leading roles in propelling China's economy into the twenty-first century. The companies were the "big three" internet firms Alibaba, Baidu, and Tencent, which had grown large and highly diversified around their initial core businesses, plus the digital camera and electronics maker Xiaomi, the large telecom company Huawei and, notably, the global appliance company Haier. The common feature among them at the time of the research was a corporate culture and management model that departed dramatically from the typical state-run Chinese bureaucracies. Further, the companies' basic management principles were found to clearly parallel those of the Silicon Valley Model.

Dr. Steiber systematically compared the Chinese firms to her Silicon Valley case companies in the 2018 book *Management in the Digital Age: Will China Surpass Silicon Valley?* Their fundamental principles turned out to match closely along a series of dimensions. Examples included the external focus of the CEOs, and a cultural and organizational emphasis on innovation, speed, adaptability, and continual learning. To quote directly from that book:

> The Chinese firms are flexible and fast-moving due to the mandate of the top leader, their flexible organizational structure, based on many smaller independent businesses, rather than one or a few large units, and less formalized processes. Here our data indicates that the Chinese firms might even be more flexible and faster than the Silicon Valley firms ...[35]

In terms of the kinds of people that the companies sought to employ, the recruiting ads for one Chinese firm, Xiaomi, even looked as if they had been lifted from the "special breed of people" descriptions provided by our Silicon Valley case companies. Xiaomi's qualifications for numerous positions stated the candidate must have an "entrepreneurial spirit" and a "passion" for excellent products, not be a conventional "company person," and so forth.[36]

Of course, there were some differences between the Chinese and Silicon Valley companies at the time of the study. For example, the Chinese management models tended to have a hybrid leadership style, in which top-down vision and management was combined with a significant amount of cross-functional horizontal communication on projects, and with increased autonomy for employees and teams. And while the Chinese firms, like Silicon Valley firms, wanted to employ highly entrepreneurial people, they also placed "great emphasis on 'loyalty' to the leader and the company."[37]

Additionally, the research found one of the Chinese firms standing out from the rest. That firm was (and is) Haier. Whereas the majority of the other companies were digital natives founded in the late 1990s or the 2000s, Haier was in a traditional

---

[35] Steiber (2018), Chapter 7.
[36] Steiber (2018), Chapter 6.
[37] Steiber (2018), Chapter 7.

10.4 Recent Developments: Further Dissemination of the Silicon Valley Model

industry — home appliances — and had emerged from humble origins as a formerly failing regional refrigerator factory. After longtime CEO Zhang Ruimin took over the factory in 1984, Haier adopted higher standards of quality and efficiency, eventually growing into the world's largest supplier of appliances and smart-home systems.

Moreover, during its recent decades of growth, Haier developed a radically new management model that continues to evolve over time. The Rendanheyi model deserves a closer look in its own right.

10.4.2 Case Study: RenDanHeYi at Haier and GE Appliances

Asked to define "RenDanHeYi" for speakers of English, Haier's Zhang Ruimin replied as follows.

> *Ren* is a Chinese word that means people or person. We mainly use it to refer to employees within an organization. *Dan* means orders, and here it represents the needs or demand of users. *HeYi* means integration. So, we're talking about the fact that everyone, every employee, gets to create value for users … [The result is] a virtuous circle built around creating value for users.[38]

The RenDanHeYi system in its current form, as of this writing, is developed and refined in such detail that it almost defies a simple summary description. However, Dr. Steiber has had the opportunity to study RenDanHeYi intimately on more than one occasion, from which some general findings can be drawn.

The RenDanHeYi model is grounded in the same basic meta-principles as the Silicon Valley Model but applies these principles in some ways that appear to be more advanced and more disruptive of the usual norms. Vast amounts of middle management and hierarchy are stripped away. Employees are organized into microenterprises (MEs), which do not necessarily remain micro-small in size, but which operate and innovate with high degrees of autonomy. Customer-facing MEs interact directly with end users of Haier products and its members are paid according to the measurable value they create for them (the "pay by user" concept). Other MEs perform support functions, and the MEs that they serve are seen as *their* customers, to the extent that formal contracts are drawn up and pay is again determined accordingly. In addition, several MEs collaborate and support each other in delivering great customer experience. This format of collaboration is called an ecosystem micro community (EMC), and tasks and incoming profit are regulated by using an EMC contract. Further, the entire system runs on advanced digital communications, with the overall goal of creating "zero distance" between Haier, the EMC, and its customers/users. Ideally, users then become true partners in the enterprise. This enables seamlessly interactive development of new products and services which either meet or anticipate customer needs, and which satisfy people so well that they become lifetime customers.

---

[38] McKinsey & Company (2021).

A very interesting case of RenDanHeYi implementation came when Haier acquired U.S.-based GE Appliances (GEA) in 2016. As a long-standing division of the General Electric Company, GEA had been home to the experimental FirstBuild unit, mentioned in Chap. 8 and this chapter as an example of innovative approaches to developing new products. Aside from occasional flashes of promise at the FirstBuild facility, however, GEA had been under-performing, with stagnant growth and loss of market share. The division was managed under bureaucratic methods imposed by General Electric and had been given the uninspiring mandates to "do no harm" to the corporate brand while controlling costs to increase short-term returns.[39]

All of this changed following the Haier acquisition. GEA's top executives chose to phase in Rendanheyi principles and methods company-wide. After 5 years, although the transition was not yet complete, GEA was reporting substantial growth in revenues, profits, and market share while rolling out valuable new products.[40] Moreover GEA's work environment had changed dramatically, as described in Dr. Steiber's 2022 book *Leadership for a Digital World: The Transformation of GE Appliances*.

In interviews for that book, senior executives at GEA compared GEA's pre-acquisition mode of operation in 2016 to its status in 2021. After being told the key features of Henry Mintzberg's "machine bureaucracy" model — and also the contrasting features of the Silicon Valley Model — the executives were asked to rate GEA for each time period on a scale of 0–6, with 0 representing a total machine bureaucracy and 6 a fully realized Silicon Valley approach. Composite results of their ratings are shown in Fig. 10.1.

As can be seen from the figure, executives who were directly involved with GEA perceived the company to be evolving noticeably toward the Silicon Valley Model — even though they were implementing the RenDanHeYi model! This, we believe, illustrates the common validity of the underlying design principles represented by both models. Now let's consider three recent cases from various industries.

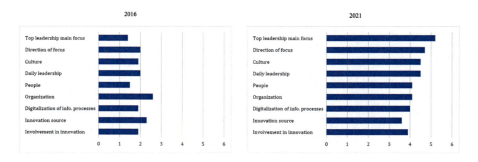

Fig. 10.1 Combined executive ratings of GEA in 2016 (top) versus 2021 (bottom), where 0 = total bureaucracy and 6 = total Silicon Valley Model (Steiber, 2022)

---

[39] Steiber (2022).
[40] See for example Zohar (2022).

10.4 Recent Developments: Further Dissemination of the Silicon Valley Model   191

10.4.3 Case Study: Fidelity Investments

Fidelity Investments, founded in 1946, is a U.S.-based multinational active in financial products and services from mutual funds to wealth management. In the mid-2010s, Fidelity's Personal Investments group was facing increased competition from digitally based fintech (financial technology) startups. The president of Personal Investments saw that her business was not optimally organized to keep pace. Each person worked on isolated parts of multiple, unrelated projects, and layers of middle management were needed to coordinate everyone's efforts. Bureaucratic silos made it hard for different functional units to work together efficiently on new product or service features that customer were starting to want.[41]

In a series of steps, this Fidelity business transformed to a flatter and more responsive management model. People were organized into integrated, cross-functional teams, with each team focused on a specific customer-oriented objective. Teams could be formed, dissolved, or changed as desired. The results were striking:

> Compared with the conventional model, the integrated teams reduced the time it would normally take to deliver a feature by 75% ... [T]eam assignments were driven by customer insights, decisions were made within the teams, and many coordination and approval steps were eliminated. At any one time there could be as many as 187 groups of people with decision rights. This system replaced a system of control in which there could be as many as eight organizational layers. The number of layers collapsed to three, even as the number of decision-makers increased dramatically.[42]

Furthermore, the team approach created a valuable new product line: a set of zero-fee mutual funds targeted to young and first-time investors. These funds brought in potential long-term customers and have helped Fidelity remain a market leader despite fierce competition.[43]

10.4.4 Case Study: Bosch Power Tools

Robert Bosch GmbH is a German engineering and technology firm with multiple businesses worldwide. The Power Tools division makes handheld electric tools such as drills, saws, and grinders, which are bought by individual consumers and are also used in the construction and fabrication industries. Several trends drove the division to re-think its management model. Although most power tools have been sold through physical retail outlets, which traditionally meant that retailers were seen as the division's key "customers," the growth of online sales called for a greater emphasis on relating directly (and digitally) to end users. Bosch Power Tools also

---

[41] McGrath and Charan (2023).
[42] Ibid.
[43] Ibid.

wanted to pursue growth in emerging markets in developing countries, and to compete better with tech companies in attracting skilled employees.[44]

Seeking improvement in these areas, the division in 2016 launched a self-designed transformation project that borrowed and adapted methods from a variety of sources including Agile, Rendanheyi, and more.[45] The overall effect was a move toward a model that closely resembles the Silicon Valley Model. Structurally, six functional silos were replaced by more than 50 cross-functional business teams. Rather than being managed top-down, the teams were given general guidelines within which to operate. Teams strategized and innovated on the basis of user scenarios, with increased reliance on user feedback. A culture of transparency — along with supportive top leadership — enabled inter-team communication and learning.[46]

By the 2020s, Bosch Power Tools had markedly increased its scores in measures of both user satisfaction and employee satisfaction. The transformation leader saw this latter development as crucial: "Creating an environment where people love to work creates the highest impact on the market for us as a company … [and helps with] attracting new talent from outside."[47]

10.4.5 Case Study: Fujitsu Western Europe

Fujitsu, founded in 1935 in Japan, is a global IT firm providing digital infrastructure and solutions to business clients. In 2019, João Domingos, Fujitsu's top VP for Western Europe, saw clear signs that his organization had stagnated. Penetration into key growth areas was unsatisfactory. Customer NPS (Net Promoter Score) ratings were negative. Then, at a conference where delegates from Haier were present, Domingos learned that one of Haier's microenterprises had grown itself to unicorn size in the same length of time that it had taken Fujitsu Western Europe to *lose* a potential contract by responding too slowly to the client's needs.[48]

The Fujitsu unit then embarked on a cultural and structural transformation. In 2020, the first microenterprise was established. By 2021 there were 14 microenterprises, trying different strategies for different market segments and producing measurable gains: one microenterprise grew by 5× in about a year. Fujitsu Western Europe also increased its employee engagement score from 64% to 73% and flipped the customer NPS from negative to positive. Other effects of the transformation included: less bureaucracy, with a decentralized organization. Greater openness to new talents and skill sets. An increased focus on entrepreneurship and experimentation, to learn new things quickly. A more supportive top leadership, with middle managers and other employees turned into decision-makers rather than followers of

---

[44] de Morree (2021) and Quintarelli (2021).
[45] Quintarelli (2021).
[46] de Morree (2021) and Quintarelli (2021).
[47] Quintarelli (2021).
[48] Minnaar (2021).

10.4.6 A Growing Force for Change: Digital Transformation

Finally, we wish to call attention to a trend that is motivating many companies to re-think their management models. As noted in Chap. 6, over the past decade or so, growing numbers of firms in traditional industries have attempted digital transformation projects. Typically, the projects involve upgrading or replacing legacy IT systems, while installing new digital capabilities meant to boost the company's performance. These capabilities may include (but are not limited to) sophisticated data mining and analysis, various uses of advanced AI, building new online platforms, and exploiting the possibilities of IT-based phenomena that range from social media to blockchain. To quote one brief definition,

> Digital transformation is the fundamental rewiring of how an organization operates. The goal of a digital transformation ... should be to build a competitive advantage by continuously deploying tech at scale to improve customer experience and lower costs.[50]

However, an important fact is gradually coming to be recognized. Digital transformation isn't only about adding new technology. As one executive stated, "Culture change is a prerequisite of digital transformation," and to achieve good results, *the organization itself must be transformed.*[51] A global study by Capgemini identified "cultural issues" as the most common barrier to digital progress. According to the study, success in digital transformation depends on either having or developing a culture marked by seven key characteristics. Along with a digital-first mindset and data-driven decision-making, the desired qualities are: agility and flexibility, collaboration, customer centricity, innovation, and openness.[52] These findings are also supported by scholarly research. To the qualities just listed, Roman Teichert added: failure tolerance, risk affinity, participation, organizational learning, and encouragement of entrepreneurship.[53]

It should not be surprising that all these qualities align strongly with elements of the Silicon Valley Model. Chapter 3 of this book, an in-depth look at the Silicon Valley ecosystem, showed that technological innovation and management innovation go hand in hand. New technologies both enable and require new ways of working — and the Silicon Valley Model evolved from precisely such a combination of influences.

---

[49] Ibid.
[50] McKinsey & Company (2023).
[51] Buvat et al. (2018).
[52] Ibid.
[53] Teichert (2019).

More recently, failures in digital transformation have shown that technical tools alone can't make a company fit for the digital age, just as a state-of-the-art bicycle can't make a person fit for the Tour de France. A significant amount of research and consulting practice is now aimed at helping companies migrate to an appropriate "digital culture" and management model. For example, the researcher Carsten Lund Pedersen notes that "finding the right balance between continuity and change" can empower a company to transform without losing its identity,[54] while the digital consultant Anand Inamdar advises "treating digital transformation as a cultural change" from the start.[55] In our view, all advice of this type builds momentum for an ongoing movement to management approaches that are congruent with the Silicon Valley Model.

10.5 Ultimate Conclusions

The end of this final chapter also marks the end of the book. We hope that throughout the book, several messages have become clear, and they will be summarized briefly here.

At the end of the first edition in 2016 we asked:

> What is the future of the Silicon Valley Model? Will it become more widely used in industries beyond the Valley? Will it serve as a helpful template for re-inventing management generally?

Now more than ever, these questions can be answered with "yes." Consider first that the model is not just a recent or a strictly localized invention. As we saw in Chap. 9, the Silicon Valley Model appears to be a highly developed form of the Adhocracy model, which has been evolving since the post-World War II era. The need for a model *of this kind* was recognized long ago. It has the force of history behind it, and it is passing the test of the present—as shown by the achievements our original case companies, along with the results produced by others.

Second, the need for such a model continues to grow. As demonstrated in Chap. 1, the forces of change in our world are constantly growing and multiplying. In part this is due to the rest of the business world starting to look more and more like Silicon Valley: increasingly driven by fast-changing information technologies, increasingly globalized and thus open to new ideas from everywhere. *But the mounting forces of change are also coming from directions that we do not yet fully comprehend or know how to deal with.*

Certainly, it seems evident that advanced forms of AI will be truly disruptive technologies. And yet no one knows for certain exactly what they will disrupt, or how, or what the ripple effects could look like. All we have so far are speculation

---

[54] Pedersen (2022).
[55] Inamdar (2022).

10.5 Ultimate Conclusions

and prognosis. Meanwhile, given the ominous rise of climate-related disasters, the challenges of sustainability alone are immense. Nor is it clear whether the so-called "world order" that we are accustomed to will persist into the future. In countries around the world, demographics and economies are changing rapidly, as are both domestic and international political dynamics.

For business firms in various places — as well as for nonprofit organizations and government agencies — tomorrow may bring new threats to confront or new opportunities to pursue. Probably plenty of both. The result is a growing demand for fast-moving, dynamic and ambidextrous organizations. These organizations must be able to operate reliably and efficiently at scale, while also freeing up the talents of entrepreneurial people to explore new directions and new solutions.

Therefore, considering all of the evidence presented in the new edition of this book, we come to the following conclusions.

- Old, bureaucratic ways of managing are no longer fit for today's world. The pace and impacts of change often exceed the ability of traditionally managed companies to respond well. In Chap. 1, we saw stories of long-established firms that lost their market leadership by failure to respond. Conversely, in that same chapter as well as in the present Chap. 10 and elsewhere, we saw cases of established companies *pivoting to success* by adopting a new management approach.
- And the new approach is the one we've called the Silicon Valley Model. It has repeatedly met the reality test of being applied in practice and producing results. This model is now *proved* to be useful in many industries, and in locations worldwide that lie far from Silicon Valley.
- Specific features of the model may change, and it may be given names other than "the Silicon Valley Model," depending on where and how it is implemented. It is also possible to implement some but not all features of the model. Or to iterate the model in new ways. However, in case after case, the underlying principles turn out to be very similar to (or even the same as) those we identified at six case companies in Silicon Valley in 2016.

Our current age places huge demands on all of us. We, the co-authors, believe that ongoing innovation and experimentation in management is urgently needed. But we are also convinced that a template to guide these efforts has now been identified. The meta-principles of the Silicon Valley Model have moved far past the stage of being hypothetical solutions. They actually work. They are well worth trying in any organization, anywhere.

We therefore offer this book in the hope that it can serve as an inspiration and a guide. The future is in your hands. If each of us, in our own ways, can embrace the dynamic entrepreneurial capabilities needed for exploring and innovating new pathways, that future may begin to look brighter for everyone.

References

Alänge, S. (1992). What role do QC-circles play in Sweden? *Total Quality Management, 3*(2), 157–163.

Alänge, S., & Miconnet, P. (2001, October). Nokia: An 'old' company in a 'new' economy. Paper presented at the 21st *Strategic Management Society Conference* in San Francisco, pp. 21–24.

Alänge, S., & Steiber, A. (2009). The board's role in sustaining major organizational change. *International Journal of Quality and Service Sciences, 1*(3), 280–293.

Alänge, S., & Steiber, A. (2015). The best of both worlds: Combining the strengths of small start-ups with a large corporation's advantages. Draft.

Birkinshaw, J. (2010). *Reinventing management: Making smarter choices for getting work done*. Wiley.

Buvat, J., Crummineri, C., Kar, K., Sengupta, A., Solis, B., Aboud, C., & El Aoufi, H. (2018). The digital culture challenge: Closing the employee-leadership gap. Capgemini white paper report, version 2. https://www.capgemini.com/wp-content/uploads/2017/06/dti-digitalculture_report_v2.pdf

Dahmén, E. (1950). *Svensk industriell företagarverksamhet*. IUI/Almgvist & Wiksell. In English translation: (1970) *Entrepreneurial activity and the development of Swedish industry, 1919–1939*. Homewood.

de Morree, P. (2021, September 8). Reinventing Bosch: A radically new way of working. Corporate Rebels. https://www.corporate-rebels.com/blog/transforming-bosch

Garud, R., Gehman, J., & Kumaraswamy, A. (2011). Complexity arrangements for sustained innovation: Lessons from 3M corporation. *Organization Studies, 32*(6), 737–767.

Gawer, A., & Cusumano, M. A. (2014). Industry platforms and ecosystem innovation. *The Journal of Product Innovation Management, 31*(3), 417–433.

General Electric Company. (2015a). Ecomagination web page: http://www.ge.com/about-us/ecomagination. Accessed 23 July 2015.

General Electric Company. (2015b). Healthymagination overview: http://www.ge.com/globalimpact2013/#/healthymagination. Accessed 23 July 2015.

Hounshell, D. A., & Kenly Smith, J. (1988). *Science and corporate strategy: DuPont R&D, 1902–1980*. Cambridge University Press.

IKEA. (2015). Our business idea: http://www.ikea.com/ms/en_IE/about_ikea/the_ikea_way/our_business_idea/index.html. Accessed 25 July 2015.

Inamdar, A. (2022, July 22). Digital transformation and its impact on digital culture. Forbes.com. https://www.forbes.com/sites/forbeshumanresourcescouncil/2022/07/22/digital-transformation-and-its-impact-on-organizational-culture

Johnson & Johnson. (2014, May 14). Janssen labs expanding and accelerating coast to coast. https://www.jnj.com/news/all/Janssen-Labs-Expanding-and-Accelerating-Coast-to-Coast-Unveils-Plan-to-Enhance-the-Innovation-Ecosystem-with-New-Incubator-in-South-San-Francisco-and-Awards-One-Year-of-Lab-Space-to-Three-Innovative-Healthcare-Companies-in-Boston. Accessed 29 July 2015.

Kling, K., & Goteman, I. (2003). IKEA CEO Anders Dahlvig on international growth and IKEA's unique corporate culture and brand identity. *Academy of Management Executive, 17*(1), 31–37.

Lundberg, A. (2015, July 12). *Entreprenörskap på jobbet ska locka fram nya idé'er* [Entrepreneurship at work will elicit new ideas]. Dagens Nyheter, http://www.pressreader.com/sweden/dagens-nyhetenweekend/20150712/281754152997343/TextView. Accessed 26 July 2015.

Manz, C. C., Shipper, F., & Stewart, G. L. (2009). Everyone a team leader: Shared influence at W.L. Gore & associates. *Organizational Dynamics, 38*(3), 239–244.

Marshall, A. (1892). *Elements of economics*. Macmillan.

McGrath, R. & Charan, R. (2023, January–February). The permissionless corporation. *Harvard Business Review*. https://hbr.org/2023/01/the-permissionless-corporation

McKinsey & Company. (2021, July 27). Shattering the status quo: A conversation with Haier's Zhang Ruimin. McKinsey Quarterly. https://www.mckinsey.com/capabilities/people-and-organizational-performance/our-insights/shattering-the-status-quo-a-conversation-with-haiers-zhang-ruimin

McKinsey & Company. (2023, June 14). What is digital transformation? McKinsey website. https://www.mckinsey.com/featured-insights/mckinsey-explainers/what-is-digital-transformation

Minnaar, J. (2021, March 20). How Fujitsu is successfully reinventing its way of working. Corporate Rebels. https://www.corporate-rebels.com/blog/fujitsu-europe-microenterprises

Mintzberg, H. (1980). Structure in 5's: A synthesis of the research on organization design. *Management Science, 26*(3), 322–341.

Owens, B. (2014). Digital resource productivity: Ecomagination, the industrial internet, and the Global Resource Challenge. General Electric Company white paper. http://www.ge.com/sites/default/files/ge_digital_resource_productivity_whitepaper.pdf. Accessed 23 July 2015.

Pedersen, C. L. (2022). Cracking the culture code for successful digital transformation. *MIT Sloan Management Review, 63*(3), 1–4. https://sloanreview.mit.edu/article/cracking-the-culture-code-for-successful-digital-transformation/

Philips Research. (2015). High Tech Campus Eindhoven. http://www.hightechcampus.com/about_the_campus/#article/ecosystem/. Accessed 25 July 2015.

Quintarelli, E. (2021). Going beyond Agile through the Rendanheyi at Bosch. Medium, 31 December 2021. https://stories.platformdesigntoolkit.com/going-beyond-agile-through-the-rendanheyi-at-bosch-917b69ce966a

Ries, E. (2011). *The lean startup: How constant innovation creates radically successful businesses*. Portfolio Penguin.

Schmidt, E., & Rosenberg, J. (2014). *How Google works*. Grand Central Publishing.

Sidhu, I. (2010). *Doing both: How Cisco captures today's profit and drives tomorrow's growth*. FT Press.

Steiber, A. (2018). *Management in the digital age: Will China surpass silicon valley?* Springer Briefs in Business.

Steiber, A. (2022). *Leadership for a digital world: The transformation of GE appliances*. Springer Management for Professionals.

Sull, D., & Eisenhardt, K. M. (2015). *Simple rules: How to thrive in a complex world*. John Murray.

Teichert, R. (2019). Digital transformation maturity: A systematic review of the literature. *Acta Universitatis Agriculturae et Silviculturae Mendelianae Brunensis, 67*(6), 1673–1687. https://doi.org/10.11118/actaun201967061673

Totrakarntrakul, R., & Lang, Y. S. (2008). *Leadership influencing organisational creativity: The case of IKEA*. Baltic Business School.

Zohar, D. (2022). GE appliances: An American catalyst. In *Zero distance*. Palgrave Macmillan. https://doi.org/10.1007/978-981-16-7849-3_18

Index

A
Alphabet Inc., xv, 10, 38, 57, 154
Ambidextrous, xiv, 24, 32–34, 36, 45, 53, 74, 135–156, 159, 167–169, 176, 180–181, 195

D
Digital age/era, xiii, 1, 15, 113, 156, 188, 194
Dynamic capabilities, xiv, 24–27, 38, 53, 56, 74, 91, 135–139, 153–155, 163, 165, 168, 169, 176, 177, 181, 185, 186

E
Entrepreneurial culture, 46, 56, 58, 162, 167, 177
Entrepreneurial leadership, 177–178
Entrepreneurial management, 16, 20, 69
Entrepreneurial organization, 135–156
Entrepreneurial people, xiii, 2, 8, 39, 53, 54, 61, 70, 75, 79, 86, 87, 139, 153, 175, 178–180, 188, 195

F
Facebook/Meta, xv, 92
Fairchild Semiconductor, 51
Federal Telegraph Company (FTC), 44, 48, 49
Fidelity Investment, xiii, 16, 191
Fujitsu, 16, 192–193

G
GE Appliances (GEA), xiii, xvi, 16, 147, 180, 186, 189–190

Google, xii, xv, xvi, 1, 10–14, 17, 23, 24, 35, 38, 43, 46, 52, 57, 64, 67, 73–77, 83–85, 87, 88, 90–92, 98, 100–111, 119–125, 136, 139–146, 149, 150, 152–154, 161, 164, 178, 181

H
Haier, xiii, xvi, 16, 173, 188–190, 192
HP, 16, 49

I
Innovation management, 38
Intel, 28, 34, 44, 49, 51, 105, 162, 183

K
Kleiner Perkins, 51
Kodak, 15–16

L
LinkedIn, xii, xv, xvi, 1, 13, 73, 77, 85, 89–91, 98–100, 103, 106, 108, 120, 124, 136, 141, 142, 152–154, 164

O
Open innovation, 34, 38, 124, 135, 139, 149–155, 163, 164, 168, 176, 181–182, 187

P
People-centric, xiv, 24, 30–32, 38, 43, 53, 74, 169

R
RenDanHeYi, xiii, 189–190, 192

S
Silicon Valley Model, xi–xv, 2, 93, 159–173, 175–195
Special breed of people, xiv, 54, 71, 73–93, 135, 188
Sustainable age/era, 156
Systems approach, xiv, 24, 35–38, 165, 169, 185, 186

T
Tesla, xii, xv, xvi, 1, 13, 14, 56, 73, 77, 98, 100–102, 106, 111, 120, 122, 125, 136, 139, 148, 150, 152, 154
Twitter/X, xii, xv, xvi, 1, 13, 73, 77, 79, 82, 99, 100, 103, 106, 110, 111, 120, 127, 136, 152–154, 164

V
Varian Associates, 45, 51

Printed in the United States
by Baker & Taylor Publisher Services